T0191598

Lecture Notes in Computer Science 13775

More information about this series at https://link.springer.com/bookseries/558

Nikolos Gurney · Gita Sukthankar (Eds.)

Computational Theory of Mind for Human-Machine Teams

First International Symposium, ToM for Teams 2021
Virtual Event, November 4–6, 2021
Revised Selected Papers

 Springer

Editors
Nikolos Gurney 🆔
University of Southern California
Los Angeles, CA, USA

Gita Sukthankar 🆔
University of Central Florida
Orlando, FL, USA

ISSN 0302-9743 ISSN 1611-3349 (electronic)
Lecture Notes in Computer Science
ISBN 978-3-031-21670-1 ISBN 978-3-031-21671-8 (eBook)
https://doi.org/10.1007/978-3-031-21671-8

This Springer imprint is published by the registered company Springer Nature Switzerland AG
The registered company address is: Gewerbestrasse 11, 6330 Cham, Switzerland

Preface

People rely on a skill commonly referred to as *theory of mind* (ToM) to infer the mental states, e.g. beliefs, of others. It is widely believed that ToM inference is a key element to the alchemy that humans employ when they make predictions about other agents. Critically, ToM inferences, as well as the associated models and predictions, can become extremely complex when made in team settings. This is particularly true when a human must form n-level beliefs about other agents and their interactions. Extensive research posits that high-performing teams naturally align key aspects of their individual models, including social models based on ToM, to create shared mental models of their environment, equipment, strategies, and, of course, the relevant agents. Thus, ToM and the ability to create shared mental models are key elements of human social intelligence. Together, these two skills may form the basis for human collaboration at all scales, whether the setting is a playing field or a military mission. It follows that artificial intelligence-based machines would benefit from the ability to model human ToM and shared mental models.

Artificial intelligence (AI) technologies have made little progress in understanding the most important component of the environments in which they operate: humans. This lack of understanding stymies efforts to create safe, efficient, and productive human-machine teams. This volume curates state-of-the-art, peer-reviewed research from computer science, cognitive science, and social science examining the development of artificial intelligence systems capable of theory of mind, exhibiting social intelligence, and using these skills in human-machine teams—i.e. **artificial social intelligence** (ASI). TOM for Teams 2021 received 22 submissions. Each submission received a minimum of three reviews in a single-blind peer review process. In the end, 11 papers were accepted for publication with minor revisions (50%) and 9 accepted with major revisions (40.9%); in total, 14 papers completed the review process and were included in this volume. The 2021 edition of this conference was held as an virtual event.

Section I: Theory of Mind

Theory of mind (ToM) is a term used to reference the ability to infer the mental states, that is, beliefs, desires, emotions, etc., of others and then use those inferences for other cognitive purposes. Modern efforts to understand the phenomenon are commonly traced back to seminal work in the social lives of primates [3] (which is where the term *theory of mind* took hold) and how situational features influence social perception [2]. That does not mean the idea is a modern invention. The idea that others have distinct minds that we can perceive and use as information is littered throughout philosophy: Descartes tried to establish a mind-body distinction for this purpose during the Renaissance, Plato used the horses and chariot analogy in the *Phaedrus* to describe conflicting internal drives and how they influence people, and the ancient Buddhist philosopher Vasubandhu described the basic factors of experience and behavior in an effort to uncover the internal states of others.

The first section of this volume presents foundational surveys that provide important background on computational ToM. Modern theories about ToM are reviewed in the chapter *Operationalizing Theories of Theory of Mind: A Survey*, which discusses competing theories, their implementation in computational agents, and what computer scientists and psychologists can collectively learn from doing so. The chapter *Knowledge of Self and Other Within a Broader Commonsense Setting* digs deeper with a look at the knowledge representations and reasoning abilities that an agent in a team needs in order for it to have ToM. The last chapter in this section, *Constructivist Approaches for Computational Emotions: A Systematic Survey*, introduces readers to three approaches to modeling emotions, a core element of ToM, and their representation in the affective computing literature.

Section II: Methodological Advances

As important as clarifying **what** is being studied is establishing best practices for **how** it is studied. Studying how people interact with intelligent machines has a rich, storied history. One of the earliest and most famous examples paired people with a natural language processing program, ELIZA, which ran a script that simulated a Rogerian psychotherapist (it simply parroted what people said) [4]. Not only did people believe that the program was intelligent, they anthropomorphized it. Joseph Weizenbaum, the author of the program, reflecting on it in the introduction to his book said [5]:

> I was startled to see how quickly and how very deeply people conversing with [ELIZA] became emotionally involved with the computer and how unequivocally they anthropomorphized it.

It seemed to him that people were forming an emotional relationship with the machine, treating it as if it had a mind and understood their plight—i.e. they assumed it was an ASI.

In the half century since Weizenbaum created ELIZA and Premack and Woodruff popularized the term ToM, vast amounts of effort has gone into developing artificial intelligence and improving our understanding of social cognition. Section II opens up with *Social Cognition Paradigms ex Machinas*, which surveys experimental methods from psychology and cognitive science and translates them for AI-settings. This survey is followed by four chapters, each introducing a state-of-the-art technology for studying and developing ASI. *Evaluating Artificial Social Intelligence in an Urban Search and Rescue Task Environment* introduces a simulated USAR testbed, data from teams of human participants performing search and rescue tasks, and evaluation of ASIs performing post hoc interpretation of the data. The next chapter, *Modular Procedural Generation for Voxel Maps*, introduces a new technology developed to drastically simplify the creation of virtual environments, such as the one in the preceding chapter, while ensuring that the environment is readily processed by artificial intelligence. An important question when developing new methods and approaches to studying any teaming task, but particularly human-machine ones, is what role does task complexity play? *Task Complexity and Performance in Individuals and Groups Without Communication* asks this question and provides relevant, guiding insights to the ASI research community. The section closes with

Development of Emergent Leadership Measurement: Implications for Human-Machine Teams, which tackles one of the biggest challenges in ASI development: digesting natural language and using it to identify emergent roles in human-machine teams.

Section III: Translating and Modeling Human Theory of Mind for ASI

This section presents work addressing the meat of the topic: endowing ASI with human-like social intelligence. This is no small task, if for no other reason because there is considerable disagreement in the cognitive science community about what exactly *is* ToM [1]. A perusal of the first two sections underscores this reality.

Each chapter in this section tackles a different aspect of AI representing the thoughts and beliefs of human agents. The section opens with *Should Agents Have Two Systems to Track Beliefs and Belief-Like States?*, which posits a new take on how to achieve human-like ToM without relying on a complex, dual-system model (one system being efficient but inflexible, the other cumbersome and flexible). The next chapter, *Sequential Theory of Mind Modeling in Team Search and Rescue Tasks*, introduces a state-of-the-art computational model for ASI that is capable of inferring ToM states from natural language. One of the biggest challenges faced by ASI researchers is staying true to the cognitive models of ToM while using the best technology available: *Integrating Machine Learning and Cognitive Modeling of Decision Making* demonstrates that a hybrid approach to modeling ToM, which implements both cognitive models and machine learning models, is not only feasible, but capable and efficient. The section wraps up with *Overgenerality from Inference in Perspective-Taking*, which establishes important perspective taking boundaries for computational ToM.

Section IV: Tools for Improving ASI

This volume closes with two chapters introducing state-of-the-art approaches to achieving human-level skills that are essential to ToM capabilities. *Using Features at Multiple Temporal and Spatial Resolutions to Predict Human Behavior in Real Time* shows that integrating a low-resolution approach to data interpretation along with the typical high-resolution approach can produce significant prediction accuracy (i.e., better ToM). The closing chapter, *Route Optimization in Service of a Search and Rescue Artificial Social Intelligence Agent*, presents a state-of-the-art learning pipeline designed to aid ASI in understanding its environment. Specifically, it empowers the ASI to assess the quality of routes that a person may follow in an environment which the ASI can later use in reasoning about the person's beliefs about the task and environment.

Closing Remarks

The mental representations that we maintain of what is happening in the minds of others is a core aspect of human cognition. As set out in the opening chapter of this volume, the scientific community has yet to fully describe this very human experience or replicate it in machines. Doing so is, arguably, one of the tallest hurdles along the path to artificial general intelligence. The authors represented in this volume also hold a strong conviction that ASI is a critical element to helping humans more fully accept and integrate computational agents into teams as well as their lives more generally. The work presented herein represents our collective efforts to better understand ToM, develop AI with ToM capabilities (ASI), and study how to integrate such systems into human teams.

Acknowledgements Part of the effort depicted is sponsored by the Defense Advanced Research Projects Agency (DARPA) under contract number W911NF2010011, and that the content of the information does not necessarily reflect the position or the policy of the US Government or the Defense Advanced Research Projects Agency, and no official endorsements should be inferred.

October 2022

Nikolos Gurney
David V. Pynadath
Gita Sukthankar
Volkan Ustun

References

1. Gurney, N., Marsella, S., Ustun, V., Pynadath, D.: Operationalizing theories of theory of mind: a survey. In Press, AAAI Fall Symposium (2022)
2. Heider, F., Simmel, M.: An experimental study of apparent behavior. Am. J. Psychol. **57**(2), 243–259 (1944)
3. Premack, D., Woodruff, G.: Does the chimpanzee have a theory of mind? Behavioral Brain Sci. **1**(4), 515–526 (1978)
4. Weizenbaum, J.: Eliza—a computer program for the study of natural language communication between man and machine. Commun. ACM **9**(1), 36–45 (1966)
5. Weizenbaum, J.: Computer power and human reason: from judgment to calculation (1976)

Organization

General Chair

Gita Sukthankar   University of Central Florida, USA

Program Committee Chairs

Joshua Elliott   DARPA, USA
Nikolos Gurney   University of Southern California, USA
Guy Hoffman   Cornell University, USA
Lixiao Huang   Arizona State University, USA
Ellyn Maese   Gallup, USA
Ngoc Nguyen   Carnegie Mellon University, USA
Katia Sycara   Carnegie Mellon University, USA

Additional Reviewers

Pavan Kantharaju
Ji Hyun Jeong
David Grethlein
Rhyse Bendell
Verica Buchanan
Lydia Tapia
Peta Masters
Christopher Corral
Chase McDonald
Kobus Barnard
Myounghoon Jeon
Yun Kang
Matt Law
Matt Wood
Stephen Cauffman

Muhammad Junaid Khan
Shengnan Hu
Ramya Akula
David Grethlein
Jared Freeman
Suresh Jayaraman
Sebastian Sardina
Ashish Amresh
Paulo Ricardo da Silva Soares
Sarit Adhikari
Deepayan Sanyal
Duy Nhat Phan
Joseph Lyons
Yun Kang

Contents

Theory of Mind

Operationalizing Theories of Theory of Mind: A Survey 3
    Nikolos Gurney, Stacy Marsella, Volkan Ustun, and David V. Pynadath

Knowledge of Self and Other Within a Broader Commonsense Setting 21
    Darsana P. Josyula, Matthew Goldberg, Anthony Herron,
    Christopher Maxey, Paul Zaidins, Timothy Clausner, Justin Brody,
    and Don Perlis

Constructivist Approaches for Computational Emotions: A Systematic
Survey 30
    Alexander Viola, Vladimir Pavlovic, and Sejong Yoon

Methodological Advances

Social Cognition Paradigms *ex Machinas* 53
    Joel Michelson, Deepayan Sanyal, James Ainooson, Yuan Yang,
    and Maithilee Kunda

Evaluating Artificial Social Intelligence in an Urban Search and Rescue
Task Environment 72
    Jared Freeman, Lixiao Huang, Matt Wood, and Stephen J. Cauffman

Modular Procedural Generation for Voxel Maps 85
    Adarsh Pyarelal, Aditya Banerjee, and Kobus Barnard

Task Complexity and Performance in Individuals and Groups Without
Communication 102
    Aditya Gulati, Thuy Ngoc Nguyen, and Cleotilde Gonzalez

Development of Emergent Leadership Measurement: Implications
for Human-Machine Teams 118
    Ellyn Maese, Pablo Diego-Rosell, Les Debusk-Lane, and Nathan Kress

Translating and Modeling Human Theory of Mind for ASI

Should Agents Have Two Systems to Track Beliefs and Belief-Like States? 149
    Irina Rabkina and Clifton McFate

Sequential Theory of Mind Modeling in Team Search and Rescue Tasks 158
  Huao Li, Long Le, Max Chis, Keyang Zheng, Dana Hughes,
  Michael Lewis, and Katia Sycara

Integrating Machine Learning and Cognitive Modeling of Decision Making 173
  Taher Rahgooy, K. Brent Venable, and Jennifer S. Trueblood

Overgenerality from Inference in Perspective-Taking 194
  Timothy Clausner, Christopher Maxey, Matthew D. Goldberg,
  Paul Zaidins, Justin Brody, Darsana Josyula, and Don Perlis

Tools for Improving ASI

Using Features at Multiple Temporal and Spatial Resolutions to Predict
Human Behavior in Real Time 205
  Liang Zhang, Justin Lieffers, and Adarsh Pyarelal

Route Optimization in Service of a Search and Rescue Artificial Social
Intelligence Agent 220
  Yunzhe Wang, Nikolos Gurney, Jincheng Zhou, David V. Pynadath,
  and Volkan Ustun

Author Index 229

Theory of Mind

Operationalizing Theories of Theory of Mind: A Survey

Nikolos Gurney[2]([✉])[ID], Stacy Marsella[3][ID], Volkan Ustun[2][ID],
and David V. Pynadath[1,2][ID]

[1] USC Viterbi School of Engineering, Computer Science Department,
Los Angeles, USA
[2] USC Institute for Creative Technologies, Los Angeles, USA
{gurney,ustun,pynadath}@ict.usc.edu
[3] Northeastern University Khoury College of Computer Sciences, Boston, USA
s.marsella@northeastern.edu

Abstract. Human social interaction hinges on the ability to interpret
and predict the actions of others. The most valuable explanatory variable
of these actions, more important than environmental or social factors, is
the one that we do not have direct access to: the mind. This lack of access
leaves us to impute the mental states—beliefs, desires, emotions, intentions, etc.—of others before we can explain their behaviors. Studying
our ability to do so, our Theory of Mind, has long been the province of
psychologists and philosophers. Computational scientists are increasingly
joining this research space as they strive to imbue artificial intelligences
with human-like characteristics. We provide a high-level review of Theory of Mind research across several domains, with the goal of mapping
between theory and recursive agent models. We illustrate this mapping
using a specific recursive agent architecture, PsychSim, and discuss how
it addresses many of the open issues in Theory of Mind research by
enforcing a set of minimal requirements.

Keywords: Artificial social intelligence · Theory of mind ·
Human-machine teams

1 Introduction

Our goal is to communicate to you a set of propositional attitudes (cognitive
states such as beliefs or desires) related to developing an artificial intelligence
helper agent (AI helper). Philosophers and psychologists have long posited that
such communication requires knowing the mental states of both the listener *and*
oneself. As convenient as it would be, we do not have direct access to your mental
states nor our own. This means that if our goal is to communicate our position

N. Gurney and G. Sukthankar (Eds.): AAAI-FSS 2021, LNCS 13775, pp. 3–20, 2022.
https://doi.org/10.1007/978-3-031-21671-8_1

effectively (it is) we must impute these states. The capacity to do so is commonly known as *Theory of Mind* (ToM; [63]).[1]

Imagine that we were slightly more intrepid authors who thought it would be easier to enlist an AI helper to author our manuscript. The fundamental communication problem, that of understanding the mental states of its readers and the author team, would persist for the AI helper. Moreover, we believe that it is reasonable to assume that access to its own mental states would make the AI helper better at its task (because then it could consider how its beliefs about you or us might factor into its work). When the helper explains a technical term, for example, it may want to assess the accuracy of its belief of your degree of belief that it has accurately depicted the term. In other words, the AI helper needs a ToM.

We are academics and as such it behooves us to share our opinions. It is only natural then that we would not just turn the AI helper loose and accept whatever it produced. We undoubtedly would find ways to insert ourselves into its process, to team with it as a sort of human-AI collective intelligence [33], in hopes of producing a high quality paper that reflects our positions. The success of our human-AI team largely hinges on trust [6,35,81,82]. For the human members of our team, trust is grounded in our assessment of the AI's abilities—critically, its level of intelligence [22]. Again, we believe that a robust theory of mind, in this instance for its human teammates, will facilitate the AI's success. Herein we review a subset of the vast literature on human social cognition, specifically focusing on ToM, and discuss implementation of myriad theories and models in such an AI helper using PsychSim, a recursive agent architecture. Critically, the PsychSim implementation enforces a set of minimal requirements that we believe reveals the strengths and weaknesses of different ToM theories.

2   PsychSim

This basic description of a PsychSim agent and its machinery will serve as a framework for comparing ToM theories. PsychSim is a social simulation platform with the capacity to implement psychologically valid theories of human behavior [66]. It uses a recursive architecture, meaning that it applies the same rules repeatedly to generate outputs [24]. Each agent in a PsychSim simulation possesses a fully specified decision-theoretic model, i.e. model of choices based on a utility framework, of itself and the other agents in its environment. Most importantly, the platform readily facilitates modeling beliefs, including those related to ToM [53]. A PsychSim-based AI helper thus has a model of itself, for each of its teammates, and potentially for the team holistically which it can use to simulate different scenarios and base recommendations on, just like our hypothetical paper mill agent.

---

[1] This name is somewhat fraught due to its implication that the development of an explicit theory is part of the underlying cognitive process. Adding to the confusion, cognitive and computational scientists often refer to how researchers have a theory of mind about how the mind works [59]. We adopt it, nevertheless, due to its universal recognition.

The minimal requirements for creating an AI helper with ToM using a recursive agent architecture, such as PsychSim, are:

(i) A framework for inferring beliefs, from observations, about others.
(ii) A means of translating these beliefs into predictions about behaviors.
(iii) A way of handling higher order reasoning (you believe that he believes that she believes...).

Partially observable Markov decision processes (POMDPs) are the backbone of PsychSim and fill each of these requirements. The POMDP framework posits that an agent assumes system variables, such as other agents, follow stochastic processes (MDPs) which it cannot fully observe. MDPs are characterized by a set of states, actions, probabilities of given actions for each state, and rewards associated with arriving in particular states. The task of an agent in an environment modeled by an MDP is simply observing the current state and potential rewards of each available action then selecting the best option given the data. States are not directly observable in the partially observable generalization of MDPs, so the agent must gather outcome information. The agent maintains models of itself and the other agents that it updates based on this information to overcome the observability obstacle. Similar to the use of recursive models in *interactive* POMDPs (I-POMDPs) [23], these models take the form of probability distributions for its observations given the state of the system and models of the stochastic processes followed by the agents in the system. The POMDPs of an agent generally rely on utility-based functions to model behavior.

3 Theories About Theory of Mind

Humans gather, process, and create information about the actions of other agents in their environment—a set of information processing behaviors collectively called social cognition [15]. Like most domains of human cognition, that is where the consensus on social cognition ends and debate begins. In the case of ToM, which is widely considered a subdomain of social cognition, there are at least three theoretical explanations of human ToM: theory, simulation theory, and more recently, arguments for social cognition without ToM. Recursive agent models, including PsychSim, share many features with all of these explanations.

A set of minimal requirements for ToM reasoning will help illustrate the strengths and weaknesses of each theoretical position as well as clarify the approaches that recursive agent models take. It is our argument that the three requirements of developing a recursive agent architecture that we enumerated above can also serve as coarse but critical requirements for ToM theories.

3.1 Theory-Theory

Modern inquiry into how humans think about and represent the mental states of others is frequently traced back to Heider and Simmel's [37] famous geometric shapes experiment. The basic paradigm involves participants watching interacting geometric shapes and reporting what they saw. In a classic scene, three shapes move around the screen. One shape quickly moves towards another shape while a third shape later moves in between them. This ground breaking experiment revealed that participants, almost universally, ascribed agency to the shapes. For example, participants said that the above scenario depicted an aggressor, victim, and third party who intervened to stop the aggression (Fig. 1).

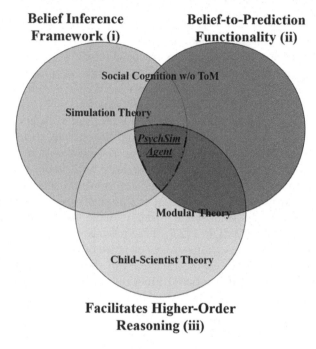

Fig. 1. The three minimal requirements of implementing ToM reasoning in a PsychSim agent and our subjective assessment of where major ToM theories fall in the space of these requirements. We argue that these requirements are also applicable to actual ToM reasoning and can serve as a means of evaluating theories and models.

Although Heider faltered in arguing that such abilities result from direct access to our own internal mental states [36], his work with Simmel precipitated the first recognizable version of theory-theory from the philosopher Wilfred Sellars [73]. Sellars took the position that we develop, via experiences and enculturation, a naive theory to explain the mental states of our peers. In other words, we function as lay scientists developing and testing tacit theories about our social world based on input from the people around us, social observations, and even rudimentary experimentation. This position would eventually come to be known as theory-theory and finds most of its empirical support in adaptions of Wimmer and Perner's false belief task [83].[2]

---

[2] The false belief task has proven extremely productive for the scientific community. Review of experimental methods is not in the scope of this paper, however it is worth noting that the false belief task and the empirical designs that followed in its footsteps likely have numerous flaws [5,38,67,80].

The conceptual account of theory-theory maps relatively cleanly to a PsychSim agent. As will become clear, PsychSim offers a formalization of ToM requirements i and ii where theory-theorists do not. Using the lay scientist analogy, the PsychSim agent's research methods, or the ways in which it formalizes and answers hypotheses, are POMDPs. A PsychSim agent typically assumes that other agents in its environment are using POMDPs for their decision-making as well. Each time a PsychSim agent makes an observation, it updates it beliefs about how the agents and environment work. In the case of agents, it assumes that they are trying to maximize their utility. This renders the accuracy of its model, which determines its ability to predict how another agent will respond to a stimulus, contingent on its prior experiences. Importantly, any interpretation it makes of a person's behavior is thus circumscribed to be goal-driven via the maximization of some utility function. Even if the observed behavior is generated by an arbitrary stochastic process, the PsychSim agent will form posterior beliefs over a candidate set of POMDPs based on how well their corresponding behaviors would match the observed behavior.

Child-Scientists. The child-scientist theory for ToM development is arguably the truest to Sellars' original vision and the most common among theory-theorist. Like many scientific perspectives, it started as an analogy to better understand how humans might develop the ability to represent others' minds. Its most ardent supporters, however, take it beyond the analogical insights and argue that philosophy of science's theory development processes are actual blueprints for how cognition transpires [27,30,44,62]. Theories are viewed as systems that assign specific representations to inputs, similar to how the visual system assigns representations to input. These systems are not rigid, particularly in early development. Just like a young child refines her interpretation of visual input from a single representation for fuzzy, four-legged creatures (dog) to a multitude of representations (cat, horse, sheep, etc.), she refines her representations for the various processes that underpin the behavior of agents in her social world.

Proponents of the child-scientist view generally subscribe to one of two explanations for the brain's ToM mechanism: a general purpose (domain-general) or modular (domain-specific) learning mechanism. The child-scientist perspective adopts the former, i.e. there is a generalized psychological structure that supports learning across domains. This general purpose learning mechanism is supported by a suite of reflexes, or cognitive capabilities, that are present from birth [29]. Together, the learning mechanism and reflexes exploit sensorimotor interactions with the environment to form theories, or models, of how the world works. These theories empower a child to not only understand her environment, but also solve increasingly complex prediction problems, including those that are classically social. The Bayesian flavor of all this is no fluke. Formalizations of domain-general mechanisms frequently take Bayesian forms [18,28,52].

Theory theorists can readily handle our requirement iii. A lay ToM scientist trying to workout higher-order beliefs simply needs to establish a hypothesis, test it, and update accordingly. The testing can even happen in situ by imagining various outcomes given a set of beliefs. Items i and ii present bigger challenges. The child-scientist approach is to assume that ToM is handled by a learning mechanism used in other types of learning, like the statistical learning mechanism proposed for vision and audition [43]. There is reasonable evidence that suggests domain-general mechanisms support ToM reasoning. For example, when a person is under cognitive load their performance in social reasoning tasks may decrease [54]. This is, of course, only correlational and not causal.

The PsychSim agent uses maximum expected utility as its domain-independent theory of reasoning, one that also acts as a constraint on its theory of others. Within that constraint, it is free to choose an arbitrary set of (possibly recursive) POMDPs as its model of those others. Like a developing human, it is possible to specify a PsychSim agent that starts with a small set of simple (e.g., short horizon, few goals) POMDPs. These are analogous to the child's theories for how the world works. Experience allows it to continually expand that set when none of its current candidates satisfactorily explain its experiences in social interaction.

Modular Theory. Cognitive modularity suggests that the brain has a fixed architecture. One perspective argues that this structure limits the flow and processing of information. The edges of modules, or regions, in the brain function as filters that can be uni- or bi-directional. That is, some of the information inside the module may not be available outside or vice versa [16]. Although theorists conceptualize the modules as rigid units, they generally offer a bit of hand waving when pressed on the actual degree of modularity [16,71]. The alternative view of modularity is knowledge-centric, meaning that rather than the brain having distinct modules for processing information, they store it. This allows for flexible skill and belief systems to process across these core systems of object representation [77]. Modular explanations for ToM generally adopt the former position and posit a distinct functional system in the brain which comes online during childhood development [47,48,50,71].

Alan Leslie's Theory of Mind Mechanism/Selection Processing is arguably the dominant modular explanation [46,47,49,72]. Leslie and colleagues argue that ToM is innate and that there is a unique mechanism which yields representations solely for related reasoning. This mechanism, much like puberty, is genetically present (innate) and activated by environmental factors. They do not, however, argue that this mechanism is responsible for all ToM abilities—just that it has a specific innate basis and a function unique to ToM reasoning. The mechanism part of the theory stipulates that the ToM module automatically processes perceptual information about behaviors and computes what mental states may have produced them. Because this process is algorithmic and spontaneous, it is prone to errors, be they from biased learning or learned heuristics. This necessitates a supplemental, executive system that overrides the module's salient outputs when they are unwanted. In the case of a false belief task, the mechanism yields a true belief about the state of the world (the actual location of the hidden object). The selection processing overrides this belief to yield an accurate ToM for the target (who has a false belief about the object location).

Modular theorists attempt a more direct approach to meeting requirements ii and iii than their child-scientists counterparts, but stop short of pointing to an actual module in the brain that handles inference (i) or prediction (ii). The ToM module handles belief inference and the translation of these beliefs into predictions, both of which can be exported to other regions of the brain for various purposes. Unlike vision or audition researchers, however, modular theorists offer inconclusive evidence for where in the brain the module exists and about the algorithmic way in which perceptual information about behaviors is processed [70].

Most recursive agent models are modular, in an information processing sense, by default. PsychSim encapsulate the models of different agents and at different recursive depths so that information cannot flow between the models except along edges in the corresponding influence diagram. This means that a unique model exists for processing information about each agent and these models output information that flows between them to account for their interactions. Furthermore, while both the agent's decision-making and its ToM models of others use the same decision-theoretic algorithms, there are typically computational shortcuts taken in the ToM models that are not used for the agent's own more thorough reasoning. For example, PsychSim ToM POMDPs are usually more abstract than the actual POMDPs used for behavior generation. This abstraction can be achieved by removing variables from the POMDP that have limited or no influence on the modeling agent's utility [64]. Removing these variables, however, does introduce uncertainty. PsychSim usually handles this by implementing a softmax, instead of strict maximization function, which is more forgiving of any errors that may result of the uncertainty. The resulting POMDP is smaller (and thus faster) than the original.

3.2   Simulation Theory

In its simplest form, simulation theory says that we understand and predict the mental states of others by trying to simulate them within ourselves [31]. This yields a very straightforward means of achieving ToM: repurposing the psychological machinery used for our own cognition to gain insight into the cognition of others. Doing so implies a two part process: first, generate imaginary mental states that correspond to the target's mental states, and second, feed those mental states into the appropriate mechanism(s) to generate an output. The simulator is thus capable of producing feasible explanations of behavior whenever they make decisions in a manner roughly similar to the target [25]. Simulation theorists argue that this yields a much more efficient ToM than any proposed by theory-theorists.

Theory-theory is constrained by high-level reasoning: the need to actively think about the cognitive state of another person to test and validate a naive theory about their every behavior is likely intractable for humans. Because of this, theory-theory is a poor candidate for explaining the seemingly automatic human capacity for detecting subtle social cues. If we had to stop to ponder on the expression of emotions, like a slight twitch in the face that is indicative of anger, we would frequently find ourselves in grave danger. Simulation theorist argue, however, that it is very capable of explaining low-level phenomena, like automatic detection of a fear response in another person. It is plausible that mirror neurons are the basis for this capability [19], but the evidence for mirror neurons in humans is largely inferred rather than observed. Invasive procedures are necessary to observe mirror neurons, which is why the vast majority of studies reporting on them appear in the animal literature [69], save a single notable example in humans [58].

It is very plausible that ToM involves two (or more) distinct systems, possibly both theory-theory and simulation theory processes [1,12,25,39,51,56,61]. Goldman [25], for example, suggests that theorizing might play an important, even dominant, role in "high-level mind reading," which he defines as imaginative simulation that is conscious, actively controlled imputation of others' mental states. This supplements unconscious, simulation-based mind reading that handles simple mental states (e.g. detecting emotional states such as fear from facial expressions). Heyes and Frith [39] adopt the terms implicit and explicit to describe neurocognitively inherited and encultured skills respectively. The implicit mechanisms are present from birth and play a vital role in formulating accurate expectations about the behavior of agents. Further, they accept that the outputs of an implicit system may inform the explicit system by preprocessing observed behavior in a way that facilitates categorization. They make clear, however, that they do not believe this to be sufficient for the sort of complex ToM observed in mature humans.

Whereas theory-theory explanations are vague about the mechanism that handles inferences, requirement i, simulation theory is much more direct: the mechanisms that we use for our own behavior are repurposed for ToM. Predictions about behavior then become a simple task of running the belief outputs through the same system that determines our behavior. This account implies that we can, in a sense, re-enter the machinery we use for our own cognition. Before the discovery of mirror neurons this was pure speculation, and to a large extent it still is given the lack of human evidence related to mirror neurons.

Unlike a human, there is a clear way for a PsychSim agent to re-enter the machinery that it uses to understand its social world. PsychSim agents explicitly use their POMDP models of others to generate expectations of their behavior. In particular, they apply their own POMDP solution algorithms to the variables, graph structures, and parameters they (possibly incorrectly) ascribe to others' POMDPs. An agent will use this capability to simulate the outcomes of each of its alternate actions, evaluating those outcomes against their utility function, and choosing the behavior that maximizes that expectation. It will also use this simulation capability to evaluate alternate explanations of observed behaviors in terms of their likelihood, which in turn causes its update its belief in those explanations.

3.3   First-Person ToM and Introspection

Both theory-theory and simulation theory posit that first-person ToM plays an important role in our social capabilities [25, 26]. There is division, however, over whether we have direct access to our internal states to make use of during first-person ToM reasoning. Gopnik [26] argues that even though people may believe their first-person knowledge is derived from experience, it actually comes from the same theory of mind system that explains the behaviors of other agents. This is because, as she argues, we lack direct access to the psychological process underlying out own behavior. Goldman [25], on the other hand, claims that we do have direct access to the psychological processes behind our behaviors. Moreover, it is his position that first-person theory of mind development precedes and is necessary for third-person abilities. An alternative simulation account is that ToM always has a "target" agent and the simulation is the same whether it is first or third person, implying that there is no direct access to internal mental states [32].

PsychSim is equipped to do all the above. First, it has two mechanisms for an agent to reason about its own behavior: via direct access to its "true" POMDP, or via a perceived POMDP. The latter may deviate from the former, just as its POMDP models of others can deviate from their true models. It is agnostic, however, about the timing of when a first-person ToM comes online. In theory, it could be inhibited or prioritized, but PsychSim implementations generally have everything happen simultaneously.

3.4   Social Cognition Without ToM

There are numerous, defensible explanations of how humans anticipate and respond to other agents that do not involve any of the classic ToM processes. Game Theory supplies many examples and one of the most recognizable: the tit-for-tat strategy [2, 68]. An agent who uses this strategy in a social interaction first cooperates and then in every subsequent interaction simply replicates the behavior of the other agent(s). The tit-for-tat model of behavior easily explains complex human behavior, such as reciprocal altruism [9, 79], without appealing to complex ToM processes. Economic theorists have posited rich social behaviors, including cooperation, emerge from learned and automated rules, i.e. social norm heuristics [8, 13]. Such heuristics may circumvent the need for deliberate self constraint—which would need to emerge from ToM reasoning—when an agent faces no risks from taking advantage of another agent [21, 57].

Other behaviors are executed according to what psychologist call scripts [7] and artificial intelligence researchers call frames [55]. A script (frame) includes a set of elements, descriptions of what those elements can do, outcomes given combinations of the various elements, and is composed of scenes. Walking into a corner market, picking up a package of candy, and paying for it at the register can all happen without explicit ToM when a script is in place. You do not have to reason about the attendant wanting money from you in exchange for your snack—the script dictates all the necessary behaviors for the social interaction.

While POMDPs are the core part of PsychSim's base architecture, there are occasions where it has been convenient to bypass decision-theoretic reasoning altogether and directly encode an agent's policy. The form of this policy is a piecewise-linear decision tree. It can capture behaviors that are reminiscent of ToM, but do not require the complete machinery. Although these sort of policies are closer in spirit to frames, they are conceptually the same thing as a script and can be implemented in recursive agents when warranted [65].

4   Modeling Theory of Mind

A complete model of ToM reasoning will have a framework for inferring beliefs about others, a way to translate those beliefs into predictions, and the capacity to handle higher order reasoning. Researchers have formalized the proposed theoretical structures of ToM in a diversity of ways. Many models are grounded in paradigms with rich histories in computational research including reinforcement learning (RL), partially observable Markov decision processes (POMDPs), utility maximization, and Bayesian inference. Additionally, modelers take both-model based and model-free approaches [17, 20, 40]. Model-based approaches are prospective, meaning that they assume a goal and active cognition, often referred to as system II thinking [41]. Model-free approaches, on the other hand, are retrospective and capable of capturing habitual cognition, i.e. Kahneman's system I thinking. Each modeling approach comes packaged with a suite of benefits and laundry list of short comings that effect its ability to capture the nuances of ToM reasoning. Moreover, there are costs and benefits when implementing the myriad models in an AI helper. The shortlist of exemplars included here is far from exhaustive, but we believe each merits consideration when designing AI helpers for human-machine teams.

4.1   Bayesian Inference

Bayesian approaches to ToM often conceptualize the observing agent as forming a hypothesis about the target's behavior. This hypothesis is evaluated given observable data and under the constraints of an underlying theory of behavior in a very theory-theory fashion [3, 4, 28, 78]. This allows for ToM to be cast as an inverse planning and inference task. When a person observes another's actions, she answers the ToM problem (implicitly) by assuming that the other person made the decision based on data, that likely includes beliefs, and according to some model of how to act in the world which approximates rationality. Next she attempts to invert this model of how to act by applying Bayesian inference: integrate the likelihood of her observations with a prior over mental states. The output becomes her ToM for the other's behavior. In one computational example of this, a target agent's plans and inferences are formalized as POMDPs that capture propositional attitudes (e.g. desires and beliefs) via utility functions and probability distributions respectively [4]. The target is assumed to be approximately rational, i.e. the target is utility maximizing. Inverting the target's forward model using Bayesian inference yields the observer's ToM model of the target.

Bayesian models of ToM not only offer a handy way of operationalizing an opaque set of cognitive processes, they also facilitate other important capabilities for adaptive agents. For example, if an observer has reason to believe that a target is knowledgeable, then she can adapt the Bayesian process used for ToM reasoning to learn how to act or refine her beliefs [74]. Or, if an observer is observing a group of targets, rather than attempting to compute a ToM for each target, she can adopt a model that represents the "average" member of the group and rely on it to make inferences and predictions about how the individuals within the group may act [42]. Importantly, the same Bayesian machinery used to model basic social cognitive processes can be used in modeling affective cognition [14,60].

POMDPs are one of the most common means of capturing the prior-observation-update-posterior belief pipeline of reasoning depicted by Bayesian ToM theories. One of the earliest examples of a Bayesian theory of mind also used a POMDP-based architecture [75]. And, as we have explictly noted, this is what PsychSim implements for its agent models.

4.2 Game Theory and Economics

Economists use game theory to model how economic agents think about and respond to the mental states of others [11]. For a given model, the "game" is captured by a mathematical description of the strategies and associated payoffs available to each agent. Games often have multiple stages during which agents choose actions to execute from a limited set, can be competitive or cooperative, and range in length from a single shot to (theoretically) infinite number of rounds. Every agent is assumed to hold beliefs, which are captured as probability distributions, about the available actions, progress of the game, and even beliefs of other agents. Importantly, games are structured such that predictions about a player's behavior can be derived without any observations.

In game-theoretic approaches to modeling ToM, each agent generally has a policy over strategies that dictate how it will behave given a set of conditions—including inferences of other agents' policies and observed behaviors. This policy is subject to a state-dependent value that the agent is attempting to optimize for in a particular game setting. Each agent has a level of *sophistication* that describes the degree to which it considers the depth of other agents' models of it [11,84].

Rousseau's stag hunt problem is a classic example of a social dilemma easily captured by game theory. Two hunters must independently decide whether to hunt a stag or hare. Hunting a stag successfully requires input form both hunters and results in each hunter garnering a greater reward (more meat). Hunting a hare can be accomplished without coordination, but also has a lower payoff. There is a risk to choosing to hunt a stag in that if the other hunter pursues hare, you will go hungry. This simplified game has two strategies (hunting a hare or stag) and the value function hinges on the amount of meat from each strategy. Each hunter has a model of the other hunter's likelihood of selecting stag that includes the other's beliefs about herself. The concept of sophistication captures how many recursions an agent considers in her model. In line with Herbert Simon's famous work on the bounds of human rationality, people generally do not go much beyond two-step logic [10, 76].

Game theoretic models can capture a number of interesting social behaviors, but they fall short of explaining the rich set of mental gymnastics that comprises social cognition. That does not mean that these models are out of place in recursive agent architectures. Situations arise when the decision-theoretic models are overly cumbersome and a simple heuristic, like tit-for-tat, is warranted. In practice, these are implemented as explicit policies [65].

4.3   Reinforcement Learning

The basic concept of model-based RL is to combine a world model and reward function to produce a policy. The world model is a learned, simplified model of an agent's environment and used to make predictions about future states of the world. Reward functions can take many forms, but frequently a cost minimization or benefit maximization function of the world model's accuracy is implemented. In essence, these are models of what an agent "ought" to do. If a food item tastes good (bad), it ought (not) to eat it and (or) be rewarded with the good (bad) flavor. The policy is the sequence of actions that an agent uses in pursuit of a goal and generated, or learned, from the repeated combination of the world model and reward function. If we assume that a mind functions via model-based RL, then predicting mental states from observable behavior can take the same form as *inverse* RL.

IRL involves an observer agent that tries to learn a target's utility function given repeated decision observations. In its simplest form, this requires a state space, an action space, and transition function which are modeled as a Markov decision process. Although powerful, this is computationally expensive—vast numbers of labeled training examples are required in order to infer a reward function from a policy (set of observed states and actions) and transition function, which is frequently a researcher degree of freedom [45]. A human infant with an IRL-based ToM would need hundreds of thousands of labeled training examples a day [40].

5   Discussion

Evaluating, especially comparing, theory about and modeling approaches to ToM reasoning is challenging. We believe that this challenge arises because theorists and modelers approach ToM without a unifying set of requirements for ToM reasoning. This leads to the value of their unique perspectives being lost to the variance in their interpretation of the problem. As we have illustrated, such a set of requirements is indispensable when comparing different approaches and perspectives. Theories that only focus on how humans handle higher order reasoning, for example, are hard to compare to those that are primarily concerned with a framework for inferring beliefs. Developing and deploying artificial agent systems, such as PsychSim, forces not only acknowledging the need to take a stance on the minimal requirements of ToM reasoning, but implementing and validating them as well.

Theory-theory approaches that do not specify a belief inference framework or its origin are incomplete. Without a framework, it is not possible to falsify a theory because simple adjustments to the mechanism that produces inputs, i.e. beliefs, that support ToM reasoning alter the theory's accuracy. This is particularly important for accounts that claim ToM is acquired rather than innate. ToM input-output data are scarce. This leaves researchers in the position of being able to select from a vast array of candidate functions the one that best fits the data and their theory. Validating their selection from the legions of alternatives is not possible, however, given the data paucity. Thus their claim becomes this is the acquired function because it fits the data and our model.

If ToM is innate, then the fundamental difference between the theory and simulation perspective is simply the inference mechanism. All that the theory-theorists are saying is that we do not know the mechanism, however it is not *that* mechanism. This again leaves them in a position to select whatever mechanism works with the data and their theory. Meanwhile, the simulation account of a repurposed mechanism leads to a paradox. If it is the same mechanism that we use for our own behavior, it must be one which can be re-entered or that supports recursion. This is necessary for the third item in our list, higher order reasoning, but not necessarily for behavior. This suggests that the mechanism was not repurposed, but designed/evolved with the capability for ToM.

A theory without a belief translation mechanism is also hard to falsify. This is because, like not having a belief inference framework, all it takes is a convenient function to make your theory valid. And again, the lack of data makes it challenging, if not impossible, to validate whether a given functional form is correct. This makes it impossible to validate the entire pipeline. A model that lacks the first or second item and only specifies a way of handling higher order reasoning, like many perspectives in the theory-theory camp do, lacks the needed structure to test its validity.

Explanations for social cognition without the higher order reasoning that typifies ToM face the challenge of exploding complexity and generalization. Scripts and frames can account for social interactions and do not need higher order reasoning, but scripting every class of social interaction would quickly become intractable for humans as the number agents and levels of reasoning increase.

All of these challenges to existing modeling and theoretical approaches to ToM reasoning point to the need for a more holistic account. Recursive agent models, like PsychSim, force researchers into taking a position on each requirement. PsychSim assumes that ToM reasoning follows a POMDP framework. The same framework is repurposed for learning about the environment, making predictions about behaviors, and higher order reasoning. Game Theory and reinforcement learning offer framework alternatives, but we believe each has a fundamental flaw. If an agent implemented a pure reinforcement learning approach, like direct policy search, it would need a way to down select to a good set of candidate policies from the vast set of possible policies. This adds a new requirement for ToM reasoning and it is possibly intractable as each new variable for consideration increases the complexity of the policy selection task. A purely game-theoretic approach would mean specifying the details for each game that an agent may enter and knowing when to use each unique game, i.e. belief inference framework. Again, the complexity of a system based entirely on this approach quickly grows intractable.

Lastly, PsychSim is more than just an approach to modeling ToM. Because it is modular, adding additional capabilities becomes trivial, which renders it a general mechanism for artificial cognition and makes it a good candidate for a unifying modeling tool [34]. This is already demonstrated in the literature. The PsychSim approach, for example, can implicitly generate the appraisals found in appraisal theories of emotion [75]. Also, its decision theoretic approach to ToM constrained mental models of others into exhibiting preference ordering [66].

6   Conclusion

There are numerous theories and modeling approaches that attempt to capture the essence of human theory of mind. The development of an agent capable of a similar level of ToM reasoning reveals where each theory and approach may falter. The requirements of creating such an agent, we believe, are also minimal requirements for actual ToM reasoning. Combining these requirements with lessons learned from attempts to explain and model ToM holds the potential of producing a more complete, viable theory.

Acknowledgements. Part of the effort depicted is sponsored by the U.S. Defense Advanced Research Projects Agency (DARPA) under contract number W911NF2010011, and that the content of the information does not necessarily reflect the position or the policy of the Government or the Defense Advanced Research Projects Agency, and no official endorsements should be inferred.

References

1. Apperly, I.A., Butterfill, S.A.: Do humans have two systems to track beliefs and belief-like states? Psychol. Rev. **116**(4), 953 (2009)
2. Axelrod, R., Hamilton, W.D.: The evolution of cooperation. Science **211**(4489), 1390–1396 (1981)
3. Baker, C.L., Saxe, R., Tenenbaum, J.B.: Action understanding as inverse planning. Cognition **113**(3), 329–349 (2009)
4. Baker, C.L., Tenenbaum, J.B., Saxe, R.: Bayesian models of human action understanding. In: Advances in Neural Information Processing Systems, vol. 18, p. 99 (2006)

5. Bloom, P., German, T.P.: Two reasons to abandon the false belief task as a test of theory of mind. Cognition **77**(1), B25–B31 (2000)
6. Bonaccio, S., Dalal, R.S.: Advice taking and decision-making: an integrative literature review, and implications for the organizational sciences. Organ. Behav. Hum. Decis. Process. **101**(2), 127–151 (2006)
7. Bower, G.H., Black, J.B., Turner, T.J.: Scripts in memory for text. Cogn. Psychol. **11**(2), 177–220 (1979)
8. Bowles, S., Gintis, H.: The origins of human cooperation. In: Hammerstein, P. (ed.) The Genetic and Cultural Origins of Cooperation (2003)
9. Brosnan, S.F., De Waal, F.B.: A proximate perspective on reciprocal altruism. Hum. Nat. **13**(1), 129–152 (2002)
10. Camerer, C.F.: Behavioural studies of strategic thinking in games. Trends Cogn. Sci. **7**(5), 225–231 (2003)
11. Camerer, C.F.: Behavioral Game Theory: Experiments in Strategic Interaction. Princeton University Press (2011)
12. Carruthers, P.: Two systems for mindreading? Rev. Philos. Psychol. **7**(1), 141–162 (2016)
13. Chudek, M., Henrich, J.: Culture-gene coevolution, norm-psychology and the emergence of human prosociality. Trends Cogn. Sci. **15**(5), 218–226 (2011)
14. D'Mello, S., Kappas, A., Gratch, J.: The affective computing approach to affect measurement. Emot. Rev. **10**(2), 174–183 (2018)
15. Fiske, S.T., Taylor, S.E.: Social Cognition: From Brains to Culture. Sage (2021)
16. Fodor, J.A.: The Modularity of Mind. MIT Press (1983)
17. Friston, K., FitzGerald, T., Rigoli, F., Schwartenbeck, P., Pezzulo, G., et al.: Active inference and learning. Neurosci. Biobehav. Rev. **68**, 862–879 (2016)
18. Frost, R., Armstrong, B.C., Siegelman, N., Christiansen, M.H.: Domain generality versus modality specificity: the paradox of statistical learning. Trends Cogn. Sci. **19**(3), 117–125 (2015)
19. Gallese, V., Goldman, A.: Mirror neurons and the simulation theory of mind-reading. Trends Cogn. Sci. **2**(12), 493–501 (1998)
20. Gershman, S.J., Gerstenberg, T., Baker, C.L., Cushman, F.A.: Plans, habits, and theory of mind. PLoS ONE **11**(9), e0162246 (2016)
21. Gigerenzer, G., Gaissmaier, W.: Heuristic decision making. Annu. Rev. Psychol. **62**, 451–482 (2011)
22. Glikson, E., Woolley, A.W.: Human trust in artificial intelligence: review of empirical research. Acad. Manag. Ann. **14**(2), 627–660 (2020)
23. Gmytrasiewicz, P.J., Doshi, P.: A framework for sequential planning in multi-agent settings. J. Artif. Intell. Res. **24**, 49–79 (2005)
24. Gmytrasiewicz, P.J., Durfee, E.H.: A rigorous, operational formalization of recursive modeling. In: ICMAS, pp. 125–132 (1995)
25. Goldman, A.: Simulating Minds: The Philosophy, Psychology, and Neuroscience of Mindreading. Oxford University Press on Demand (2006)
26. Gopnik, A.: How we know our minds: the illusion of·first-person knowledge of intentionality. Behav. Brain Sci. **16**(1), 1–14 (1993)
27. Gopnik, A.: The scientist as child. Philos. Sci. **63**(4), 485–514 (1996)
28. Gopnik, A., Glymour, C., Sobel, D.M., Schulz, L.E., Kushnir, T., Danks, D.: A theory of causal learning in children: causal maps and bayes nets. Psychol. Rev. **111**(1), 3 (2004)
29. Gopnik, A., Meltzoff, A.N.: Minds, bodies and persons: young children's understanding of the self and others as reflected in imitation and theory of mind

research, pp. 166–186. Cambridge University Press (1994). https://doi.org/10.1017/CBO9780511565526.012

30. Gopnik, A., Meltzoff, A.N., Kuhl, P.K.: The Scientist in the Crib: Minds, Brains, and How Children Learn. William Morrow & Co. (1999)

31. Gordon, R.M.: Folk psychology as simulation. Mind Lang. **1**(2), 158–171 (1986)

32. Gordon, R.M.: Simulation without introspection or inference from me to you. In: Davies, M., Stone, T. (eds.) Mental Simulation. Blackwell (1995)

33. Gupta, P., Woolley, A.W.: Articulating the role of artificial intelligence in collective intelligence: a transactive systems framework. In: Proceedings of the Human Factors and Ergonomics Society (Forthcoming)

34. Gurney, N., Pynadath, D.V.: Robots with theory of mind for humans: a survey. In: 20212 31st IEEE International Conference on Robot & Human Interactive Communication (RO-MAN). IEEE (2022)

35. Gurney, N., Pynadath, D.V., Wang, N.: Measuring and predicting human trust in recommendations from an AI teammate. In: Degen, H., Ntoa, S. (eds.) HCII 2022. LNCS, vol. 13336, pp. 22–34. Springer, Cham (2022). https://doi.org/10.1007/978-3-031-05643-7_2

36. Heider, F.: The Psychology of Interpersonal Relations. Lawrence Erlbaum Associates, Inc. (1958)

37. Heider, F., Simmel, M.: An experimental study of apparent behavior. Am. J. Psychol. **57**(2), 243–259 (1944)

38. Heyes, C.: Submentalizing: I am not really reading your mind. Perspect. Psychol. Sci. **9**(2), 131–143 (2014)

39. Heyes, C.M., Frith, C.D.: The cultural evolution of mind reading. Science **344**(6190) (2014)

40. Jara-Ettinger, J.: Theory of mind as inverse reinforcement learning. Curr. Opin. Behav. Sci. **29**, 105–110 (2019)

41. Kahneman, D.: Thinking, Fast and Slow. Macmillan (2011)

42. Khalvati, K., et al.: Modeling other minds: Bayesian inference explains human choices in group decision-making. Sci. Adv. **5**(11), eaax8783 (2019)

43. Kirkham, N.Z., Slemmer, J.A., Johnson, S.P.: Visual statistical learning in infancy: evidence for a domain general learning mechanism. Cognition **83**(2), B35–B42 (2002)

44. Kuhn, D.: Children and adults as intuitive scientists. Psychol. Rev. **96**(4), 674 (1989)

45. Lake, B.M., Ullman, T.D., Tenenbaum, J.B., Gershman, S.J.: Building machines that learn and think like people. Behav. Brain Sci. **40** (2017)

46. Leslie, A.M.: Pretense and representation: the origins of "theory of mind". Psychol. Rev. **94**(4), 412 (1987)

47. Leslie, A.M.: Pretending and believing: issues in the theory of ToMM. Cognition **50**(1–3), 211–238 (1994)

48. Leslie, A.M.: ToMM, ToBy, and agency: core architecture and domain specificity. Mapp. Mind Domain Specificity Cogn. Cult. **29**, 119–148 (1994)

49. Leslie, A.M.: How to acquire a 'representational theory of mind'. metarepresentations: a multidisciplinary perspective, pp. 197–223 (2000)

50. Leslie, A.M., Friedman, O., German, T.P.: Core mechanisms in 'theory of mind'. Trends Cogn. Sci. **8**(12), 528–533 (2004)

51. Low, J., Apperly, I.A., Butterfill, S.A., Rakoczy, H.: Cognitive architecture of belief reasoning in children and adults: a primer on the two-systems account. Child Dev. Perspect. **10**(3), 184–189 (2016)

52. Lu, H., Yuille, A.L., Liljeholm, M., Cheng, P.W., Holyoak, K.J.: Bayesian generic priors for causal learning. Psychol. Rev. **115**(4), 955 (2008)
53. Marsella, S.C., Pynadath, D.V., Read, S.J.: PsychSim: agent-based modeling of social interactions and influence. In: Proceedings of the International Conference on Cognitive Modeling, vol. 36, pp. 243–248 (2004)
54. McKinnon, M.C., Moscovitch, M.: Domain-general contributions to social reasoning: theory of mind and deontic reasoning re-explored. Cognition **102**(2), 179–218 (2007)
55. Minsky, M.: A Framework for Representing Knowledge. de Gruyter (2019)
56. Mitchell, J.P.: The false dichotomy between simulation and theory-theory: the argument's error. Trends Cogn. Sci. **9**(8), 363–364 (2005)
57. Molnar, A., Loewenstein, G.: Thoughts and players: an introduction to old and new economic perspectives on beliefs. In: Musolino, J., Sommer, J., Hemmer, P. (eds.) The Science of Beliefs: A Multidisciplinary Approach (Provisional Title, to be published in October 2021). Cambridge University Press (2021)
58. Mukamel, R., Ekstrom, A.D., Kaplan, J., Iacoboni, M., Fried, I.: Single-neuron responses in humans during execution and observation of actions. Curr. Biol. **20**(8), 750–756 (2010)
59. Newell, A.: Unified Theories of Cognition. Harvard University Press (1994)
60. Ong, D.C., Zaki, J., Goodman, N.D.: Computational models of emotion inference in theory of mind: a review and roadmap. Top. Cogn. Sci. **11**(2), 338–357 (2019)
61. Perner, J., Kühberger, A.: Mental simulation. In: Other Minds: How Humans Bridge the Divide Between Self and Others, pp. 174–189. The Guilfod Press, New York (2005)
62. Perner, J., Lang, B.: Development of theory of mind and executive control. Trends Cogn. Sci. **3**(9), 337–344 (1999)
63. Premack, D., Woodruff, G.: Does the chimpanzee have a theory of mind? Behav. Brain Sci. **1**(4), 515–526 (1978)
64. Pynadath, D.V., Marsella, S.: Minimal mental models. In: AAAI, pp. 1038–1044 (2007)
65. Pynadath, D.V., Marsella, S.C.: Fitting and compilation of multiagent models through piecewise linear functions. In: International Conference on Autonomous Agents: Proceedings of the Third International Joint Conference on Autonomous Agents and Multiagent Systems, vol. 3, pp. 1197–1204 (2004)
66. Pynadath, D.V., Marsella, S.C.: Psychsim: modeling theory of mind with decision-theoretic agents. In: IJCAI, vol. 5, pp. 1181–1186 (2005)
67. Quesque, F., Rossetti, Y.: What do theory-of-mind tasks actually measure? Theory and practice. Perspect. Psychol. Sci. **15**(2), 384–396 (2020)
68. Rabin, M.: Incorporating fairness into game theory and economics. Am. Econ. Rev. 1281–1302 (1993)
69. Rizzolatti, G., Craighero, L.: The mirror-neuron system. Annu. Rev. Neurosci. **27**, 169–192 (2004)
70. Saxe, R., Wexler, A.: Making sense of another mind: the role of the right temporo-parietal junction. Neuropsychologia **43**(10), 1391–1399 (2005)
71. Scholl, B.J., Leslie, A.M.: Modularity, development and 'theory of mind'. Mind Lang. **14**(1), 131–153 (1999)
72. Scholl, B.J., Leslie, A.M.: Minds, modules, and meta-analysis. Child Dev. **72**(3), 696–701 (2001)
73. Sellars, W., et al.: Empiricism and the philosophy of mind. Minn. Stud. Philos. Sci. **1**(19), 253–329 (1956)

74. Shafto, P., Goodman, N.D., Frank, M.C.: Learning from others: the consequences of psychological reasoning for human learning. Perspect. Psychol. Sci. **7**(4), 341–351 (2012)
75. Si, M., Marsella, S.C., Pynadath, D.V.: Modeling appraisal in theory of mind reasoning. Auton. Agent. Multi-Agent Syst. **20**(1), 14–31 (2010)
76. Simon, H.A.: Models of Bounded Rationality: Empirically Grounded Economic Reason, vol. 3. MIT Press (1997)
77. Spelke, E.S., Kinzler, K.D.: Core knowledge. Dev. Sci. **10**(1), 89–96 (2007)
78. Tenenbaum, J.B., Griffiths, T.L., Kemp, C.: Theory-based Bayesian models of inductive learning and reasoning. Trends Cogn. Sci. **10**(7), 309–318 (2006)
79. Trivers, R.L.: The evolution of reciprocal altruism. Q. Rev. Biol. **46**(1), 35–57 (1971)
80. Turner, R., Felisberti, F.M.: Measuring mindreading: a review of behavioral approaches to testing cognitive and affective mental state attribution in neurologically typical adults. Front. Psychol. **8**, 47 (2017)
81. Wang, N., Pynadath, D.V., Hill, S.G.: The impact of POMDP-generated explanations on trust and performance in human-robot teams. In: AAMAS, pp. 997–1005 (2016)
82. Wang, N., Pynadath, D.V., Rovira, E., Barnes, M.J., Hill, S.G.: Is it my looks? Or something I said? The impact of explanations, embodiment, and expectations on trust and performance in human-robot teams. In: Ham, J., Karapanos, E., Morita, P.P., Burns, C.M. (eds.) PERSUASIVE 2018. LNCS, vol. 10809, pp. 56–69. Springer, Cham (2018). https://doi.org/10.1007/978-3-319-78978-1_5
83. Wimmer, H., Perner, J.: Beliefs about beliefs: representation and constraining function of wrong beliefs in young children's understanding of deception. Cognition **13**(1), 103–128 (1983)
84. Yoshida, W., Dolan, R.J., Friston, K.J.: Game theory of mind. PLoS Comput. Biol. **4**(12), e1000254 (2008)

Knowledge of Self and Other Within a Broader Commonsense Setting

Darsana P. Josyula[1]([✉]) [iD], Matthew Goldberg[2] [iD], Anthony Herron[1] [iD],
Christopher Maxey[2] [iD], Paul Zaidins[2] [iD], Timothy Clausner[2] [iD], Justin Brody[3] [iD],
and Don Perlis[2] [iD]

[1] Bowie State University, Bowie, MD 20715, USA
darsana@cs.umd.edu, herrona0814@students.bowiestate.edu
[2] University of Maryland, College Park, MD 20742, USA
{mdgold,clausner,perlis}@umd.edu
[3] Franklin and Marshall College, Lancaster, PA 17603, USA

Abstract. We examine some formal-reasoning aspects of Theory of Mind (ToM) from the perspective of an agent teaming with others, in a broad (active logic) setting that includes a commonsense-reasoning context. Our emphasis is on how to represent time-evolving inferences by an agent about what it and other agents do or don't know. Specifically, what sorts of knowledge representation and reasoning are needed for an agent in a team to capture ToM in a formal time-evolving commonsense-reasoning setting, especially with regard to introspection, presence of direct contradictions, inference about another's knowledge or lack (e.g., on their asking a question, and on being told an answer), and quotation mechanisms for representing beliefs about beliefs.

Keywords: Theory of mind · Active logic · Commonsense reasoning · Quasi-quotation

1 Introduction

Theory of Mind (ToM) refers to an agent's ability to ascribe evolving knowledge (and lack of knowledge) to itself and others [12, 16]. Thus, it is the ability to represent and reason about minds (one's own and that of others), and in particular to distinguish what knowledge/belief at a given time is in any given mind, from what is not in that mind (but may be in another mind) [2]. As such, ToM is related to so-called meta-reasoning (about self and other).

Much recent work on ToM focuses more specifically on: (i) distinctions of perspective between agents, i.e., between the content of one's own mind and that of another – often assessed in terms of whether one can attribute a belief to another that one does not belief oneself ("false-belief"); and (ii) developmental stages in children. For AI purposes,

© The Author(s), under exclusive license to Springer Nature Switzerland AG 2022
N. Gurney and G. Sukthankar (Eds.): AAAI-FSS 2021, LNCS 13775, pp. 21–29, 2022.
https://doi.org/10.1007/978-3-031-21671-8_2

however, there may be little consequence in distinguishing among aspects of ToM. In this paper, we will view all these as aspects of an underlying ability to represent and reason about the content of one's own mind (or knowledge base – KB) and that of another as they vary over time as a result of reasoning and observation. We will use "belief" and "knowledge" interchangeably in what follows.

Surprisingly, even very simple team interactions seem to require a substantial amount of knowledge, not only about the environment and tasks but also about the changing knowledge within oneself and others as agents interact with their environment and perform tasks. Even informing based on reasoning (e.g., that hearing the utterance will add a new belief to the hearer's KB) involves knowledge and inference about the hearer's KB. Similarly, the knowledge that one (self) has encountered contradictory information involves reasoning about the contents of one's own KB.

Here, we explore knowledge of self and other that applies to robotic agents interacting in real time either with humans or with other robotic agents. Potential axioms will be illustrated using our own time-sensitive reasoning formalism of active logic. We begin with an informal example, then quickly review related work, observe some needed adjustments for interacting agents, and then sketch a formal approach and some technical issues involving quotation. Our outlook is to employ highly general axioms as much as possible, rather than ones geared to a single narrow application.

2   Informal Example

Many actions tacitly involve knowledge. An agent that does not know it has performed an action may blindly perform it again (under the misimpression that it has not been performed). Actions have consequences. Smart agents should know this about any given action that might be taken, and expect the consequences, including about how the action would alter one's knowledge. Some actions are even done to gain knowledge; e.g., opening a tool-cabinet may result in A's KB having the information as to whether a particular flashlight is inside. A goal to open the cabinet can be adopted for the very purpose of gaining this knowledge.

Consider one agent A (a robot) being asked by another agent B (a human), "Is the flashlight in the tool-cabinet?"—a mere "yes," "no," or "I don't know" by A seems enough of a reply. However, the reasoning that goes into the response-generation – if based on general principles that can apply broadly across domains – will depend on a considerable amount of knowledge that A has, including knowing:

- that it is being addressed and asked a yes-no question
- that the questioner B desires to be informed of a reliable answer
- whether it knows about the flashlight
- that if it does not know, then it might easily find out by opening the cabinet
- what to expect while undertaking actions like opening the cabinet
- that an action has been initiated, is being performed, has been completed successfully, or has failed
- that it would know the answer to the original question if it sees the flashlight in the toolbox

- that if the flashlight is not immediately visible upon opening the cabinet, one may have to move items that occlude the vision
- that if it (now) knows the answer, it can tell it to B
- that B will have the information that A has given it
- that then B will no longer desire/need to be informed

The (incomplete) list above illustrates that there is a great deal of hidden knowledge behind commonsense behaviors and this knowledge is needed for reasoning about own-knowledge and own-action for active engagement with the environment, for even simple-seeming team behaviors.

3 Related Work

A key starting point for us is related theories [4] for expressing and reasoning with knowledge about others, events, and communication. The other theories that we examined do not specify how the agent's own knowledge evolves over time; instead, they show how the agent's knowledge base evolves from an external viewer's perspective. In short, each is an *external* logic that specifies how the agent should reason rather than an *internal* logic that an agent uses directly for its own reasoning [11].

Davis [3] incorporates a situation-based, possible-worlds theory of knowledge and a branching time structure with an interval-based theory for multi-agent actions. Davis [3] and Davis and Morgenstern [5] handle time using a sort for clock-times and a time structure that incorporates every feasible action and possible consequences as a separate branch, but the time model does not single out a timeline or branch as a history that will actually happen. Thus, from a real-time agent's perspective, time is at stand-still during the agent's reasoning. The agent believes the logical closure of its knowledge in each situation without consideration of the time taken to derive the closure in an implemented real-time agent. Thus, in Davis' theory, though actions occur in time, reasoning occurs outside the time structure.

Davis uses a meta-theorem to prove the consistency of the presented theory. For agent implementations working with evolving time and knowledge, inconsistencies are bound to happen; therefore, the question arises as to whether consistency is even possible. Rather, the ability to note and reason about the inevitable inconsistencies becomes very relevant for real-time agents. Additionally, Davis' theory deals only with informative acts with the implicit assumption that the hearer has knowledge of when the speaker initiated the communication, and the speaker has knowledge about when the hearer has received the communication. Such knowledge may not be available for a real-time agent's theory.

Jiao [8] uses a "transpositional thinking" principle for an agent to reason about the knowledge of others based on their behaviors and to predict their behavior based on its acquired knowledge about others. Inconsistencies between expected and observed behaviors are used to amend the understanding about others. This then becomes the new foundation for agents to reason about future behavior of others. But this theory is also presented as an external logic to describe how the reasoning of teaming agents should proceed.

Another theory for reasoning about knowledge by matching agents' expectations to their observations is presented by van Ditmarsch, et al. [17]. They describe a semantics-driven propositional dynamic epistemic logic for specifying observations and protocols. Epistemic expectation models obtained from epistemic protocols describe the agents' expected observations, which in turn influence their reasoning about their own knowledge and other agents' epistemic attitudes. As in prior references, this is an external approach.

The recent book by Gordon and Hobbs [7] presents an even more ambitious undertaking than Davis. They attempt a full-blown formalization of "commonsense psychology", largely as a massive representation of theory of mind. This external theory again contrasts with a theory *internal* to an agent about how people think (and how machines can represent such).

The above approaches do not address real-time issues associated with internal and changing beliefs, inconsistencies, and imperfect knowledge within an evolving time setting in an implemented system. Rather, they describe an external representation for an agent's knowledge that allows symbolic reasoning in an omniscient setting.

4   Active Logic

Unlike a number of representative formal treatments [3, 7, 8, 14, 17] which are essentially external logics, active logic [1, 9, 10] is an "internal" logic that an agent uses for onboard reasoning. It has a clock rule that allows keeping track of the evolving time as reasoning proceeds. The clock rule infers now(t+1) at time t+1 from knowing now(t) at time t. Reasoning proceeds in recorded time-steps. Only sentences that are entailed by applying the inference rules once to the sentences present at a given step, are added to the KB in the next step. Any derivation takes time, and therefore, there is no issue of omniscience. Observations can come in at any step and be incorporated into the ongoing reasoning in the next time step.

If an agent's KB has the belief/knowledge φ at time t, then at $t + 1$, it can infer that it believes/knows φ, denoted as K(self, φ, t) by introspecting for φ (i.e., pos_int(φ)). This is "positive introspection". Similarly, there is a negative introspection rule for inferring what it doesn't know. Introspecting for φ at time t, when φ is *not* present in the KB, (i.e. neg_int(φ)) leads to ~K(self, φ, t) being asserted in the KB.

As reasoning proceeds, a direct contradiction at time t between P and ~P is noted at time t as contra(P, ~P, t) and both P and ~P are distrusted and retracted using the contradiction detection rule. Contradiction-handling axioms can allow assessing and reinstating one of the contradictands when the agent has adequate knowledge to conclude that for a given case.

Active logic provides the possibility to incorporate new observations, new constraints, new goals, and changes in reward structure into the reasoning process. Like online planning methods [6, 15, 18], active logic provides for planning and acting to occur together in an interleaved manner rather than all the planning happening before acting. The key benefit of active logic is its ability to account for the passage of time through every step of the planning and execution, which allows it to interject these processes as deadlines pass, goals change, or dangerous observations occur. Active logic's ability to track and access its history allows it to use the knowledge of when specific observations, beliefs revisions, or inconsistencies occurred in the past in the ongoing reasoning.

5 Toward a Formal Approach

Our preliminary work has involved the following fifteen commonsense inferences to endow individual agents with the capacity to reason in real time about changing beliefs, observations, and actions of both themselves and other agents. These are to be understood as defaults which can be overridden for abnormal cases. Note that these rules are not task-specific, and in principle could apply to a wide range of scenarios and tasks. In an active logic-based agent, these rules are internal to an agent's own knowledge base.

1. If an event (typically agent-caused) occurs and I do not know that I caused it, then it is not my action (hence another agent's action) that caused it; i.e., I did not cause it.
2. If another agent asks me for φ, then I know that the other agent doesn't have φ.
3. If φ is in my KB, then I can infer that I know φ. This is the *positive introspection rule* (via a *pos_int* predicate) that states that an agent knows what it knows.
4. If φ is not in my KB, then I can infer that I do not know φ. This uses the *negative introspection rule* (via a *neg_int* predicate) that states that an agent doesn't know/believe a given item at a given time.
5. If I know that another agent doesn't know/have φ and I do know/have φ, then I can provide φ to the other agent.
6. If I don't have φ and I know that doing α will provide me φ, initiate action α when I want φ to hold.
7. If I initiate an action α at time t, then do(α, t) is recorded in my KB. An agent knows which actions it initiated.
8. If I know that action α has consequence γ, then I expect the consequence γ to hold when α is completed.

   a. If I inform another agent of φ, then I record in my KB that the other agent will have φ in its KB.
   b. If I ask another agent a question Q, then I record in my KB that the other agent will attempt to provide me an answer ϕ.

9. From do(α, t), I infer doing(α) and record it in the KB until the action is observed to terminate (successfully or not). An agent knows which actions it is doing
10. If my action α terminates at t, then I assert done(α, t) in the KB. An agent knows which actions it completed.
11. If I expect the consequence γ to hold when α is completed, and γ does hold once I have done(α, t) in my KB, then assert succeeded(α).
12. If I expect the consequence γ to hold when α is completed, but γ does not hold once I have done(α, t) in my KB, then assert failed(α).
13. If another agent asks me a question Q and I can't find an answer ϕ for Q in a reasonable amount of time, respond to the agent "I don't know" with a tell action.

14. If I hear φ from another agent, then I know that the other agent knows φ holds and I record φ holds in my KB.
15. If there is a contradiction between my not knowing φ earlier and knowing φ now, reinstate that I know φ.

6 Formalism Using Quotation

Although we began with high-level natural language rules, we also must handle the formal issue of representing these in active logic and making inferences using them. Many of the above defaults are meant to represent not only beliefs of an active logic agent pertaining to other agents' beliefs, but also to quantify over the beliefs of others. For example, a formalized rule 14 must quantify over all beliefs that may be substituted for φ. We also have used formulas nested inside other formulas, such as for various arguments to meta-predicates (e.g., the contra predicate, indicating the presence of contradiction, and the neg_int predicate, for negative introspection on an agent's lack of a belief). To enable this kind of formula nesting, active logic has been extended to incorporate a syntactic theory of belief. The active logic mechanism for this syntactic theory uses a special kind of quotation term to represent a quoted formula, allowing it to nest inside of other terms in the language. Quotation terms are thus a novel sort of term that we employ, which is distinct from a constant term. Quotations may be unified with and substituted for variables and do not take active logic beyond a first-order system.

As an example, a ground instance of rule 5 above might be the following (1) for agent A's belief regarding agent B:

$$\sim K(agent\_B, \text{``}at(flashlight, cabinet)\text{''}) \wedge pos\_int(\text{``}at(flashlight, cabinet)\text{''}) \quad (1)$$
$$\rightarrow tell(\text{``}at(flashlight, cabinet)\text{''}, agent\_B)$$

However, the basic mechanism of a quotation term is not sufficient for reasoning with nested beliefs with generality. Consider a version of rule 8a above: *If I tell "P(x)" to agent B, then B will know "P(x)"*. Here the *x* is intended as a variable, so the quotes should not apply to *x* itself, but rather to whatever *x* is replaced by in an individual inference such as: *I told "P(c)" to B, so now B knows "P(c)"*. We address this next, but a bit more tailored to our working example.

If agent A were to represent a belief such as "If I tell an object's location to agent B, then B will know this object's location," a formula such as the following (2) would *not* accomplish this effectively:

$$tell(\text{``}at(Object, Location)\text{''}, agent\_B) \rightarrow K(agent\_B, \text{``}at(Object, Location)\text{''}) \quad (2)$$

The variables *Object* and *Location* are intended to quantify over possible objects and locations, and so the quotes should not apply to them directly, but instead to whatever constants (such as flashlight and cabinet) might replace them in individual inferences. To allow a type of variable that may substitute into the context of quotation terms, we use the syntactic device of quasi-quotation (which was originally introduced by Quine [13]) for such quantifying into quotation.

Our intended meaning of the quoted formula would make use of quasi-quotation (indicated with the backtick character '), to unquote these variables as shown below (3):

$$tell(\text{``}at(\text{`}Object, \text{`}Location)\text{''}, agent\_B) \rightarrow K(agent\_B, \text{``}at(\text{`}Object, \text{`}Location)\text{''}) \quad (3)$$

With the formula modified to utilize these unquotes, if the quantifiers of *Object* and *Location* were written explicitly, they would now have scope over the whole formula. Agent A would thus hold the desired belief, which is now general enough to quantify over the sets of locations about which it may inform agent B.[1]

Our preliminary work revealing the high-level inferences has been the subject of ongoing research on reasoning, using quotation and quasi-quotation, in the software artifacts implementing active logic inference. We anticipate that this progress is well-suited to apply active logic to ToM.

7 Agent Reasoning for the Informal Example

Making use of the commonsensical general knowledge for inference discussed earlier, A's reasoning might proceed along the following lines (where numbers refer to items 1–15 in Sect. 5):

- On detecting an utterance, infer using 1 above, that the heard utterance is not my own and is that of B.
- Infer that B is unaware of whether the flashlight is in the cabinet, using 2.
- If I know that the flashlight is in the cabinet, infer that I know something that I can provide B using 3 and 5.
- If I don't know if the flashlight is in the cabinet, and I know that I can search for it there, I can initiate searching the cabinet action using 4 and 6.
- I record that I initiated an action to search the cabinet for a flashlight using 7.
- I record that I expect to know if the flashlight is in the cabinet when the search action is completed using 8.
- I record the fact that the search is progressing using 9.
- I note the completion of search using 10.
- I infer that my action succeeded when an action is done and the expectation is met using 11.
- I infer that my action failed when an action is done but the expectation is not met using 12
- If I find the flashlight in the cabinet, I infer that I can convey "Yes" to B using 5.
- If I do not find the flashlight in the cabinet, I infer that I can convey "No" to B using 5.

---

[1] We note that the memory requirements for quotation terms are of the same computational complexity as for formulas in a first-order language without quotation, as any formula using quotation may be converted into a first-order formula with size of the same order, by replacing quotation marks with a unary function "quote", quasi-quotation marks with a function "quasi-quote", quoted predicate symbols with function symbols of the same name, and quoted logical operators with binary or unary function symbols naming the operators.

- If I cannot find the answer to B's query in a reasonable time, I respond to B "I don't know" using 13.
- Once an inference/decision is made to inform B, I initiate a tell action to respond with an answer and infer that it has been initiated using 7.
- As I execute the tell action, I infer the action is being done using 9 and expect B to then have the information using 8a.
- I note the contradiction between not knowing whether the flashlight is in the cabinet initially, and now knowing that it is there. I also distrust both formulas in the same time step using the contradiction detection rule. At the next time step, I reinstate that I know that there is a flashlight using 15. Similarly, I resolve the contradiction between B's not knowing and now knowing.

In our discussion so far, A has been considered as a robot and B as a human. Similar reasoning can happen even when both A and B are robotic agents. When B is an artificially intelligent agent, the reasoning *in agent B* may proceed along the following lines:

- I do not know if the flashlight is in the cabinet.
- I initiate an action to ask A if the flashlight is in the cabinet using 6.
- I record that I initiated the ask action using 7 and expect a response from A using 8b.
- While I ask, I record that I am asking using 9.
- Once I ask, I record that I asked using 10.
- If I get a response "Yes", I record in my KB that A knows the flashlight is in the cabinet, and that the flashlight is in fact there, using 14.

8 Conclusion

We have outlined a knowledge-rich, time-sensitive, and contradiction-tolerant approach to internal ToM-like reasoning in a team setting, where quasi-quotation is needed to allow representation of nested beliefs. Ongoing work is expected to lead to effective computational mechanisms that can be applied within robotic and other automated systems, whether in robot-robot or robot-human teams.

Acknowledgement. This work was supported by DARPA CREATE program grant# DARPA-PA-19-03-01-FP-037, "Towards Knowledge of Cooperative Agency: A Foundation for Task-General Teaming".

References

1. Anderson, M., Josyula, D., Perlis, D., Purang, K.: Active logic for more effective human-computer interaction and other commonsense applications. In: Workshop for Empirically Successful First-Order Reasoning, International Joint Conference on Automated Reasoning. IJCAR, Cork (2004)
2. Butterfill, S.A., Apperly, I.A.: How to construct a minimal theory of mind. Mind Lang. **28**(5), 606–637 (2013)

3. Davis, E.: Knowledge and communication: a first-order theory. Artif. Intell. **166**(1–2), 81–139 (2005)
4. Davis, E.: Logical formalizations of commonsense reasoning: a survey. J. Artif. Intell. Res. **59**(1), 651–723 (2017)
5. Davis, E., Morgenstern, L.: A first-order theory of communication and multi-agent plans. J. Log. Comput. **15**(5), 701–749 (2005)
6. Ghallab, M., Nau, D., Traverso, P.: Automated Planning: Theory & Practice (The Morgan Kaufmann Series in Artificial Intelligence), 1st edn. Morgan Kaufmann, Burlington (2004)
7. Gordon, A., Hobbs, J.: A Formal Theory of Commonsense Psychology: How People Think People Think, 1st edn. Cambridge University Press, Cambridge (2017)
8. Jiao, W.: Multi-agent cooperation via reasoning about the behavior of others. Comput. Intell. **26**(1), 57–83 (2010)
9. Josyula, D.: A unified theory of acting and agency for a universal interfacing agent. UMD Theses and Dissertations. University of Maryland, Department of Computer Science, College Park, MD (2005)
10. Josyula, D., Anderson, M., Perlis, D.: Metacognition for dropping and reconsidering intentions. In: AAAI Spring Symposium on Metacognition in Computation, pp. 62–67. AAAI Press, Menlo Park (2005)
11. Perlis, D., Brody, J., Kraus, S., Miller, M.: The internal reasoning of robots. In: Thirteenth International Symposium on Commonsense Reasoning. Association of Computational Logic, London (2017)
12. Premack, D., Woodruff, G.: Does the chimpanzee have a theory of mind? Behav. Brain Sci. **1**(4), 515–526 (1978)
13. Quine, W.: Mathematical Logic, Revised Harvard University Press, Cambridge (1981)
14. Reiter, R.: Knowledge in Action - Logical Foundations for Specifying and Implementing Dynamical Systems. MIT Press, Cambridge (2001)
15. Ross, S., Pineau, J., Paquet, S., Chaib-draa, B.: Online planning algorithms for POMDPs. J. Artif. Intell. Res. **32**(2), 663–704 (2008)
16. Tomasello, M.: How children come to understand false beliefs: a shared intentionality account. In: Proceedings of the National Academy of Sciences, vol. 115, no. 34, pp. 8491–8498. National Academy of Sciences, Washington, D.C, 21 August 2018
17. van Ditmarsch, H., Ghosh, S., Verbrugge, R., Wang, Y.: Hidden protocols: modifying our expectations in an evolving world. Artif. Intell. **208**(1), 18–40 (2014)
18. Ye, N., Somani, A., Hsu, D., Lee, W.S.: DESPOT: online POMDP planning with regularization. J. Artif. Intell. Res. **58**(1), 31–266 (2017)

Constructivist Approaches
for Computational Emotions:
A Systematic Survey

Alexander Viola[1], Vladimir Pavlovic[2], and Sejong Yoon[1]([✉])

[1] The College of New Jersey, Ewing, NJ 08628, USA
{violaa1,yoons}@tcnj.edu
[2] Rutgers University, Piscataway, NJ 08854, USA
vladimir@cs.rutgers.edu

Abstract. Computational emotion, is naturally predicated on an operating theory of emotion. This paper seeks to explore the prevalence of three different approaches in the literature, namely basic emotion, dimensional emotion, and constructed emotion. Basic emotion maintains that there exists a discrete set of primitive emotions evolved as responses to certain stimuli; dimensional emotion sees different emotions as systematically related by two or more dimensions (typically valence and arousal); and constructed emotion describes emotional experience as a function of the brain's general predictive faculties applied to learned social concepts of different emotions. In order to see how these approaches are represented in affective computing literature, we conduct a systematic survey spanning the IEEE, ACM, ScienceDirect, and Engineering Village databases. Out of 204 selected papers, 151 apply basic emotion theory, 48 apply dimensional emotion, and 5 apply constructed emotion. We find promising representation of the constructed emotion theory in the affective computing literature and conclude that it provides a theoretical basis worth pursuing for affective engagement human computer interaction (HCI) applications.

Keywords: Constructed emotion · Affective computing · Systematic survey

1 Introduction

The very idea of affective computing, that is, the capacity for computers to perceive or express emotion, took off in Picard's seminal 1995 paper titled *Affective Computing* [43]. In it, she saw the technology of the time and imagined it would soon be capable of reckoning with human emotion in a robust way, imbuing it all with importance with an observation from the field of psychology: emotion is fundamental to the decision-making of all kinds, minor and major, frivolous and life-changing; it undergirds our values and impacts, literally, how we see the world; and at last, it is essential to communication. The idea is, if a computer could develop a sort of *empathy*, an awareness of the moods of its users, it could

N. Gurney and G. Sukthankar (Eds.): AAAI-FSS 2021, LNCS 13775, pp. 30–50, 2022.
https://doi.org/10.1007/978-3-031-21671-8_3

become a more helpful tool for a great number of applications. Suppose learning software could detect the interest or frustration of a student and modify a lesson to suit that. Or consider a computer as a tool for those whose jobs are to play with emotion: computer-aided composing, visual art, clip selection. Even entertainment that can swell and recede and shift with its' viewers participation and emotion, or, perhaps, simply giving synthesized speech its proper tonality to convey subtle meaning. You can even find applications in health and safety – suppose a system could determine if a driver was angry and prone to aggressive driving or if a driver was inattentive and liable to cause an accident. These are all examples where computational emotion models can help human-machine interactions in various ways.

Applications of affective computing are so numerous by virtue that emotion is an undercurrent that influences nearly everything in our lives. The practice of affective computing is inherently multidisciplinary, drawing from psychology, neurology, mathematics, computer science, sociology, and linguistics [6] and so can be challenging – but potentially enriching – pursuit. Evidently, many see that potential. In the decades following Picard's paper, we see affective computing applied in as many ways she foresaw and more. We see papers pursuing emotion recognition in faces, speech, and gestures [28,38,58], or in brain scans, heart rates, or skin conductance [3,33,39], emotionality and other subjective attribute detection in music, movies, and visual art [40,54]. There are strides being made in artificial affective agents [34,60,61], and in sentiment analysis of forums, blogs, and social media posts [20,41,63]. The field is lush with a variety of diverse applications and holds promise in expanding the range of computers' usefulness and perhaps someday fundamentally changing the way we interact with them.

As affective computing grows in popularity and as machine learning has become ascendant, the ultimate aim of creating silicon systems that can effectively grasp at and reckon with human emotion seems ever more attainable. Amidst this promise and excitement, however, we argue that it is important to step back and examine the theoretical foundations of our very idea of emotion: how we think about these things informs how we develop affective systems, what we expect from them, how we conceptualize them, and ultimately, how we use them.

The predominant theory of emotion that largely guides current affective computing, **basic emotion**, holds that there are fundamental emotional experiences that a computer (or an observer) can correctly and objectively *detect* in a person. The underdog theory of **constructed emotion**, however, posits that emotion is inherently subjective, impossible to accurately *detect* in a person's face, behavior, or neural activity. It may seem, then, like the very concept of computational emotion prediction is wholly incompatible with this theory. Yet, we seek to find applications that reimagine the roles of these predictive systems in affective application design, creating programs that enhance a user's ability to examine the personal feelings only they are truly equipped to determine. As the main contribution, this paper puts forth the idea that affective computing informed by the *constructed theory of emotion* holds promise in creating systems that a user feels emotionally empowered by, rather than unsettlingly analyzed by, with a systematic survey of the theories.

2   Computational Models of Emotion

Before we discuss the survey methodology and results about various computational emotion models, it would be good to examine these theories more in-depth and grasp at the general form of affective computing papers that apply each of them. As reflected in the results above, both basic emotion and dimensional emotion share the lion's portion of guiding thought in the field. Affective computing has historically accommodated both of these competing approaches and continues to do so. Picard's paper over two decades ago mentions this capacity to pursue useful affective research in either vein of theory [43], and the significant presence of both basic and dimensional emotion papers to this day offers testament to this fact. Planting the seeds of constructed emotion in this fertile field very well may yield new, interesting, and applicable research.

2.1   Basic Emotion

The theory of basic emotion has enjoyed prevalence in the literature, introductory psychology courses, and the public's general science consciousness. Its premise is intuitive and offers a digestible origin story to the sometimes primal-feeling emotions that color our lives in alternately beautiful, tragic, and frightening hues. One of its fundamental premises, universally understood emotion, is also a pleasing and hopeful conclusion to arrive at – it's something exciting to communicate. In affective computing, its taxonomy of discrete emotions is also pleasantly well-suited for classification models of all stripes.

Summary. Most popular as Ekman's theory of basic emotion, this approach maintains the existence of six emotions with distinct causal neurology and unique physical expression, developed in response to frequently-encountered situations in our evolutionary history [15]. Namely, the six emotions are anger, disgust, fear, surprise, happiness, sadness, and surprise. The classification of "basic" requires that these responses exhibit aforementioned causal circuits and, ideally, exist in other species as well; among other requirements, these rules differentiate these six from the myriad non-basic emotions that can be considered various modulations or alternations of these basic components. Given an evolutionary basis, this theory also goes hand-in-hand with the concept of universal emotion, i.e., that particular facial configurations and situations can be reliably and consistently classified as evoking one of these six emotions, especially across highly differing cultures. This theory evidently informs affective computing approaches that aim to classify "emotion signals" into corresponding discrete categories, often a subset of the above six emotions. A clear example would be a facial emotion classification model trained on emotion-labeled face images that considers success as an objective detection of emotion as it adheres to these labels (Fig. 1).

Example. *Image based Static Facial Expression Recognition with Multiple Deep Network Learning* is a paper published in 2015 by Yu and Zhang [58] for the Emotion Recognition in the Wild Challenge of that same year. They propose a model

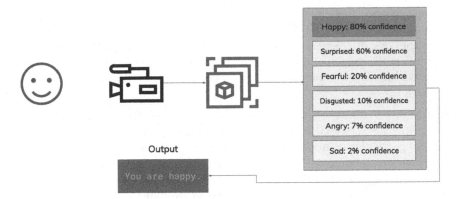

Fig. 1. An illustration of a sample basic emotion approach applied to a facial expression recognition task. A face being examined with a camera attached to an FER model, with outputs showing confidence levels for a variety of emotion classes. The label with the highest confidence is taken as the answer.

to perform an emotion categorization task on the Static Facial Expression in the Wild (SFEW) dataset, placing movie frames of human faces into seven categories, namely *Angry, Disgust, Fear, Happy, Neutral, Sad, and Surprise.* This model is first built on a robust, multi-level facial detection system, with the largest detected area across all levels being used as input for prediction. The highest level is a joint cascade detection and alignment detector, as it is reasonably robust to image perturbations and offers better face localization, the second level a deep CNN detector that offers more robustness in the case of occluded or sharply angled faces, and the last a mixture of trees detector. The prediction model itself is formed by five convolutional layers with three stochastic pooling layers interspersed between to reduce overfitting, three final densely connected layers, and a softmax layer followed with negative log-likelihood loss. For robustness, the paper also generates randomly perturbed images as a part of the input. It considers both the original and perturbed images in prediction and outputs the average voting response of all forms of the image. To further improve performance, multiple differently initialized copies of the model are ensembled, with learned ensemble weights using either optimal ensembled log-likelihood loss or optimal ensembled hinge loss. The network pre-trains on the FER dataset and is fine-tuned on the SFEW training set to the tune of 61.29% accuracy on the challenge's SFEW test set. This significantly surpasses the challenge baseline accuracy of 39.13% and so proves to be an effective basic emotion classification model that improves on its predecessors via a variety of smart changes.

2.2   Dimensional Emotion

A dimensional representation of emotion aims largely to address perceived shortcomings in a discrete basic emotion approach, primarily issues of applicability to actual emotion experience due to a lack of nuance [24]. Proponents believe that breaking emotion down into two (or more) dimensions provides such nuance and creates room to render systematic relationships between emotions in the space. Papers applying dimensional theory are free to predict continuous values for various emotion dimensions and leave that as is or may use those values to place a reading within discrete emotion regions in the emotional dimension space [43].

Summary. A dimensional emotion approach relies on Russell's circumplex model of affect [47], which is based on the hypothesis that emotions may be represented by particular combinations of various dimensions. Russell's model focuses particularly on the dimensions of valence and arousal (or activity). For example, a state assessed as highly negative (i.e., low valence) with low arousal might be classed as a depressive state; a state assessed as more or less neutral (i.e., moderate valence) with high arousal might be classed as a state of surprise. These states are not entirely independent as in basic emotion, instead of exhibiting systematic relationships to one another – in comparing, say, fear (negative, high arousal) and contentment (positive, lower arousal), they can be considered opposites. Optionally, a dimensional model in this vein may include additional dimensions such as dominance (a Pleasure-Arousal-Dominance (PAD) model), expectation, or intensity depending on desired complexity and nuance (Fig. 2).

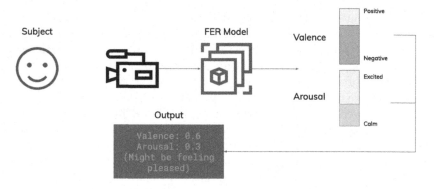

Fig. 2. An illustration of a sample dimensional emotion approach applied to an FER task. A face being examined with a camera attached to an FER model, with outputs showing meters that display valence and arousal levels. This is connected to a terminal "reading" these results and inferring an emotion label.

Example. *Continuous Prediction of Spontaneous Affect from Multiple Cues and Modalities in Valence-Arousal Space* is a 2011 paper written by Nicolaou, et al. that "presents the first approach in the literature towards automatic, *dimensional* and continuous affect prediction in terms of arousal and valence based on facial expressions, shoulder gesture, and audio cues" [38]. The model operates on the *Sensitive Artificial Listener Database* (SAL-DB), which contains spontaneously-elicited emotion data in the form of audio/video samples with continuous human-generated annotations. Based on these annotations, the data has been normalized to account for positive emotion bias in the dataset and segmented into roughly equal quantities of positive and negative emotion clips. The authors designed features for this data in three separate modalities: for audio, Mel-frequency cepstral (MFC) coefficients over time, and prosody features like energy and pitch; for the face, a mapping of 20 facial feature points represented by video frame-based vectors of the 2D coordinates of these points; and for the shoulders, there are similar sets of points, two on each shoulder and one on a stable central point. Comparing the performance of SVMs for regression and Bidirectional LSTMs (BLSTMs), the authors find better affect prediction performance from the BLSTMs on all input modalities (audio, video) and for all emotion dimensions (valence, arousal), suggesting the importance of the proper representation of temporal data in continuous prediction. Also comparing feature fusion (feature concatenation as input into a single model), model-level fusion (fusion of individual predictions of a particular emotion dimension from facial expression cues and audio cues into another LSTM for final prediction of the same dimension), and output-associative fusion (the combination of both valence/arousal predictions for all cues into another model to yield a single prediction for valence or arousal), they find the best performance out of output-associative fusion. This output-associative fusion appropriately represents observed systematic relationships between valence and arousal values, i.e., the model changes its final arousal prediction based on its prior valence predictions. Improved performance, in this case, suggests the importance of representing this relationship in effective dimensional emotion prediction. Overall, the paper finds promise in the temporal representation of affect via LSTMs and in the representation of these systematic relationships between valence and arousal.

2.3   Constructed Emotion

Constructed emotion, compared to basic emotion and dimensional emotion represents something of a paradigm shift. It aims to bring emotion theory up-to-date with modern neurology research, dispelling outdated ideas of 'regions' of emotions and fully dissolving the arbitrary philosophical barrier between "thought" and "emotion" [9]. Emotion becomes a complex but almost romantic process of social construction, with sophisticated neural predictive processes opening up potentially infinite varieties of affective experience. It remains a minority theory, especially in affective computing where it has scarcely penetrated, but it has its growing, enthusiastic supporters [7–9, 19].

Summary. In simplest terms, the theory of constructed emotion holds that emotion is in the eye of the beholder and in the heart of the feeler. Emotion is held to be an experience created within and between human beings through complex predictive processes, and so is something sheerly subjective. The theory suggests, then, that it is impossible to objectively detect emotion as a predictable, well-formed response to certain stimuli.

This approach refutes the idea of basic emotions with distinct mechanisms or expressive "fingerprints," instead maintaining that emotions, in the confluence of context, verbal emotion conceptualization, interoception, social agreement, and personal history, are constructed by the brain into a unique experience. These influences feed into the brain's default mode of prediction, where input is constantly presaged (and corrected, if it varies from what's predicted), and appropriate responses occur based on these predictions. This general mechanism may be taken as the evolutionary development of a highly efficient, highly flexible response system to an infinite variety of situations. Like experiences of emotion, perceptions of others' emotional displays are based upon prediction and thus are not infallible and rely extensively on context. In another sense, emotions do not exist objectively to be reliably "detected," rather, they are powerful instances of human-created social reality. In this vein of logic, the constructivist approach calls emotion universality into doubt, often citing flaws in the methodology of universality research.

Example. *Mirror Ritual: An Affective Interface for Emotional Self-Reflection,* a 2020 paper written by Rajcic and McCormack [46], describes work done on an affective interface that integrates existing emotion perception and text generation technologies to create emotionally meaningful experiences for users. The system takes on the external appearance of a smart mirror with a concealed camera and a reflective display. A user looks at the mirror, and the system uses OpenCV's Haar cascade classifier to detect their face. The affective mirror then performs real-time facial emotion detection based on a CNN trained on the FER-2013 dataset and generates an emotional seed-word based on perceived emotion and intensity. A mild grimace and furrowed brow, for example, might generate the seed-word "irritated," and a beaming grin might generate the seed-word "ecstatic." After the seed-word is generated, it is then fed into a fine-tuned GPT-2-345M text generation model from OpenAI to generate brief, user-engaging poetry based on their perceived emotion. This text generation model

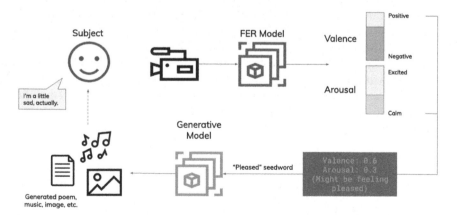

Fig. 3. An illustration of a sample constructivist approach that uses a FER model. A face being examined with a camera attached to a FER model, with outputs showing valence and arousal levels. These levels are used to generate an appropriate emotion seed word for another model that will generate affective content for the subject. The subject reflects on this content and arrives at their own assessment of their emotion.

is trained on a variety of sources, including postmodern poetry, in order to yield poetry that's accessible but still open to interpretation in order to best facilitate a sort of affective relationship between the mirror and a user. User assessment of the mirror described moments of uncanny appropriateness and great relevance to personal events, though on occasion, users reported a dip in their affective engagement when poems did not seem relevant (Fig. 3).

This affective mirror paper describes an imperfect but still quite promising HCI application that successfully integrates Barrett's theory of constructed emotion with existing AI and affective computing technologies, like FER and text generation. Importantly, it reconciles the apparent conflict between the constructed emotion theory and the prescriptive nature of most emotion assessment systems. Simply put, Rajcic and McCormack relegate the emotion perception and subsequent poetry generation to a position of non-authority in the overall design of the mirror. Ultimately, the mirror's capabilities are tools for humans to make sense of their own emotions and relationships – the agency and interpretive work is given to the users. The emotion prediction aspect refrains from acting as an authoritative, correct *recognition* of human emotions as is common in other applications like surveillance. Given a poem instead, a user is free to reject or accept its implications. The tool combines constructed emotion with affective computing in a truly inspiring way.

3   Systematic Survey

The aim of a systematic survey is to provide a reproducible, rigorous, and accountable process for creating questions and finding answers in related literature. The purpose of these questions may be to inquire about the effectiveness of relevant technologies, to provide a valuable introductory summary to the surveyed field, or to suggest an area worthy of additional research. To achieve reproducibility and accountability, a systematic survey publishes its database search queries and

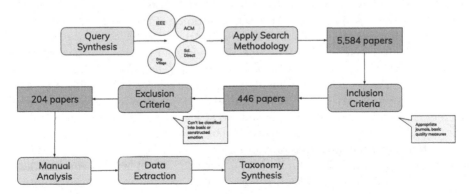

Fig. 4. An illustration of the sequence of paper gathering and selection. After search string generation and database querying, a series of selections reduces the number of papers to an amount tractable for manual analysis.

maintains consistent and documented criteria by which papers are deemed pertinent or impertinent. Following these overarching steps of search and then selection, finally qualitative and/or quantitative analysis in service of the survey's purpose is performed on the remaining papers (Fig. 4).

To substantiate our claims on the status quo of affective computing and the promise of constructivist-inspired program design, we have conducted a systematic survey of the field and found a crucial representation of constructivist approaches in recent papers. The primary impetus for conducting this survey is to get a grasp on the field of affective computing as a whole, especially as it applies emotion theory to various applications. This is a crucial part of our research that's been conducted so far because our aim is to reconsider existing practices and offer a constructivist-based approach that has the potential to create novel experiences of affective engagement in Human-Computer Interaction (HCI).

3.1   Description

The following section includes a breakdown of our key systematic literature review steps as they appear in Silva and Neiva's guide to the practice [50]. Grouping minor and similar tasks for the sake of organization, these include: formulating the research question(s); generating, testing, and refining search strings, conducting the searches and storing data, and finally parsing through the data to select and then analyze relevant papers. In each of these, we will briefly introduce the task, discuss methods, and offer an evaluation on the process and results.

3.2   Methodology

Problem Formulation. In some ways, the questions we posit reflect the suspicions we have about the topic. Our paper primarily seeks to examine the efficacy of existing emotion inference methods, ponder the potential effectiveness of constructivist methods, and question whether emotion inference technologies will provide lasting value in in-the-wild settings. These topics and rationale for asking them will be discussed in greater detail below. Some of them arise in part due to conclusions drawn in Barrett's *How Emotions Are Made* [9].

Our first overarching question: *How effective are existing emotion inference methods based on basic emotion theory, and how well will they generalize to real-world, in-the-wild applications?* Though, say, facial expression classification may be growing increasingly robust, it is reasonable to question whether or not these discrete classification models will be able to classify less well-formed facial input well. In addition, generalizability gets called into question if models are trained on acted, stereotypical expressions of emotion– these are clear signals, but in actual scenarios, you are unlikely to find these perfect matches. When systems like these are integrated into aspects of HCI (robot or apps), will the user find the classification of their feelings into six firm categories robust or reductive? If overly reductive, an application integrating such technology may seem either toy-like or at worst presumptive, and in either case, will fail to be useful. This question plays the role of acting as a primary impetus for our research. It represents one of the key questions that we are overall seeking to prove or disprove.

The above question presumes some level of widespread adoption of basic emotion-based inference techniques, however, and so we are also responsible for confirming this presumption. We therefore have a few more key questions on our plate. *What does the field of affective computing look like? Are approaches either explicitly or implicitly based on basic emotion theory very prevalent, to begin with? Are there other, more widespread approaches that we should instead ask questions of? What are typical applications for these affective computing technologies?* Seeking an answer to these questions acts as a key grounding element that ensures we have an accurate and less-skewed perspective of the field. If basic emotion approaches turn out to be relatively uncommon, or applications largely shy away from actually predicting emotions, then perhaps there is less of a need for our question to be asked in the first place. Perhaps others have had the same hypothesis and arrived at the same conclusion already. Essentially, this question helps ensure that our research is relevant, representative, and fair.

Our second big question: *Would a constructivist (or some other) approach be more effective than the dominating approaches? Would this approach capture more nuance in an emotion prediction system?* Of course, we must also examine whether or not a system guided by the constructivist approach would be better to begin with–regardless of our hypotheses, we can't in good faith assume so. This question essentially asks us to justify the inclinations we may have towards the approach and asks us to provide a basis for arguing for the pursuit of constructivist-based affective computing. If we can find no compelling reasons or promises, then there would be no point in encouraging computing research based on this approach.

At last, we must ask: *What does affective computing informed by a constructivist approach even look like?* This is a key question for two reasons: (a) we may lack examples because systems following the constructivist approach are relatively few; and (b), Barrett's theory posits ideas that may fundamentally conflict with the idea of computational emotion prediction. In simplest terms, the theory of constructed emotion holds that emotion is in the eye of the beholder and in the heart of the feeler. Emotion is held to be **an experience created within and between human beings through complex predictive processes**, and so is something sheerly subjective. The theory suggests, then, that it is impossible to objectively detect emotion as a predictable, well-formed response to certain stimuli. Barring completely abandoning the premise of affective emotion prediction, then, how do we reconcile the practice to this theory? Could a predictive agent act like another subjective observer of others' emotions, with biases based on training data instead of human experience? There seems to be an added complexity to designing a constructivist-based emotion perceiver or seems to require some re-conceptualization. These questions serve to explore what practical implementation might look like, as well as to consider how a "paradigm shift" might be necessary to attain the benefits of a constructivist-based approach.

Search Methodology. With the above questions in mind, the next task is to create the search string that will be used to query various published-paper databases, and we focused on the computer science literature.

The first step is to consider our research questions and create a preliminary search string that may lead us to papers that can answer these questions. We then take this string and query three databases, recommended by Silva and Neiva's guide [50] for their prevalence in computer science and overall comprehensiveness: *IEEE Explore* [26], *ACM Library* [1], and *Elsevier ScienceDirect* [16]. Examining the quality, quantity, and relevance of results each round, the string is iteratively revised to yield a set of more promising results. With each revision, we also take care to ensure that the string is properly adapted to the syntax of each database we query, so it retains the same search semantics. For reference, the aim was to retrieve approximately 3,000 to 5,000 papers on the topic of various approaches (basic emotion, constructivist, dimensional) in the field of affective computing. In particular, we wanted to ensure that any constructivist approaches are represented and so take additional care to modify our search accordingly.

Between each iteration of the string was a process of experimenting with syntax, search parameters, and sample searches to get ideas of how different keywords were represented in the databases. For example, searches of just *"affect"* and *"affect NOT affective"* were compared to get an idea of how many papers might be captured by the homonym verb "affect" but not be related to emotion. This assumes that a paper containing "affect" but not "affective" is less likely to be about emotion and more likely to include the word as an incidental verb. Respectively, *"affect"* alone returned 57k results in the IEEE database, and *"affect NOT affective"* returned 56k, suggesting that the majority of papers included by the term "affect" was probably not related to emotion or affective computing. This informed the change from querying for "affect" to "affective." Similarly, searches of the names representing various emotion theories (i.e., Ekman for basic emotion, Barrett for constructed emotion) returned very few results and so informed additional changes. We arrive at the following string and have used it to conduct our search: *("affective" OR emotion OR mood) AND (prediction OR inference) AND ("basic emotion" OR "theory of constructed emotion" OR constructivist OR Plutchik).*

With the search strings finalized and the searches complete, we must proceed with passing eyes over our results to begin collecting information and start answering the questions we posed in earlier steps of the survey process. This proves to be an intensive process that examines papers in rounds with increasing levels of detail. This and other ancillary tasks are as follows.

Table 1. Papers by Category. *Theoretical* papers are those that discuss applying a given theory of emotion to affective computing. *Implementation* papers refer to those that explicitly or implicitly use a theory of emotion in the creation of an affective computing application. *Datasets/Other* refer to training data created for model prediction in a particular vein of emotion theory. Irrelevant papers and those whose theory is not apparent have been omitted for clarity.

Category	Number of papers
Basic Emotion	–
Theoretical	38
Implementation	106
Datasets/Other	6
Subtotal	150
Dimensional Emotion	–
Theoretical	18
Implementation	30
Datasets/Other	1
Subtotal	49
Constructed Emotion	–
Theoretical	1
Implementation	2
Datasets/Other	2
Subtotal	5
Total	204

The first step to this larger task was exporting all of the 5500+ results from our databases–often requiring page-by-page exporting–and saving them to a local archive. A reference management software [29] was used extensively for this purpose, as we were able to easily import paper metadata and abstracts in the bibtex format into it. Once imported, then began the task of broadly classifying all of the papers as irrelevant or relevant. If relevant, a paper was also organized by the apparent theory of emotion the paper's method ascribes to, based on the title and abstract, and whether a paper appears to be implementation-based or theoretical. If a paper was decidedly relevant but didn't ascribe to either basic or constructed emotion theory, it was placed in the Relevant/Other category. When classified, a paper was marked as'skimmed' to indicate completion and facilitate useful grouping and sorting functionality in JabRef. Table 1 summarizes this step.

To narrow down 5500+ papers manually tractable, some heuristics were applied to classify papers as irrelevant. If a paper is: a) older than 2004, b) not in English, c) lacking title or abstract, d) is an inaccessible book, or e) published in a most likely irrelevant journal, it is classified as out-of-scope for this survey. Note that we post-processed the resulting list to include some key papers published before 2004. To illustrate the last criterion, an article published in *Poultry*

Science or *Poetics*, for example, is most likely not relevant to our survey. These heuristics a) and e) mostly culled results in pure psychology or neurobiology, as well as other miscellany venues. Roughly four thousand results were culled from our pool of 5,583 via these heuristics.

After irrelevant papers were sorted away and relevant papers coarsely classified into emotion theory groups, the relevant papers were passed over once more to gather additional useful information. To gauge the relative popularity and importance of a paper in its field, we used citation counts. To accomplish this, paper titles were used as queries into Google Scholar, and the citation count was gathered into our JabRef archive as additional metadata.

Beyond coarse classifications, the second pass over relevant results involved scanning titles and abstracts once more, with an eye on two particular aspects, namely, the affective computing method used and its application, if one is apparent (e.g., for gauging student interest in a virtual classroom setting). These two aspects were concatenated and appended as additional metadata to relevant results, in the form of the string, e.g., *"artificial affective agents for human-robot interaction,"* for example. The purpose of this step was to get an idea of where and how affective computing is frequently applied and what technologies are frequently pursued.

Search Results. Final searches also included results from *Engineering Village* [17], rounding out results with an additional 42 papers and completing the list of databases that were recommended by Silva and Neiva [50] and were accessible through our institutional resources. The final tally of results are as follows: 4,846 papers from *ScienceDirect*, 92 from *IEEE*, 604 from *ACM Library*, and 42 from *Engineering Village*, for a total of 5,584 papers. Trimming the irrelevant papers using the method explained in the preivous section, we ended up with **204** papers as shown in Table 1 and Table 2.

As a qualitative overview, a couple of applications saw considerable representation in this survey, particularly facial emotion recognition (FER) and textual emotion recognition (TER), the latter primarily for sentiment analysis applications. Interestingly, a non-negligible amount of papers discussed the application of affect modeling for the sake of artificial affective agents, like game AI or human-robot interaction. Another common application was multimedia sentiment analysis, mostly of videos and images, but occasionally of music, as shown in Table 2.

Outcomes. General classifications of papers into emotion theory groups followed most of the original hypotheses. A significant portion of the relevant papers fell under the basic emotion category (151 of 204 papers, nearly three quarters). However, a significant amount fell under the "Other" category. A good amount of these fell under a **dimensional emotion** approach, which assessed emotions based on several dimensions – typically, but not always, these were of valence (positive/negative) and arousal (high energy/low energy). Despite not explicitly addressing dimensional approaches in our search string, this is a surprising turnout that suggests that dimensional approaches are another popular con-

Table 2. Papers by Application. A breakdown of collected papers by applied field. Papers in the "other" category frequently discuss theory of applying a given emotion theory to affective computing, as well as includes miscellaneous singleton applications.

Category	Number of papers
Facial expression recognition	64
Textual emotion recognition	56
Speech-based emotion recognition	27
Biometric emotion recognition	22
Multimedia emotion classification	22
Multimodal emotion recognition	14
Other	8
Total	204

tender. The majority of the "Other"-categorized papers fell under "unspecified other," however, mostly because many papers made no implicit or explicit mention of their approach for their emotion models. Many of them had ambiguous or brief abstracts and titles that made categorization difficult from this short passover and so have been dropped from the results to preserve a list of papers with definitely known emotion theories. A closer reading of these papers yield mostly basic emotion and dimensional emotion categorizations, and constructivist papers represented only a little over 2 percent of all relevant papers.

Yet, finding even a few papers that fall under this non-prescriptivist constructed emotion heading is an important result that suggests interest in a constructivist-informed approach to affective computing, especially in HCI. Below we will summarize this particularly relevant paper as well as prominent and illustrative examples applying the other theories of emotion for future references. Table 3 shows representative samples from the resulting survey database.

4   Discussion

After surveying the affective computing literature and examining a few notable papers in-depth, we now revisit a few of our initial questions and draw conclusions.

Broadly, what does the field of affective computing look like in terms of the theory of emotion? As initially expected, there seems to be a very significant representation of basic emotion theory at work in the field, informing many papers on a variety of tasks, particularly emotion classification. Dimensional emotion represents a significant second theory alive in the literature with a moderate showing in the survey, though it is important to consider that the final query string did not explicitly search for dimensional approaches. Having so many dimensional papers turn up without"dimensional" literally within the search string may suggest that dimensional papers represent a much greater portion than represented in this survey. Another look, next time not focusing primarily *basic emotion vs. constructed emotion* may yield an answer to this open question and provide a more

Table 3. A subset list of collected papers grouped by emotion theory category and sorted by year published. The acronym *EP* refers to emotion prediction. *BASIC* refers to Basic Emotion, *DIM.* refers to Dimensional Emotion, and *CON.* refers to Constructed Emotion. For detailed discussions on the definitions of these, please refer to the main text.

Citation	Author	Year	Category	Mode and Methodology
[14]	Domínguez-Jiménez et al.	2020	BASIC	physiological signals EP; comparison of multiple methods
[2]	Ahmad et al.	2020	BASIC	text; English to Hindi emotion embedding transfer learning, CNN/BLSTM
[54]	Yadav and Vishwakarma	2020	BASIC	movie trailer EP via ILDNet
[25]	Hameed et al.	2019	BASIC	respiration-based EP; FFT analysis
[18]	Feng	2019	BASIC	text; sentiment analysis of social media[...]
[12]	Chatterjee et al.	2019	BASIC	text; sentiment analysis using deep learning
[48]	Sajjad et al.	2019	BASIC	FER; Oriented FAST and Rotated BRIEF features supporting an SVM
[36]	Löffler et al.	2018	BASIC	affective agent; multimodal expression
[59]	Zeng et al.	2018	BASIC	FER; high-dimensional facial appearance features as input to DSAE
[5]	Arnau-González et al.	2017	BASIC	EEG EP; EEG feature combination
[65]	Zhou et al.	2015	BASIC	FER; emotion distribution learning
[58]	Yu and Zhang	2015	BASIC	FER; ensemble face detection, CNN
[30]	Khezri et al.	2015	BASIC	multimodal physiological signals, SVM/KNN
[57]	Yu and Wang	2015	BASIC	text; Twitter sentiment analysis
[40]	Orellana-Rodriguez et al.	2015	BASIC	multimedia affect contextualization
[61]	Zhang et al.	2015	BASIC	FER for AAAs, robust facial point detection
[34]	Lin et al.	2015	BASIC	AAAs for composite emotion study
[37]	Majumder et al.	2014	BASIC	FER using KSOM
[33]	Kukolja et al.	2014	BASIC	physio. EP method comparison
[60]	Zhang et al.	2013	BASIC	FER and topic analysis for affective agent
[44]	Purver and Battersby	2012	BASIC	text; automatic labelling for EP models
[27]	Ilbeygi and Shah-Hosseini	2012	BASIC	FER using fuzzy inference
[13]	Chen et al.	2012	BASIC	SER; multilevel models w/ SVMs
[52]	Wu et al.	2011	BASIC	SER using modulation spectral features
[31]	Kim et al.	2010	BASIC	text; comparison of unsupervised ER models
[28]	Iliev et al.	2010	BASIC	SER; glottal features on OPF model
[45]	Quan and Ren	2009	BASIC	text; creation of Chinese emotion corpus
[21]	Gill et al.	2008	BASIC	text; sentiment analysis via LIWC and LSA
[4]	Alm et al.	2005	BASIC	text; sentiment analysis via SNoW ML
[22]	Goldman and Sripada	2005	BASIC	FER via simulationist models
[35]	Liu et al.	2003	BASIC	text; 'common sense' affect detection
[11]	Calder et al.	2001	BASIC	FER; PCA for facial features
[42]	Pantic and Rothkrantz	2000	BASIC	FER; facial action-based EP
[49]	Scheirer et al.	1999	BASIC	wearable FER for expression detection
[51]	Wang et al.	2020	DIM	text; sentiment analysis, regional CNN-LSTM
[64]	Zhou et al.	2020	DIM	FER via bilinear CNN
[53]	Xiaohua et al.	2019	DIM	FER; two-level attention with Bi-RNN
[62]	Zhang et al.	2018	DIM	multimodal smartphone-based EP
[3]	Al Zoubi et al.	2018	DIM	EEG-based EP via liquid state machine
[55]	Yin et al.	2017	DIM	multimodal physio. EP with SAE ensembles
[20]	Giatsoglou et al.	2017	DIM	text; sentiment analysis comparison
[63]	Zhao et al.	2016	DIM	user-unique image EP
[32]	Koelstra and Patras	2013	DIM	FER and EEG fusion for affect tagging
[39]	Nogueira et al.	2013	DIM	DIM. regression to BASIC physio EP
[24]	Gunes and Schuller	2013	DIM	DIM. vs. BASIC comparison survey
[56]	Yoon and Chung	2013	DIM	EEG w/ ML classifier
[41]	Ortigosa-Hernández et al.	2012	DIM	text; sentiment analysis w/ semi-supervised models
[10]	Cai and Lin	2011	DIM	EP for driving safety analysis
[38]	Nicolau et al.	2011	DIM	multimodal EP using BLSTMS
[23]	Grimm et al.	2007	DIM	SER emotion primitive analysis
[46]	Rajcic and McCormack	2020	CON	FER for affective poem generation

accurate view of the affective computing field. As for constructed emotion, this survey found that this theory has not quite taken a significant foothold in the literature yet, though the presence of the promising *Mirror Ritual* paper [46] may be a sign of breakthrough and future growth of the theory in the literature.

What does a constructed emotion approach look like in affective computing? Mirror Ritual [46] provides one possible answer to this question. We see that this paper doesn't necessarily reject the existing methods of basic emotion classification and dimensional emotion prediction, but rather it leverages them to achieve a slightly different goal than the others. Instead of aiming to directly classify a user as experiencing a particular emotion (or as in some combination of valence and arousal), the idea is to use whatever credence existing prediction methods have to incorporate some form of generated art with the emotion the model perceives. The model may or very well may not be correct, but its direct assessment of the user is downplayed in favor of providing a tool for emotional reflection. This way, a given user retains agency and self-definition of their own internal state, choosing to integrate an emotionally relevant generated poem into their own understanding of their feelings or reject an irrelevant one. In this formulation, more accurate emotion prediction would be helpful, but if the capacity for a computer to *perceive* emotion is fundamentally limited by stipulations posed by constructed emotion theory, that is still okay. The ultimate goal is to create something evocative and emotionally salient for users, in some ways more in the wheelhouse of art than anything else. Furthering of constructivism in affective computing may very well resemble pursuits of AI art creation. This assessment provides some valuable insight into our next question.

Would a constructed emotion approach be more effective than approaches based on other theories? Given the above assessment, this question may very well have been a flawed one to ask. Ultimately, the methods are not necessarily competing, to begin with, as their goals are fundamentally different. It doesn't do much good to try and compare how accurately a basic-emotion predictive model classifies faces into emotion categories and how well a constructed-emotion approach creates opportunities for valuable emotional reflection. One may ask *"Which will ultimately prove more useful to society and helpful to human emotion modeling?"*, but it stands outside of the scope of this survey.

5   Conclusion

This survey has systematically examined over 200 papers in the field of affective computing, and in doing so, has arrived at the following conclusions: (a) Basic emotion classification and analysis tasks are presently the most popular, representing a majority of papers. (b) Facial, speech, and text-based emotion recognition tasks, regardless of emotion theory, are the most popular tasks in the field. (c) Constructed emotion in affective computing does not compete with emotion prediction methods of other stripes but instead utilizes them to achieve an entirely different goal. (d) Constructed emotion approaches represent a tiny minority of papers, but sample papers nonetheless represent potential for a new class of 'affective engagement' HCI applications. Future directions include further exploration into the potential of constructivist-based affective computing applications, the creation of a constructed emotion HCI device prototype, and the pursuit of generative art models inspired by users' emotions, as in the *Mirror Ritual* paper [46].

Acknowledgement. This work was supported in part by NSF Awards IIS 1955404 and 1955365.

References

1. ACM Digital Library (2020). https://dl.acm.org/. Accessed 19 Sept 2020
2. Ahmad, Z., Jindal, R., Ekbal, A., Bhattachharyya, P.: Borrow from rich cousin: transfer learning for emotion detection using cross lingual embedding. Expert Syst. Appl. **139**, 112851 (2020)
3. Al Zoubi, O., Awad, M., Kasabov, N.K.: Anytime multipurpose emotion recognition from EEG data using a liquid state machine based framework. Artif. Intell. Med. **86**, 1–8 (2018)
4. Alm, C.O., Roth, D., Sproat, R.: Emotions from text: machine learning for text-based emotion prediction. In: Proceedings of the Conference on Human Language Technology and Empirical Methods in Natural Language Processing, HLT 2005, pp. 579–586. Association for Computational Linguistics, USA (2005)
5. Arnau-González, P., Arevalillo-Herráez, M., Ramzan, N.: Fusing highly dimensional energy and connectivity features to identify affective states from EEG signals. Neurocomputing **244**, 81–89 (2017)
6. Arya, R., Singh, J., Kumar, A.: A survey of multidisciplinary domains contributing to affective computing. Comput. Sci. Rev. **40**, 100399 (2021)
7. Aviezer, H., et al.: Angry, disgusted, or afraid?: studies on the malleability of emotion perception. Psychol. Sci. **19**(7), 724–732 (2008)
8. Bar, M.: The proactive brain: using analogies and associations to generate predictions. Trends Cogn. Sci. **11**(7), 280–289 (2007)
9. Barrett, L.F.: How Emotions are Made. PAN Books (2018)
10. Cai, H., Lin, Y.: Modeling of operators' emotion and task performance in a virtual driving environment. Int. J. Hum. Comput. Stud. **69**(9), 571–586 (2011)
11. Calder, A.J., Burton, A., Miller, P., Young, A.W., Akamatsu, S.: A principal component analysis of facial expressions. Vis. Res. **41**(9), 1179–1208 (2001)
12. Chatterjee, A., Gupta, U., Chinnakotla, M.K., Srikanth, R., Galley, M., Agrawal, P.: Understanding emotions in text using deep learning and big data. Comput. Hum. Behav. **93**, 309–317 (2019)

13. Chen, L., Mao, X., Xue, Y., Cheng, L.L.: Speech emotion recognition: features and classification models. Digit. Signal Process. **22**(6), 1154–1160 (2012)

14. Domínguez-Jiménez, J., Campo-Landines, K., Martínez-Santos, J., Delahoz, E., Contreras-Ortiz, S.: A machine learning model for emotion recognition from physiological signals. Biomed. Signal Process. Control **55**, 101646 (2020)

15. Ekman, P.: An argument for basic emotions. Cogn. Emot. **6**(3–4), 169–200 (1992)

16. Elsevier ScienceDirect (2020). https://www.sciencedirect.com/. Accessed 19 Sept 2020

17. Engineering Village (2020). https://www.engineeringvillage.com/home.url? redir=t. Accessed 19 Sept 2020

18. Feng, Z.: Hot news mining and public opinion guidance analysis based on sentiment computing in network social media. Pers. Ubiquit. Comput. **23**(3–4), 373–381 (2019)

19. Gendron, M., Roberson, D., Vyver, J., Barrett, L.: Perceptions of emotion from facial expressions are not culturally universal: evidence from a remote culture. Emotion (Washington, D.C.) **14**, 251–62 (2014)

20. Giatsoglou, M., Vozalis, M.G., Diamantaras, K., Vakali, A., Sarigiannidis, G., Chatzisavvas, K.C.: Sentiment analysis leveraging emotions and word embeddings. Expert Syst. Appl. **69**, 214–224 (2017)

21. Gill, A.J., French, R.M., Gergle, D., Oberlander, J.: The language of emotion in short blog texts. In: Proceedings of the 2008 ACM Conference on Computer Supported Cooperative Work, CSCW 2008, pp. 299–302. Association for Computing Machinery, New York (2008)

22. Goldman, A.I., Sripada, C.S.: Simulationist models of face-based emotion recognition. Cognition **94**(3), 193–213 (2005)

23. Grimm, M., Kroschel, K., Mower, E., Narayanan, S.: Primitives-based evaluation and estimation of emotions in speech. Speech Commun. **49**(10), 787–800 (2007)

24. Gunes, H., Schuller, B.: Categorical and dimensional affect analysis in continuous input: current trends and future directions. Image Vis. Comput. **31**(2), 120–136 (2013)

25. Hameed, R.A., Sabir, M.K., Fadhel, M.A., Al-Shamma, O., Alzubaidi, L.: Human emotion classification based on respiration signal. In: Proceedings of the International Conference on Information and Communication Technology, ICICT 2019, pp. 239–245. Association for Computing Machinery, New York (2019)

26. IEEE Explore Database (2020). https://ieeexplore.ieee.org/Xplore/home.jsp. Accessed 9 Sept 2020

27. Ilbeygi, M., Shah-Hosseini, H.: A novel fuzzy facial expression recognition system based on facial feature extraction from color face images. Eng. Appl. Artif. Intell. **25**(1), 130–146 (2012)

28. Iliev, A.I., Scordilis, M.S., Papa, J.P., Falcão, A.X.: Spoken emotion recognition through optimum-path forest classification using glottal features. Comput. Speech Lang. **24**(3), 445–460 (2010)

29. JabRef - Free Reference Manager (2020). https://www.jabref.org/. Accessed 8 Sept 2020

30. Khezri, M., Firoozabadi, M., Sharafat, A.R.: Reliable emotion recognition system based on dynamic adaptive fusion of forehead biopotentials and physiological signals. Comput. Methods Programs Biomed. **122**(2), 149–164 (2015)

31. Kim, S.M., Valitutti, A., Calvo, R.A.: Evaluation of unsupervised emotion models to textual affect recognition. In: Proceedings of the NAACL HLT 2010 Workshop on Computational Approaches to Analysis and Generation of Emotion in Text,

CAAGET 2010, pp. 62–70. Association for Computational Linguistics, USA (2010). 125, textual affect recognition; survey

32. Koelstra, S., Patras, I.: Fusion of facial expressions and EEG for implicit affective tagging. Image Vis. Comput. **31**(2), 164–174 (2013)
33. Kukolja, D., Popović, S., Horvat, M., Kovač, B., Ćosić, K.: Comparative analysis of emotion estimation methods based on physiological measurements for real-time applications. Int. J. Hum. Comput. Stud. **72**(10), 717–727 (2014)
34. Lin, J., Yu, H., Miao, C., Shen, Z.: An affective agent for studying composite emotions. In: Proceedings of the 2015 International Conference on Autonomous Agents and Multiagent Systems, AAMAS 2015, Richland, SC, pp. 1947–1948. International Foundation for Autonomous Agents and Multiagent Systems (2015)
35. Liu, H., Lieberman, H., Selker, T.: A model of textual affect sensing using real-world knowledge. In: Proceedings of the 8th International Conference on Intelligent User Interfaces, IUI 2003, pp. 125–132. Association for Computing Machinery, New York (2003)
36. Löffler, D., Schmidt, N., Tscharn, R.: Multimodal expression of artificial emotion in social robots using color, motion and sound. In: Proceedings of the 2018 ACM/IEEE International Conference on Human-Robot Interaction, HRI 2018, pp. 334–343. Association for Computing Machinery, New York (2018)
37. Majumder, A., Behera, L., Subramanian, V.K.: Emotion recognition from geometric facial features using self-organizing map. Pattern Recogn. **47**(3), 1282–1293 (2014)
38. Nicolaou, M.A., Gunes, H., Pantic, M.: Continuous prediction of spontaneous affect from multiple cues and modalities in valence-arousal space. IEEE Trans. Affect. Comput. **2**(2), 92–105 (2011)
39. Nogueira, P.A., Rodrigues, R., Oliveira, E., Nacke, L.E.: A hybrid approach at emotional state detection: merging theoretical models of emotion with data-driven statistical classifiers. In: Proceedings of the 2013 IEEE/WIC/ACM International Joint Conferences on Web Intelligence (WI) and Intelligent Agent Technologies (IAT), WI-IAT 2013, vol. 02, pp. 253–260. IEEE Computer Society, USA (2013)
40. Orellana-Rodriguez, C., Diaz-Aviles, E., Nejdl, W.: Mining affective context in short films for emotion-aware recommendation. In: Proceedings of the 26th ACM Conference on Hypertext & Social Media, HT 2015, pp. 185–194. Association for Computing Machinery, New York (2015)
41. Ortigosa-Hernández, J., Rodríguez, J.D., Alzate, L., Lucania, M., Inza, I., Lozano, J.A.: Approaching sentiment analysis by using semi-supervised learning of multi-dimensional classifiers. Neurocomputing **92**, 98–115 (2012)
42. Pantic, M., Rothkrantz, L.: Expert system for automatic analysis of facial expressions. Image Vis. Comput. **18**(11), 881–905 (2000)
43. Picard, R.W.: Affective computing (1995)
44. Purver, M., Battersby, S.: Experimenting with distant supervision for emotion classification. In: Proceedings of the 13th Conference of the European Chapter of the Association for Computational Linguistics, EACL 2012, pp. 482–491. Association for Computational Linguistics, USA (2012)

45. Quan, C., Ren, F.: Construction of a blog emotion corpus for Chinese emotional expression analysis. In: Proceedings of the 2009 Conference on Empirical Methods in Natural Language Processing, EMNLP 2009, vol. 3, pp. 1446–1454. Association for Computational Linguistics, USA (2009). 123, textual emotion detection for analysis

46. Rajcic, N., McCormack, J.: Mirror ritual: an affective interface for emotional self-reflection. In: Proceedings of the 2020 CHI Conference on Human Factors in Computing Systems, CHI 2020, pp. 1–13. Association for Computing Machinery, New York (2020)

47. Russell, J.: A circumplex model of affect. J. Pers. Soc. Psychol. **39**, 1161–1178 (1980). https://doi.org/10.1037/h0077714

48. Sajjad, M., Nasir, M., Ullah, F.U.M., Muhammad, K., Sangaiah, A.K., Baik, S.W.: Raspberry Pi assisted facial expression recognition framework for smart security in law-enforcement services. Inf. Sci. **479**, 416–431 (2019)

49. Scheirer, J., Fernandez, R., Picard, R.W.: Expression glasses: a wearable device for facial expression recognition. In: Extended Abstracts on Human Factors in Computing Systems, CHI 1999, CHI EA 1999, pp. 262–263. Association for Computing Machinery, New York (1999)

50. Silva, R., Neiva, F.: Systematic literature review in computer science - a practical guide (2016)

51. Wang, J., Yu, L.C., Lai, K.R., Zhang, X.: Tree-structured regional CNN-LSTM model for dimensional sentiment analysis. IEEE/ACM Trans. Audio Speech Lang. Proc. **28**, 581–591 (2020)

52. Wu, S., Falk, T.H., Chan, W.Y.: Automatic speech emotion recognition using modulation spectral features. Speech Commun. **53**(5), 768–785 (2011)

53. Xiaohua, W., Muzi, P., Lijuan, P., Min, H., Chunhua, J., Fuji, R.: Two-level attention with two-stage multi-task learning for facial emotion recognition. J. Vis. Commun. Image Represent. **62**, 217–225 (2019)

54. Yadav, A., Vishwakarma, D.K.: A unified framework of deep networks for genre classification using movie trailer. Appl. Soft Comput. **96**, 106624 (2020)

55. Yin, Z., Zhao, M., Wang, Y., Yang, J., Zhang, J.: Recognition of emotions using multimodal physiological signals and an ensemble deep learning model. Comput. Methods Programs Biomed. **140**, 93–110 (2017)

56. Yoon, H.J., Chung, S.Y.: EEG-based emotion estimation using Bayesian weighted log-posterior function and perceptron convergence algorithm. Comput. Biol. Med. **43**(12), 2230–2237 (2013)

57. Yu, Y., Wang, X.: World cup 2014 in the Twitter world: a big data analysis of sentiments in U.S. sports fans' tweets. Comput. Hum. Behav. **48**, 392–400 (2015)

58. Yu, Z., Zhang, C.: Image based static facial expression recognition with multiple deep network learning. In: Proceedings of the 2015 ACM on International Conference on Multimodal Interaction, ICMI 2015, pp. 435–442. Association for Computing Machinery, New York (2015)

59. Zeng, N., Zhang, H., Song, B., Liu, W., Li, Y., Dobaie, A.M.: Facial expression recognition via learning deep sparse autoencoders. Neurocomputing **273**, 643–649 (2018)

60. Zhang, L., Jiang, M., Farid, D., Hossain, M.: Intelligent facial emotion recognition and semantic-based topic detection for a humanoid robot. Expert Syst. Appl. **40**(13), 5160–5168 (2013)

61. Zhang, L., Mistry, K., Jiang, M., Chin Neoh, S., Hossain, M.A.: Adaptive facial point detection and emotion recognition for a humanoid robot. Comput. Vis. Image Underst. **140**, 93–114 (2015)

62. Zhang, X., Li, W., Chen, X., Lu, S.: MoodExplorer: towards compound emotion detection via smartphone sensing. Proc. ACM Interact. Mob. Wearable Ubiquit. Technol. 1(4) (2018)

63. Zhao, S., et al.: Predicting personalized emotion perceptions of social images. In: Proceedings of the 24th ACM International Conference on Multimedia, MM 2016, pp. 1385–1394. Association for Computing Machinery, New York (2016)

64. Zhou, F., Kong, S., Fowlkes, C.C., Chen, T., Lei, B.: Fine-grained facial expression analysis using dimensional emotion model. Neurocomputing **392**, 38–49 (2020)

65. Zhou, Y., Xue, H., Geng, X.: Emotion distribution recognition from facial expressions. In: Proceedings of the 23rd ACM International Conference on Multimedia, MM 2015, pp. 1247–1250. Association for Computing Machinery, New York (2015)

Methodological Advances

Social Cognition Paradigms *ex Machinas*

Joel Michelson[⌧], Deepayan Sanyal, James Ainooson, Yuan Yang,
and Maithilee Kunda

Department of Computer Science, Vanderbilt University, Vanderbilt Place,
Nashville 37235, TN, USA
{joel.p.michelson,deepayan.sanyal,james.ainooson,yuan.yang,
mkunda}@vanderbilt.edu

Abstract. In this paper, we discuss the creative design of task
paradigms invented to study the social and theory-of-mind skills utilized
by humans and animals as well as the potential applications of these
paradigms in artificial intelligence research. We first present a detailed
review of 21 tasks from the cognitive literature. Next, we provide a
description of our process for translating these tasks into AI-suitable
environments, along with a detailed example using the competitive feeding task paradigm. Finally, we discuss how a battery of these tasks would
be useful for building, training, and evaluating future artificial models of
social intelligence.

Keywords: Theory of mind · Reinforcement learning · Comparative
cognition · Developmental psychology

1 Introduction

In the late 1980s ecologist James Gould performed a series of experiments to
better understand honeybees' navigational abilities [1], but these experiments
also ended up posing fascinating questions about bees' social reasoning abilities.
In the first experiment, Gould captured several foraging bees and carried them
to a boat with flowers in the middle of a lake. These foragers then returned to
their hive and indicated the flowers' location by dancing, but failed to inspire
any recruits to fly in that direction. Later, foragers were shown a new location
of flowers, in the same boat but now moved close to the opposite shoreline. This
time, their recruitment was successful.

Why did the bee recruits decide to "believe" the foragers the second time, but
not the first? While this example has a lot to do with mental maps, navigation,
and memory, it also involves bees reasoning about the beliefs of other bees in
relation to their own in a pretty sophisticated way.

"But wait!" the skeptical reader exclaims. "What if this wasn't about beliefs,
but something more basic? What if the foragers simply smelled like lakewater,
or gave off some other basic cue, and recruits merely avoided following that

---

D. Sanyal, J. Ainooson and Y. Yang—These authors contributed equally to this work.

© The Author(s), under exclusive license to Springer Nature Switzerland AG 2022
N. Gurney and G. Sukthankar (Eds.): AAAI-FSS 2021, LNCS 13775, pp. 53–71, 2022.
https://doi.org/10.1007/978-3-031-21671-8_4

smell/cue?" This very question was asked by experimenters, and they conducted a followup experiment in which the entire hive was transported to a field with flower stations at analogous relative positions.[1]

Now, while foragers enjoyed good food at both field sites and danced roughly equally for both, recruits (presumably who had "not yet been out to note that the lake has mysteriously dried up overnight" [2], p.100) still preferred the shoreline-analogous location.

This example illustrates two important points motivating our work. First: social and theory-of-mind (ToM) abilities (i.e., reasoning about the mental states of the self and others [3]) are essential for intelligence in a wide variety of contexts faced by a wide variety of species.

Second: studying these abilities requires *extremely* careful task designs. It can be easy to design tasks that look like ToM tasks but that can be solved using simple perceptual cues. The comparative cognition (nonhuman animal) literature is rife with debates about ToM tasks and what they purportedly measure versus what they actually measure e.g. [4,5].

In artificial intelligence (AI), social and ToM skills are receiving increasing attention due to their essential role in settings involving cooperation and competition, including in multi-agent settings as well as for human-machine teams. And, while AI research has begun to pull inspiration from the rich literature on biological social cognition, we propose that there is much to be learned on both sides by bridging research across cognitive and computational approaches.

In particular, AI research is often driven forward by having concrete challenge tasks in a specific domain (e.g., chess, Go, ImageNet ILSVRC). We observe that, in the current AI literature, social and ToM tasks are often studied in isolation, with different AI systems built to tackle one or a small set of related tasks, like the ToMNet system [6]. On the other hand, collections of tasks in other areas of AI have served to catalyze interesting lines of ensuing research, like ALE [7] and the Animal-AI Testbed [8] for various single-agent scenarios, or Arena [9] and MARLÖ [10] for multi-agent scenarios.

In this paper, we present our initial steps towards creating a new ToM-Testbed for AI research, inspired by the human and animal ToM literature. We envision the ToM-Testbed as containing a large suite of ToM tasks implemented in a uniform gridworld environment like those commonly used in multi-agent research. While our ToM-Testbed is still under construction, the contributions of this paper include:

- A detailed review of 21 tasks (with multiple variants per task) from the human and non-human animal ToM literature that are candidates for inclusion in our ToM-Testbed.

---

[1] How gullible are bees to this kind of house-swap? As the paper amusingly notes, "Bees readily accept a new site as the home locale if the most prominent landmarks are roughly equivalent, and substitutions of grass for water and vice versa are not the most outrageous exchanges bees will tolerate" [2, p. 100].

- A description of our process of translating tasks designed for humans and animals to gridworld environments, with a detailed example using the competitive feeding task.
- A discussion of specific ways in which the ToM-Testbed could be leveraged in computational experiments to study ToM abilities, learning, transfer, and more.

Our eventual goal is to be able to answer questions about ToM tasks and models that were previously inaccessible. For example, which tasks are readily solvable by off-the-shelf machine learning models? Does success at one set of tasks by an artificially intelligent model seem to imply success at another? If so, do models' performances replicate findings in human childhood development and the rest of the animal kingdom?

2   Background: Populations of Interest

Before diving into our review of specific tasks, we first present a high-level overview of where significant pockets of research on social and ToM reasoning are to be found: 1) typical child development; 2) atypical development (e.g., autism); 3) non-human animals; and 4) artificial agents.

2.1   Typical Child Development

Tasks involving ToM have been vital for understanding child development. In 1983, [11] designed what became known as the Sally Anne task, a test of the ability to attribute false beliefs to other people, that can be given to children. Although false belief (FB) tests are popular and useful predictors of multiple aspects of social skills' development, other aspects of social cognition are examined independently. In Beaudoin's et al. review of developmental ToM measures, skills are divided into seven categories, each referring to the inference of and reasoning about others' emotions, desires, intentions, percepts, knowledge, beliefs, and non-literal communication [12].

Numerous theories about the ontogenetic development of ToM have been proposed. Nativist theories maintain that children's learning is largely independent of environment, that evolution essentially hardwires social skills into their brains [13]. 'Theory theory' focuses on the idea of a 'conceptual revolution' in which children learn to formulate scientific theories [14]. Simulation theory is a view that highlights the importance of pretend play in children, under the assumption that the capacity for pretence is the mechanism that allows for ToM [15]. The executive function hypothesis overlaps with simulation theory, and focuses on the importance of ToM as a component of flexible planning and goal-directed behavior [16–18].

ToM tests for human children frequently involve storytelling. Many types of measurement are used, such as verbal question answering, making choices of pictures or objects, making actions within a setting, or eye-tracking.

2.2 Atypical Child Development

ToM is also a cornerstone of studying various trajectories of atypical child development. For example, ToM has long been shown to develop and present in atypical ways in autism. Many (though not all) children on the autism spectrum show difficulties in false belief tasks [19] and other areas of ToM [20], though the sources and full effects of these differences are still not well understood.

As another example, deaf children who are born to hearing parents have been observed to show ToM deficits similar to those shown by children with autism, but similar deficits were *not* seen in deaf children born to deaf parents, who presumably had the benefits of rich parent-based language exposure from early infancy [21].

Research on ToM in atypical development can not only provide clues as to ingredients and dependencies that support ToM in typical development, but also can highlight how intelligent agents can develop compensatory strategies in the absence of some of these ingredients or dependencies.

Much of this research has also yielded debates about specific ToM tasks, their design, and what they measure.

2.3 Non-human Animals

There is longstanding and vigorous debate about the higher-level social and ToM reasoning capabilities of nonhuman animals, usually studied as a function of different species. Even nonhuman primates like chimpanzees show only limited ToM abilities relative to what even young typically developing human children can do. Even so, the gulfs in social and ToM abilities among different nonhuman animal species are vast, with nonhuman primates and a handful of other species (corvids, i.e., jays and crows, dolphins, domesticated dogs, etc.) showing quite sophisticated abilities relative to other animal species.

In animals, ToM tasks are even more specific and difficult to interpret than they are in humans. As such, their design is generally incredibly strict, with researchers inventing increasingly ingenious controls to avoid null and alternate hypotheses [5], like the Clever Hans effect.[2] Furthermore, at times, animals produce puzzling results in which they succeed at one puzzle but fail at something that seems (to us) to be much simpler.

Animals' tests are restricted in form, as we cannot verbally explain rules, stories, etc. to the subjects. Only certain kinds of responses can be measured for the same reasons.

2.4 Artificial Agents

Recently, social skills have been the focus of much attention by AI researchers, so some of the ideas from human and animal tests have been adapted for machine use.

---

[2] Clever Hans was a horse who was seemingly able to solve difficult problems of arithmetic, but later found to be reliant upon his trainer's involuntary body language cues.

Rabinowitz et al. developed ToMNet, a supervised learning system designed to predict the actions, beliefs, preferences, and percepts of agents moving around a gridworld environment [6]. In their study of ToMNet's abilities, they design computational variants of the Sally Anne test, a paradigm designed to test for false-belief attribution in humans and animals [11].

Hernandez-leal et al. provide a thorough review of research in the field of multi-agent deep reinforcement learning [22], including a discussion of algorithms that perform some version of theory-of-mind reasoning in the context of adversarial games.

From a slightly different angle, the work described in this paper is heavily inspired by the Animal AI Testbed [8], which is a suite of first-person navigation challenges implemented in a three-dimensional environment modeled after studies of animal intelligence, and in which many of the tasks have specifically been deployed with animals in other research. Although it does not currently include tests of social reasoning, its repertoire of 900 sub-tasks are all variants of one of 12 animal cognition paradigms or 16 classes of environment used to teach fundamental skills like basic exploration.

3   Review of ToM Tasks

We have conducted a detailed review of numerous widely-used ToM tasks from the cognitive literature, mostly drawing from studies of non-human animals (though several of these tasks have been used in human studies as well).

We present this review as a resource for AI researchers to get a sense of the kinds of tasks used in the cognitive literature and to understand which of these tasks are more or less difficult for our various animal brethren. These tasks are also highly informative from the perspective of task designs, i.e., in identifying when and how tasks might be solved using alternative (e.g., non-ToM) methods, and how task variants can be combined to pinpoint the extent to which an individual intelligent agent truly demonstrates certain capabilities.

We present an overview of studies we reviewed in Table 1, and we also present narrative descriptions of all tasks in the Appendix. We have classified these tasks into the kinds of ToM reasoning they entail: preferences, perception, intent, knowledge, beliefs, deception, and other.

4   Translating Real-World Tasks into AI Tasks

We first describe some desiderata that we are using to guide our selection of real-world (referring here to tasks designed for humans and animals) ToM tasks and our implementation of them for AI frameworks. Then, we describe the process of implementation for one example task.

4.1 Desiderata

Just as there are almost always alternate explanations for observed animal behaviors, performing well at a given example of these tasks does not necessarily indicate success at any specific skill. We do not expect to be able to build a system for testing models with outputs as convenient as "has ToM" or even "can infer preferences of another agent". Like the paradigms' use for studying animals, any particular test is subject to interpretation and criticism. For this reason, our aim in translating these problems is to do so with a purely task-based perspective.

That said, a task for an artificially intelligent agent should be as informative and meaningful as possible. For each task variant, our goal is to create an artificial environment as close as possible to the original design. In human and animal tests, intelligent controls are implemented to help ensure the results report on their intended subject. By providing multiple variations of each task, with every reasonable control and dependent variable available, we hope to provide the most perspectives into models' reasoning processes as possible. In fact, the computational nature of the tasks and models offers novel methods of observation that are infeasible in the real world. Agents' belief states may be quantified objectively [6], their perceptions reported with perfect accuracy, and their ontological training process can be understood deeply, a stark contrast with any test performed on humans and (especially) animals.

Due to tasks' dependence on precursor knowledge, we attempt to retain commonalities between them when sensible. Tasks should involve the simplest percepts and controls possible so that a completely naïve model does not need to overcome too many unrelated learning hurdles to succeed. In Table 2, we hypothesize commonalities of selected skills that may be necessary for the completion of various tasks.

One of the benefits of using a visual task environment is the possibility of these tests (in their reimagined formulation) being run in human or animal studies for comparison. The ability to run these same benchmarks with human subjects of similar populations to previous studies will provide insight into both the adequacy of our specific implementations as well as additional data reproducing findings on the real-world versions of these tasks.

Table 1. Social Cognition Paradigms. *pret*, *ctrl*, and *test* refer to the numbers of individually defined pretraining, control, and test conditions. We consider measured exposure to most task elements to be training, but certain elements assumed to be understood (such as familiarization with the Likert scale) are not included. In several cases, pretraining involves the prior tasks in the experiment,these do not count as additional training tasks. Likewise, if a training task is used as a control condition, we only count it once as a pretraining task.

Task	Variant	Species	n	pret	ctrl	test
Preference						
Yummy-yucky [23]		14, 18 month-old children	159	2	1	1
Multiple desires [24]	Successive	5, 8 year-old children	20, 15	0	0	2
	Simultaneous	Children of various ages	75	0	0	4
	Study 3	5, 7 year-old children	25, 25	0	0	2
Perception						
Picture identification [25]	Picture task	2–3;6 year old children	16, 9	2	2	4
Appearance-reality [26]	Testing	Children of various ages	>16	0	3	5
	Teaching	3 year-olds	16	0	0	1
Intent						
Two-action [27]		Japanese quail	12	1	1	2
Distinguishing Int. [28]		2 and 3 year-old children	8, 8	1	0	2
		Chimpanzees, orangutans	5, 5	1	0	2
Rational imitation [29]	Head-touching	14-month-old children	36	0	0	2
[30]		Preverbal infants	27	0	1	2
Accidental Trans. [31]	Experiment 1	3–8-year-old children	162	0	2	2
	Experiment 2	3–8-year-old children	46	0	2	1
Knowledge						
Competitive Feeding [32]	Did	Chimpanzees	9	0	1	2
	Who	Chimpanzees	8	0	1	1
	Which	Chimpanzees	9	0	1	2
Knower-Guesser [33]	Begging	Wolves and Dogs	60	1	1	4
	Bucket training	Wolves and Dogs	8, 12	0	0	2
Goggles [34]	Gaze following	Chimpanzees	25	1	1	2
	Competitive	Chimpanzees	19	1	1	3
See-know task [35]	Experiment 1	3, 4 year-olds	16, 16	0	2	2
	Experiment 2	3 year-olds	12	0	4	4
Belief						
Sally Anne [11]	Standard	Children of various ages	36	0	2	2
	Exploration	Kindergarten children	92	0	2	3
[19]	Standard	Human children	61	0	3	1
[36]	Experiment 1	Great apes	43	1	0	2
	Experiment 2	Great apes	44	1	0	2
[37]	FB 1	2 year-old children	20	2	1	1
	FB 2	2 year-old children	20	2	1	1
Ignorance vs. FB [38]	Experiment 1	3, 4 and 5 year-old children	20, 20, 20	0	2	2
	Experiment 2	3, 4 and 5 year-old children	24 24 24	0	2	2
	Experiment 3	3;6 year-old children	22	0	2	2
	Experiment 4	3 and 4 year-old children	18 18	0	2	1
	Experiment 5	3–4 year olds	36	0	2	2
	Experiment 6	4, 5 and 6 year-olds	12 12 12	0	2	3
Inhibitory FB [39]	Negative desire	4 year-olds	16	0	3	2
	Opp. behavior	4 year-olds	16	0	3	2

(continued)

Table 1. (*continued*)

Task	Variant	Species	n	pret	ctrl	test
Deception						
Penny hiding [40]		2–7 year-old children	106	1	0	1
Box-locking sabotage [41]	One box	Human children	87	1	1	4
	Two boxes	Human children	88	1	1	4
Back/forth forage [42]		Chimpanzees	12	2	1	2
Unseen competitors [43]		Ravens	10	0	2	1
Other						
Mirror self-recog. [44]	Mirror exposure	Chimpanzees	4	1	0	1
	Marking	Chimpanzees, monkeys	4 4	1	1	1
Role-reversal [45]		Chimpanzees	4	1	0	2

Table 2. Hypothetical commonalities between selected tasks. While Memory refers to a requirement for the subject to have memory, $Desires_A$, $Sees_A$, and FB_A refer to the subject's inference of (i.e. attribution of) desires, vision, and false beliefs (FBs) in other agents present in the task's setting.

Task	Memory	$Desires_A$	$Sees_A$	FB_A
YummyYucky		x		
Two-action	x	x		
Knower-guesser	x		x	
Sally Anne	x	x	x	x

Finally, the testbed should be able to run quickly and in parallel for optimal reinforcement learning training. The battery of tasks on the testbed should be extensible, to accommodate the frequent development of new tasks by comparative and developmental psychologists. The system should be open source to enable rapid advances in social capabilities of AI.

4.2   Passive Observers and Active Participants

While some tasks involve observing and then answering questions, plenty require an agent's participation in the given setting. This requirement is not surprising, given that many social skills exhibit themselves through cooperation and competition with peers. The distinction between observational and interaction-based tasks is not always clear, and many tests may be imagined in either light.

Our selection of a two-dimensional environment allows for multiple kinds of input types (e.g. egocentric and allocentric worldviews, three-channel and 'rich' image formats), and should be amenable to both supervised and reinforcement-learning models. To maintain consistency across task implementations, we ensure that a human subject should be able to participate in all tasks with similar inputs and controls. Although certain tasks make use of objects in different ways, generally objects' representations are retained across tasks (e.g. 'food' is a green circle).

4.3   Precursor Knowledge

All of the experiments for humans and animals require a wealth of precursor 'common sense' knowledge, such as object detection, memory, navigation, etc.

Many of these experiments are intended to be performed on a subject lacking certain prior experience, but exactly what experience they can be allowed to have is not clear. In Rabinowitz' et al. implementation of Sally Anne, they account for agents having novel goal preferences by training a multitude of agents with random preferential permutations [6]. That way, ToMNet's training involves repeatedly learning other agents' preferences from recent memory (ontogenetically). But can we expect the same of novel objects, like translucent glass? In our task-based approach, we may generally approach these sorts of problems by providing a multitude of training variants, e.g. a training set that includes translucent glass and one that does not.

4.4   Implementation

Due to its ease of use, runtime speed, and imagistic representations, we opt to adapt MarlGrid [46], a multi-agent fork of MiniGrid [47], an open-source implementation of a gridworld for reinforcement learning in a setting that is compatible with the popular OpenAI Gym [48].

4.5   Task Selection

For our initial set of tasks to consider for implementation, we select those with the most apparent translations to gridworld environments. This set includes several tasks that use verbal or image-based storytelling, as many of these stories can be expressed with observable events.

As mentioned in Sect. 1, [12] divides ToM tasks into seven categories: emotions, desires, intentions, percepts, knowledge, beliefs, and mentalistic understanding of non-literal communication. Although emotional understanding is a valuable aspect of social intelligence, we opt to omit it from our tasks due to the bounty of existing work in the field of affective computing and the difficulty of translating the complexity of emotions to simplified systems. Likewise, non-literal communication is a complex concept that cannot be easily translated to toy environments due to its dependence on natural language understanding, so we omit that category as well.

4.6   Detailed Example: Competitive Feeding

The competitive feeding paradigm is a test for specific ToM skills, like attribution of seeing and knowing, to conspecifics in social hierarchies.

The competitive feeding paradigm requires two animals, one of whom—the subject—is subordinate to the other in an existing social hierarchy. The two animals are kept on opposite sides of a central enclosure, separated from the enclosure by barriers (a top-down view of this task is shown in Fig. 1). A researcher

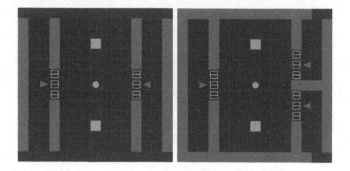

Fig. 1. General setups for experiments CF1 and CF2. Individual test conditions and probe trials differ only in the sequence of changes to the environment, including the ordering of doors opening, the opacity of the dominant's door, and the food's conditional re-positioning. During the simulated 'baiting', the food object (green circle) moves to overlap one of the green squares, where it is no longer visible to either agent. Agents and doors are depicted as red triangles and yellow-barred boxes, respectively. This specific setup differs slightly from [32] in that the subordinate cannot see the food after this stage, and must remember its location. (Color figure online)

first places food on the subordinate's side of one barrier (baiting), and later moves it to the subordinate's side of another barrier. Finally, both animals are released, with the subordinate having a slight head start. Two conditions are varied: whether the dominant's door is open or closed during the first baiting, as well as during the second baiting; and whether the subject can see the dominant during the baiting.

This test attempts to distinguish ToM in animals by showing that the subject attempts to get more food when it can see the dominant, and knows the dominant does not know the location of food; i.e. whether the dominant's door is closed during the second baiting event. In other words, the subject must generate a ToM of the dominant agent to accurately predict whether the dominant will attempt to reach food at its first location or its second.

In [32], three experiments are performed, each with its own set of testing conditions. During tests, the dominant's door opens only once the subordinate touches the floor of the central cage, or after thirty seconds, giving the subordinate a head start towards the food. Probe trials are randomly interspersed, in which food is placed in the open and both animals are released simultaneously. The purpose of these probe trials is to make sure the subordinate animal does not gain confidence in its ability to reach food before its competitor.

4.6.1   Experiment CF1a-d

The goal of experiment 1 is to test for the attribution of sight, or the answer to the question "did she see it hidden or moved?". Four testing variants are used, with names referring to the dominant's condition: Uninformed, in which the subordinate has vision of the dominant, but the dominant is unable to see the baiting; Control uninformed (competitor informed), in which both subjects may see one another and the dominant observes the baiting; Misinformed, in which subjects see one another as food is placed, but then the dominant's door is closed and the food is moved to a new location; and Control misinformed (competitor informed), in which food is moved as in Misinformed but in view of the dominant.

4.6.2   Experiment CF2a-c

Experiment 2 requires the subject to distinguish *who* saw it hidden, of multiple potential competitors. Two dominant competitors are placed in cages opposing the subject, but only one witnesses the baiting. The two test conditions are each simply releasing one of each of the competitors: the one who witnessed or the one who did not witness the baiting. It is made apparent to the subject which competitor will be released before it is released.

4.6.3   Experiment CF3a-d

Experiment 3 uses multiple food objects to study whether the subject can understand *which* piece is seen hidden by a competitor. Now, there are three food locations, and two pieces of food are placed during the baiting. The same four conditions as experiment 1 are used, except the dominant always sees the first baiting, but only conditionally witnesses the second baiting or the movement of one piece of food.

4.6.4   Experiment CF4a-i

[4] argue the competitive feeding paradigm does not distinguish theory of mind from non-mentalist problem solving. In this version, there are n (e.g., 5) lanes, each with a food bucket with hidden contents. After initial exposures, nine separate conditions are presented randomly to the subjects, eliminating the possibility of solution via a single, simple strategy.

4.6.5   Further Details

The subject should be pretrained until familiar with several concepts, including that food is hidden under similarly-colored tiles; that competitors have similar perceptions, actions, and goal-driven intentions (they will always attempt to take the food if they see it); and that doors have three distinct states that sometimes change spontaneously: open, closed (opaque), and closed (transparent). **Precursors CF0**, then, are designed to integrate all three of these concepts in randomly generated settings.

5   Discussion: Challenges and Promise

Despite its theoretical and demonstrated usefulness in both the natural world and in artificial settings, the cognitive requirements—fulfilling both necessity and sufficiency—of ToM are not well understood. These abilities are rare in the natural world, so logic dictates they must be either very difficult to create or are only useful in niche circumstances. By implementing a cognitive model that demonstrates these abilities, and by testing that model in a variety of environments, we may learn what is necessary and sufficient for the model's success, and which environmental conditions encourage agents to train and make use of such a model, even at significant cost to the agent.

We hypothesize that ToM's presence alongside other advanced cognitive abilities in the human repertoire is no coincidence; many of the abilities we consider uniquely human (e.g. compositionality, etc.) have roots in the same core mental constructs. Given the recent success of [6] at training an agent to correctly answer questions regarding other agents' false beliefs, we believe a similar implementation will provide an excellent starting point for further development.

While developmental psychology has produced evidence of somewhat-regular sequential orderings, or stages, in which skills often emerge [49], the understanding of skills' intrinsic dependencies in the field of artificial intelligence is fairly underdeveloped. Transfer and curriculum learning are already massive fields of study, but—perhaps due to AI's relatively more easily accessible nature—these studies tend to aim to capture the admittedly more alluring concept of skills themselves rather than rote task performance.

One potential direction for our ToM-Testbed will be to organize tasks according to a ladder or graph of dependencies, based on findings from the human and animal literature. Then, we can examine these dependencies in the context of transfer learning and curriculum learning. For instance, to what extent does training on precursor tasks result in more efficient or more robust higher-level ToM abilities?

6   Conclusion

In this work we addressed the immense potential in leveraging the diverse tasks invented by biologists and psychologists to study ToM in animals for AI research. The development of these tasks initially required careful planning to overcome the many alternate intelligent and unintelligent explanations of animal behavior. We examine 21 tasks from the cognitive literature, including many more subtasks, for their eligibility in a battery of tests for the training and evaluation of artificial agents. We present a brief description of the setup and goal of each task examined, found in the Appendix. After discussing the desirable properties of a ToM-Testbed, we examine the process of translating one task, competitive feeding, to a simplified multi-agent gridworld environment. Finally, we discuss how the endeavor of understanding ToM skills may present a challenging frontier, but also the promise of helping us—and our bots—better understand each other.

Acknowledgments. We extend thanks to our financial supporters at NISE and to our anonymous reviewers for their helpful criticisms, comments, and suggestions.

Declarations

Funding. This work was supported in part by the Neurodiversity Inspired Science and Engineering (NISE) NSF program grant DGE 19-22697 (K. Stassun, PI).

Appendix A ToM Task Descriptions

Preferences

Yummy-yucky. The Yummy-yucky task is designed to tell whether a subject is able to attribute preferences to an experimenter [23]. First, the subject's preferences are established by allowing them time with two bowls of different foods. An experimenter tries one food and then the other, and makes expressions of either disgust or happiness. The experimenter requests food from the subject by placing their palm halfway between the bowls.

Multiple desires[24] test for children's ability to attribute multiple desires to another being. In these tests, children are told a story, and are then asked to answer specific questions, either verbally or by choosing a picture of what might happen next. Three variants are tested: successive desires, simultaneous and contradictory desires, and scenarios involving false beliefs.

Perception

Picture Identification. The picture identification task is a simple task of perspective-taking ability [25]. A subject is shown a flat occluder with a picture on both sides. The occluder is rotated so that one side faces the subject, and one faces the experimenter. The subject is then asked questions such as what it is able to see, what the experimenter is able to see, and whether the experimenter can see the picture on the subject's side of the occluder.

Appearance-Reality. The appearance-reality task is a general framework for distinguishing whether a subject has the ability to understand that objects' appearances and true natures sometimes differ [26]. For example, a red car held behind a green pane of glass might appear black. Experimenters question subjects about their perceptual experience and reality (e.g. "What color is the car really?") under different circumstances, such as when the car is only partially occluded by the green pane.

Intent

Two-action. The two-action test is a general framework for differentiating imitation and emulation in animals [27]. Experimenters demonstrate one of two methods by which a subject may achieve a reward. The subject's behaviors are then recorded and compared with control subjects' behaviors without demonstration.

Distinguishing Intentions from Accidents. In this task, subjects choose one box out of three based on a mark placed by the experimenter. In each trial, two boxes out of the three are marked, one *intentionally* and one (by way of observed performance) *accidentally*. Subjects are rewarded for choosing the box which the experimenter marked intentionally [28].

Rational Imitation. The rational imitation task is similar to the two-action test, but in this variant the demonstrator is sometimes shown to have a reason for performing a task in an inconvenient way, e.g. using their head to flip a light switch because their hands are occupied [29,30]. Now we may compare whether a subject truly understands the demonstrator's goal-oriented behavior, as the subject might reason that they are able to use their hands to complete a task rather than directly imitating the demonstrator.

Accidental/Moral Transgression. In this task, a subject is presented with a story involving either an accidental or a moral transgression [31]. An accidental transgression would be a mistake made by a character due to their lack of understanding, i.e. a false belief. For example, a character might throw a bag in the trash without knowing it contains another character's prized possession. A moral transgression would have the same outcome in the story but is performed intentionally by the character. The subject is asked numerous questions about the scenario similar to those in the Sally–Anne task, but including additional questions about whether characters should be punished and why.

Knowledge

Competitive Feeding. The competitive feeding paradigm requires two animals, one of whom (the subject) is considered subordinate to the other in their social hierarchy [32]. The two animals are kept on opposite sides of an enclosure with two barriers. A researcher first places food on the subordinate's side of one barrier, and later moves it to the subordinate's side of another barrier. Finally, both animals are released, with the subordinate having a slight head start.

Knower-Guesser. The knower-guesser paradigm is a commonly used method for determining whether animals can attribute concepts such as 'seeing' and 'knowing' [33]. It also allows a nonverbal subject to directly participate in an interspecific exercise rather than simply observing. Two human experimenters, the Knower and the Guesser, are presented to an animal subject. The Guesser leaves the room (or has their gaze somehow occluded), while the Knower places food in some location that is not visible to the subject. The Guesser returns, and then both Knower and Guesser point to places where they think the food is located. The subject may then search one container for food and keep it as a reward.

Goggles. Because a subject of a knower-guesser test might employ a number of non-mentalistic strategies, in the goggles/visor test the difference between knower and guesser may only be correctly inferred by generalizing from first-person experience with an occluding object [34]. In this variant, the subject spends some time with an object that appears opaque from a distance, like goggles or a wire screen. This object may be either opaque or translucent. Then, a test like knower-guesser is performed, with the experimenter's vision being occluded by the object. In the test, the object is always opaque, so the experimenter is truly blind and the subject has no chance of seeing their eyes.

See-Know. This task is similar to the Knower-Guesser task, with the exception that the evaluation is verbal in nature [35]. In one version of the task, the subject is either the Knower or the Guesser, while the other role is played by a puppet. The Knower then observes the process of hiding a toy in a box and the subject is quizzed on whether they or the puppet know the color of the toy in the box. In the other variant, there are two puppets which play both roles, and the subject is asked to attribute knowledge about their knowledge and percept to either of them.

Beliefs

Sally Anne. The Sally Anne test, also referred to as the standard FB test or the change-of-location FB test, is a commonly used test for the attribution of false beliefs [11]. The prototypical Sally Anne test, first used in 1985 by [19], involves the use of puppets to tell a short story. Sally places her toy in one location, and then leaves the room. Next, unbeknownst to Sally, Anne moves the toy to a new location. Finally, Sally returns to look for her toy. Several control questions establish that the subject understands the basic story elements such as the characters' names and the toy's location. The subject is then asked: "Where will Sally look for her toy?"

Ignorance and False Belief. While false belief tasks require some form of advanced understanding of somebody else's mental state, understanding ignorance of certain knowledge in others is likely an easier task. The tasks for testing ignorance in others follow a similar pattern as False Belief tests, with the modification that the subject is directly asked if the other participant is aware of the location of the manipulated object [38].

Inhibitory FB. The inhibitory false-belief test is intended to explain successful performance at the Sally Anne test [39]. In addition to having true or false beliefs, characters might have positive or negative desires. In the negative desire condition, the Sally character wants to look in a container where the hidden object is *not* located. In the Opposite behavior condition, Sally is introduced as an odd person who always does things she does not want.

Deception

Penny-Hiding. The penny-hiding game is a simple test of deception [40]. During training, an experimenter repeatedly allows the subject to guess which of their closed hands hides a penny. Rather than leave the results to chance, in some number of trials both hands contain a penny, and in other trials neither does. For the test, the roles are reversed: the subject is asked to hide a penny in one of their hands, and the interviewer guesses which. The subject's hands are visible during the hiding, so they may only hide the penny's location by repeatedly passing it between their hands or imitating the same action. Subjects are graded by the experimenter based on their apparent use of deceptive strategies.

Box-Locking. The box-locking test examines subjects' abilities in settings that allow for sabotage and verbal deception [41]. First, puppets are introduced to the subject along with rewards for 'success': the friendly seal shares what it finds, but the thieving wolf takes everything for itself. In both settings, a reward is hidden in a box, and the subject is tasked with making sure the seal is able to find the reward, but the wolf is not. In the sabotage setting, the child is able to use a key to lock the box, physically preventing a puppet character from opening it. In the deception setting, the child is asked by the puppet character whether the box is locked, and the child may lie to prevent it from attempting to open the box. A minor variation involves the use of two boxes, so the child may lock either one, or may lie about the location of the reward.

Back-and-Forth Foraging. This task studies whether subjects are able to ascribe their own reward preferences to competitors [42]. Two rewards are hidden under boards on a platform, as viewed by the subject. One of the boards has a hole below it so that that board is flat after the reward is put under it, while the other one is slanted. The platform is then presented first to the competitor, who has to choose one of the reward items. Then, the platform is presented to the subject, who has to decide which reward to pick. In a control condition, the subjects do not display strong preference towards either reward in the absence of the competitor. The social condition tests whether the subject determines that the competitor would go for the reward under the slanted board and choose the other.

Caching Food from Unseen Competitors. While changes in food caching behavior of scrubjays in the presence of competitors has been well-documented, most experiments allow the subject direct access to the conspecific's gaze. This task seeks to test whether ravens can use the fact that unseen competitors have visual access to their food-caching behavior and alter their behavior based on that [43]. The subject is put in a room and audio recordings of other scrubjays are played from behind a closed window which has a peephole in it. The subjects are made aware to the presence of the peephole by the experimenter. The task tests whether the subjects infer the presence of competitors in the adjacent room by the sound and alter their behavior based on the assumption that the competitor can see them through the peephole.

Other

Mirror Self-recognition. Mirror self-recognition tests are generally tests for bodily self-awareness [44]. A subject is given exposure time with mirrors, with increasing proximity. In some observational variants, experimenters observe the subject and rate its behaviors as social (e.g. trying to communicate with the mirrored self), versus self-directed (e.g. using the mirror to help clean its own teeth). Often researchers will paint a marking on a subject's body in a location that would otherwise be undetectable to them, such as their forehead. The subject may then touch the mark after being exposed to it via the mirror.

Role-Reversal. The role-reversal test is similar to the penny-hiding test, but in a cooperative scenario instead of competitive [45]. Using the same apparatus as for the knower-guesser test, a subject is trained to take on one of two roles: the informant, or the operator. The other role is performed by an experimenter. The informant is able to see where food is hidden, and may communicate that information to the operator. The operator then pulls a lever and shares the food with their partner. Success is determined by the operator's correct choice of food location. After subjects learn their roles successfully, they are given the alternate role and tested for their ability to complete the new task without training.

References

1. Gould, J.L., Gould, C.G., et al.: The Honey Bee. Scientific American Library, New York, United States (1988)
2. Gould, J.L.: Honey bee cognition. Cognition **37**(1–2), 83–103 (1990)
3. Bird, G., Viding, E.: The self to other model of empathy: providing a new framework for understanding empathy impairments in psychopathy, autism, and alexithymia. Neurosci. Biobehav. Rev. **47**, 520–532 (2014)
4. Penn, D.C., Povinelli, D.J.: On the lack of evidence that non-human animals possess anything remotely resembling a 'theory of mind'. Philos. Trans. R. Soc. B: Biol. Sci. **362**(1480), 731–744 (2007)
5. Penn, D.C., Holyoak, K.J., Povinelli, D.J.: Darwin's mistake: explaining the discontinuity between human and nonhuman minds. Behav. Brain Sci. **31**(2), 109–130 (2008)
6. Rabinowitz, N., Perbet, F., Song, F., Zhang, C., Eslami, S.A., Botvinick, M.: Machine theory of mind. In: International Conference on Machine Learning, pp. 4218–4227. PMLR (2018)
7. Bellemare, M.G., Naddaf, Y., Veness, J., Bowling, M.: The arcade learning environment: an evaluation platform for general agents. J. Artif. Intell. Res. **47**, 253–279 (2013)
8. Crosby, M., Beyret, B., Shanahan, M., Hernández-Orallo, J., Cheke, L., Halina, M.: The animal-AI testbed and competition. In: Escalante, H.J., Hadsell, R. (eds.) Proceedings of the NeurIPS 2019 Competition and Demonstration Track. Proceedings of Machine Learning Research, vol. 123, pp. 164–176. PMLR, Vancouver, Canada (2020)
9. Song, Y., et al.: Arena: a general evaluation platform and building toolkit for multi-agent intelligence. Proc. AAAI Conf. Artif. Intell. **34**(05), 7253–7260 (2020)

10. Perez-Liebana, D., et al.: The multi-agent reinforcement learning in malmö (marlö) competition. arXiv preprint arXiv:1901.08129 (2019)
11. Wimmer, H., Perner, J.: Beliefs about beliefs: representation and constraining function of wrong beliefs in young children's understanding of deception. Cognition **13**(1), 103–128 (1983)
12. Beaudoin, C., Leblanc, É., Gagner, C., Beauchamp, M.H.: Systematic review and inventory of theory of mind measures for young children. Front. Psychol. **10**, 2905 (2020)
13. Leslie, A.M.: Pretending and believing: issues in the theory of ToMM. Cognition **50**(1–3), 211–238 (1994)
14. Gopnik, A., Wellman, H.M.: The theory theory. In: An Earlier Version of this Chapter Was Presented at the Society for Research in Child Development Meeting, 1991. Cambridge University Press (1994)
15. Harris, P.L.: From simulation to folk psychology: the case for development. Mind Lang. **7**, 120–144 (1992)
16. Carlson, S.M., Moses, L.J.: Individual differences in inhibitory control and children's theory of mind. Child Dev. **72**(4), 1032–1053 (2001)
17. Hughes, C.: Finding your marbles: does preschoolers' strategic behavior predict later understanding of mind? Dev. Psychol. **34**(6), 1326 (1998)
18. Russell, J.: How executive disorders can bring about an inadequate'theory of mind'. In: Autism as an Executive Disorder, pp. 256–304. Oxford University Press, New York, United States (1997)
19. Baron-Cohen, S., Leslie, A.M., Frith, U., et al.: Does the autistic child have a "theory of mind". Cognition **21**(1), 37–46 (1985)
20. Happé, F., Frith, U.: Theory of mind in autism. In: Schopler, E., Mesibov, G.B. (eds.) Learning and Cognition in Autism. Current Issues in Autism, pp. 177–197. Springer, Boston (1995). https://doi.org/10.1007/978-1-4899-1286-2_10
21. Peterson, C.C., Siegal, M.: Representing inner worlds: theory of mind in autistic, deaf, and normal hearing children. Psychol. Sci. **10**(2), 126–129 (1999)
22. Hernandez-Leal, P., Kartal, B., Taylor, M.E.: A survey and critique of multiagent deep reinforcement learning. Auton. Agent. Multi-Agent Syst. **33**(6), 750–797 (2019). https://doi.org/10.1007/s10458-019-09421-1
23. Repacholi, B.M., Gopnik, A.: Early reasoning about desires: evidence from 14-and 18-month-olds. Dev. Psychol. **33**(1), 12 (1997)
24. Bennett, M., Galpert, L.: Children's understanding of multiple desires. Int. J. Behav. Dev. **16**(1), 15–33 (1993)
25. Masangkay, Z.S., McCluskey, K.A., McIntyre, C.W., Sims-Knight, J., Vaughn, B.E., Flavell, J.H.: The early development of inferences about the visual percepts of others. Child Dev. **45**, 357–366 (1974)
26. Flavell, J.H., Green, F.L., Flavell, E.R., Watson, M.W., Campione, J.C.: Development of knowledge about the appearance-reality distinction. Monogr. Soc. Res. Child Dev. **51**, 87 (1986)
27. Akins, C.K., Zentall, T.R.: Imitative learning in male Japanese quail (coturnix japonica) using the two-action method. J. Comp. Psychol. **110**(3), 316 (1996)
28. Call, J., Tomasello, M.: Distinguishing intentional from accidental actions in orangutans (pongo pygmaeus), chimpanzees (pan troglodytes) and human children (homo sapiens). J. Comp. Psychol. **112**(2), 192 (1998)
29. Meltzoff, A.N.: Infant imitation after a 1-week delay: long-term memory for novel acts and multiple stimuli. Dev. Psychol. **24**(4), 470 (1988)
30. Gergely, G., Bekkering, H., Király, I.: Rational imitation in preverbal infants. Nature **415**(6873), 755–755 (2002)

31. Killen, M., Mulvey, K.L., Richardson, C., Jampol, N., Woodward, A.: The accidental transgressor: morally-relevant theory of mind. Cognition **119**(2), 197–215 (2011)
32. Hare, B., Call, J., Tomasello, M.: Do chimpanzees know what conspecifics know? Anim. Behav. **61**(1), 139–151 (2001)
33. Udell, M.A., Dorey, N.R., Wynne, C.D.: Can your dog read your mind? understanding the causes of canine perspective taking. Learn. Behav. **39**(4), 289–302 (2011)
34. Karg, K., Schmelz, M., Call, J., Tomasello, M.: The goggles experiment: can chimpanzees use self-experience to infer what a competitor can see? Anim. Behav. **105**, 211–221 (2015)
35. Pillow, B.H.: Early understanding of perception as a source of knowledge. J. Exp. Child Psychol. **47**(1), 116–129 (1989)
36. Krupenye, C., Kano, F., Hirata, S., Call, J., Tomasello, M.: Great apes anticipate that other individuals will act according to false beliefs. Science **354**(6308), 110–114 (2016)
37. Southgate, V., Senju, A., Csibra, G.: Action anticipation through attribution of false belief by 2-year-olds. Psychol. Sci. **18**(7), 587–592 (2007)
38. Hogrefe, G.-J., Wimmer, H., Perner, J.: Ignorance versus false belief: a developmental lag in attribution of epistemic states. Child Dev. **57**, 567–582 (1986)
39. Leslie, A.M., Polizzi, P.: Inhibitory processing in the false belief task: two conjectures. Dev. Sci. **1**(2), 247–253 (1998)
40. Gratch, G.: Response alternation in children: a developmental study of orientations to uncertainty. Vita Humana **7**, 49–60 (1964)
41. Sodian, B., Frith, U.: Deception and sabotage in autistic, retarded and normal children. J. Child Psychol. Psychiatry **33**(3), 591–605 (1992)
42. Schmelz, M., Call, J., Tomasello, M.: Chimpanzees know that others make inferences. Proc. Natl. Acad. Sci. **108**(7), 3077–3079 (2011)
43. Bugnyar, T., Reber, S.A., Buckner, C.: Ravens attribute visual access to unseen competitors. Nat. Commun. **7**(1), 1–6 (2016)
44. Gallup, G.G.: Chimpanzees: self-recognition. Science **167**(3914), 86–87 (1970)
45. Povinelli, D.J., Nelson, K.E., Boysen, S.T.: Comprehension of role reversal in chimpanzees: evidence of empathy? Anim. Behav. **43**(4), 633–640 (1992)
46. Ndousse, K.K., Eck, D., Levine, S., Jaques, N.: Emergent social learning via multi-agent reinforcement learning. In: International Conference on Machine Learning, pp. 7991–8004. PMLR (2021)
47. Chevalier-Boisvert, M., Willems, L., Pal, S.: Minimalistic gridworld environment for openai gym. GitHub (2018)
48. Brockman, G., Cheung, V., Pettersson, L., Schneider, J., Schulman, J., Tang, J., Zaremba, W.: Openai gym. arXiv preprint arXiv:1606.01540 (2016)
49. Piaget, J.: Piaget's theory. In: Inhelder, B., Chipman, H.H., Zwingmann, C. (eds.) Piaget and His School, Springer Study Edition, pp. 11–23. Springer, Heidelberg (1976)

Evaluating Artificial Social Intelligence in an Urban Search and Rescue Task Environment

Jared Freeman[1]($\boxtimes$) (iD), Lixiao Huang[2] (iD), Matt Wood[1] (iD), and Stephen J. Cauffman[2] (iD)

[1] Aptima, Inc., Woburn, MA 01801, USA
jaredtfreeman@gmail.com, wood82@gmail.com
[2] Arizona State University, Phoenix, AZ 85004, USA
{lixiao.huang, scauffma}@asu.edu

Abstract. Human team members show a remarkable ability to infer the state of their partners and anticipate their needs and actions. Prior research demonstrates that an artificial system can make some predictions accurately concerning artificial agents. This study investigated whether an artificial system could generate a robust Theory of Mind of human teammates. An urban search and rescue (USAR) task environment was developed to elicit human teamwork and evaluate inference and prediction about team members by software agents and humans. The task varied team members' roles and skills, types of task synchronization and interdependence, task risk and reward, completeness of mission planning, and information asymmetry. The task was implemented in Minecraft™ and applied in a study of 64 teams, each with three remotely distributed members. An evaluation of six Artificial Social Intelligences (ASI) and several human observers addressed the accuracy with which each predicted team performance, inferred experimentally manipulated knowledge of team members, and predicted member actions. All agents performed above chance; humans slightly outperformed ASI agents on some tasks and significantly outperformed ASI agents on others; no one ASI agent reliably outperformed the others; and the accuracy of ASI agents and human observers improved rapidly though modestly during the brief trials.

Keywords: Artificial Intelligence · Social science · Theory of Mind

1 Introduction[1]

Teams succeed through coordinated actions by members who differ in their capabilities and roles. Teams achieve this coordination using domain-specific, often mission-specific, compositions of training, talk, technology, and Theory of Mind (ToM) [1, 11]. The first three techniques help team members manage the scope of the fourth, ToM, which enables team members to infer the capabilities and goals of teammates, predict their actions, and coordinate or compensate to improve teamwork.

© The Author(s), under exclusive license to Springer Nature Switzerland AG 2022
N. Gurney and G. Sukthankar (Eds.): AAAI-FSS 2021, LNCS 13775, pp. 72–84, 2022.
https://doi.org/10.1007/978-3-031-21671-8_5

Training—by which we mean education, planning, rehearsal, and repeated mission execution—demonstrably develops members' ability to predict the responses of colleagues to challenges, coordinate actions, and improve performance [10, 14]. Such preparation is essential over all missions but typically inadequate for any given mission because training cannot perfectly anticipate a specific mission (nor should it if it is to ensure generalizability of learning across potential variants of the mission).

To compensate for the inadequacy of training, teams communicate in real time using spoken language (e.g., military air control communications protocols) and symbolic language (e.g., the marking conventions used by search and rescue teams). These communication protocols range from the formal to the informal. They convey among team members much of what any member knows, needs, or intends at the moment. However, communications are often inaccurate, incomplete, untimely, or unavailable (e.g., in military operations).

Technologies designed to improve team coordination can compensate for the inevitable inadequacies of training and talk. MacMillan et al. [9] describe applications of multi-objective optimization, simulation, and empirical research to design teams that are better sized and synchronized, and thus outperform standard teams in empirical and computational studies. The rich literatures of operations research and robotics describe techniques for making plans more efficient, robust, or resilient, and planning more rapidly [c.f., 7]. Real-time social network analysis and related techniques have been used to help military commanders assess and improve teamwork in their organizations in near real time [2]. In many military operations, sophisticated technologies represent the state of a mission on displays and recommend or enact responses to threats, thus automating what would otherwise require human coordination (c.f., Aegis doctrine for automatically executing tactical actions defined by policy). Such technologies are, however, not available in all domains at all times, nor competent or trusted by their users in all situations.

Through training, talk, and technology, team members scope, develop, and maintain mental models of their teammates, or Theory of Mind (ToM). They use these models when training, talk, and technology are insufficient to coordinate with team members. More specifically, ToM enables team members to infer the cognitive and affective state of teammates, their goals, and their needs; to predict teammates' actions; and to develop guidance and actions that coordinate work. Such inference is ineluctable, difficult, and errorful.

Recent research explores whether we can develop a Machine Theory of Mind (MToM) to offload from humans some of the burden of developing, validating, maintaining, and applying ToM of teammates. Rabinowitz et al. [12] demonstrated that meta-learning could be used by an artificial system to make accurate inferences and predictions concerning artificial agents. Such work, if extended to model multiple human team members, might be called Artificial Social Intelligence (ASI) or Machine Theory of Teams (MToT). ASI could potentially generate advice that improves teams in the most difficult of circumstances, those in which team members are highly varied in their capabilities and capacity, task synchronization is complex, there is risk of failure at high stakes, preparation and information are incomplete, communication is encumbered, and thus the necessity and difficulty of building ToM is high.

Research to develop ASI requires collaboration between computer scientists and social scientists. DARPA sponsors this research in a program called Artificial Social Intelligence for Successful Teams (ASIST). ASIST engages six teams in the development of ASI; six teams in social science research intended to improve ASI inference, prediction, and intervention; and one team (our own) that is focused on experimental design, testbed development, and evaluation. Below, we briefly describe the design of the most recent study to advance ASIST [6] and the initial findings from evaluation of the accuracy[2] of MToM applied to human teams.

2   Method

2.1   Experiment Design and Task Environment

Development and evaluation of ASI require a team task that systematically demands and complicates the generation of ToM. The domain of Urban Search and Rescue (USAR) instantiates many of the attributes of such a team task (enumerated above and in Table 1).

Table 1. Comparison of teamwork features in USAR and a Minecraft USAR simulation.

Team attributes	USAR features	Minecraft ASIST task features
Skills & roles	USAR requires heterogeneous teams (different roles); individual and team tasks	Three team members and three possible roles; individual and team tasks
Task synchronization	Temporal constraints with asynchronous, sequential, and simultaneous tasks	15 min missions to rescue victims in tasks requiring asynchronous, sequential, and simultaneous teamwork
Risk	Hazards, unexpected events for workers	Hidden freeze plate in rooms
Reward	Some victims more severe, triage necessary	Critical victims vs. regular victims (high vs. low reward)
Preparation	Planning is important	Planning session was manipulated
Information	Incomplete information on victim and blockage location	Maps are incomplete
Communication	Verbal comms & searched areas marked to communicate with team	Audio & marker blocks for comms (Divergent marker keys create conflicting mental models)

---

[2] We are agnostic to the genesis of ToM in humans, whether it be an innate capability to apply theory (the "theory theory" account of Gopnik, 1992) or mental simulation (Gordon, 1986) to infer and predict. Training, talking, and technology, discussed above, are data sources for both mechanisms, whether building theory from empirical data, or specifying input conditions and operating rules for simulation. The genesis of human ToM may be an inspiration for the design of MToM, but it is not a constraint assessment of accuracy, which is our current focus.

A USAR task environment was built using Minecraft, which provides a lightweight method to simulate the task constraints that a typical USAR team might encounter [3, 8]. A study was designed in which teams of three were tasked with finding and rescuing victims of two types, regular and critical, in 15-min missions. Each team member could choose from three roles (a searcher—finding and relocating victims, a medic—treat victims, and an engineer—removing rubble). Task costs and rewards varied: regular victims could be rescued by a single medic in 7.5 seconds for 10 points each; critical victims required three team members to join together to "wake" the victim from a coma, after which a medic could rescue the victim in 15 seconds for 50 points each. A few threat rooms had hidden freeze plates that could immobilize any team member who enters the room and require rescue by a medic teammate. Each of 64 teams of remotely distributed members executed two different missions in the same virtual building but with different victim and rubble layouts. Mission order was counterbalanced between teams.

To control the degree to which the team shared a model of roles, goals, and strategy at the start of missions, we manipulated the opportunity to plan together. 32 teams in a planning condition were given three minutes to develop a plan for approaching the task before the second trial. 32 teams in a control condition performed math problems for three minutes instead.

To control the distribution of starting knowledge over team members, we provided maps that displayed one building section to all members, a unique section to each member, and hid sections from all members (see Fig. 1). The maps accurately showed locations of fallen rubble and victims.

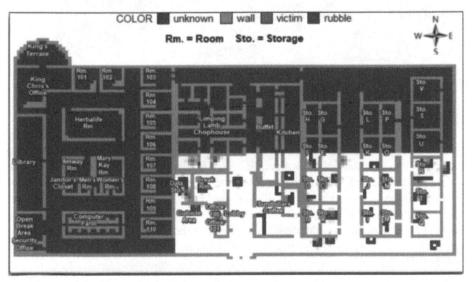

Fig. 1. An example map depicts building structure and, in two white areas, victims and rubble. Maps for two other players reveal victims and rubble in the left bottom and central bottom, and in the central top and bottom top.

To control the agreement of knowledge between team members, we provided conflicting definitions (or legends) for three marker blocks carried by all members to lay as signals to others; the colors of marker blocks designate the ownership (e.g., participant "Red" lays red marker blocks), but the symbols (1, 2, and 3) on marker blocks are the same between team members. Two members received a legend in which the marker block labelled 1 meant "no victim here", marker block 2 meant "regular victim here". One member received the same marker blocks, but the definitions were reversed in the legend (see Fig. 2). All members received a marker block 3 defined as "critical victim here". This conflict in marker block meaning enabled us to apply a variant of the "Sally-Anne" test of Theory of Mind, in which the ASI must infer whether one member will enter a room given potentially false beliefs about the meaning of another's marker block [12, 13]. Maps and marker block legends were displayed during each trial, to help participants form and execute search and rescue strategies (see Fig. 3).

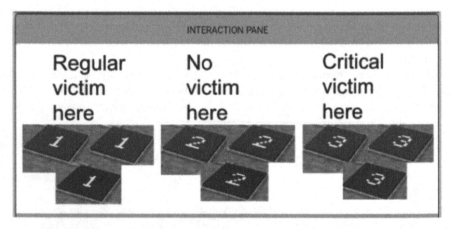

Fig. 2. A marker block legend with "reversed" meaning. (Color figure online)

In sum, we created a between-within group mixed experimental design. The between-group factor was planning (with or without) before the second trial. The within-group factor was two missions of equivalent difficulty in terms of victim and rubble layout. At the individual level, we also manipulated the three versions of information maps for different known regions, and two versions of marker block legends. Individual tasks and interdependent tasks were designed to allow us to study and ASI to model individual taskwork, two-member coordination (in response to threat rooms), three-member coordination (to rescue critical victims), as well as individual and team navigation and rescue strategies.

Fig. 3. Participant interface displays the information map (top left), marker block legend (bottom left), and Minecraft (right).

2.2 Participants

201 participants (67 teams) were recruited from Reddit, Discord, and a University list-serv with the requirement of playing Minecraft, living in the United States, speaking English, and having a normal color vision. Three teams' data were omitted due to flaws in displaying the information map and marker blocks). The remaining 64 teams (192 participants) consisted of 141 males, 49 females, and 2 individuals who declared other gender identities or preferred not to respond. The mean age of participants was 22.04 (SD = 5.22, ranging from 18 to 49). The most common ethnicities were white/Caucasian (54.2%; 104), Asian (25.8%; 49), and Hispanic or Latino (13%; 25). All participants had at least a high school level education.

2.3 Procedure

The remotely conducted two-session experiment lasted for 3.5 h. In Session 1 (one hour), participants checked in to install the required software (e.g., Minecraft, Forge mods, and Zoom™) correctly and then finished pre-dispositional surveys. In Session 2 (which ran two and a half hours), three qualified participants were required to join as a team to go through a voice-over training video, a hands-on practice of required individual actions and team interactions in the Minecraft™ world, an independent action-based Minecraft competency test, and then two formal missions. Participants filled out survey sections after each step in Session 2. Consent forms were attained at the beginning.

2.4   Data, Metrics, and Measures

The study used 469 survey items to elicit or quantify 22 constructs spanning demographics, individual differences (e.g., personality, spatial ability, game experience), accuracy of Theory of Mind, and teamwork process and climate. The testbed message bus registered all experimental metadata (e.g., the specific assignment of marker block legends and maps to participants, and identifiers of trials and teams) and all events in the Minecraft world (e.g., moving, using tools, and rescuing a victim), their timestamps, locations, and the entities involved. In addition, the study captured experimenters' Bird's-eye view videos of trials (see Fig. 4); Zoom™ videos, audio, and transcriptions; as well as various abstractions of the data (e.g., field of view, semantic translation of location, speech act classes).

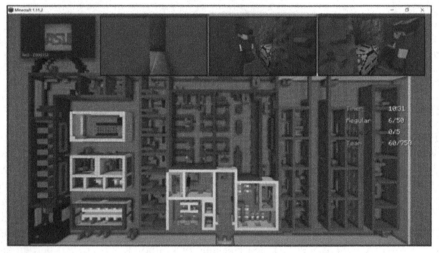

Fig. 4. Bird's-eye view displays Zoom speakers' identity and participants' game views (top) and the mission space (bottom).

ASI agents generated measurements relevant to four metrics of accuracy (see Table 2) using various combinations of the data above. Human observers generated measurements on the four metrics from Bird's-eye view videos that presented participants' locations on the building map, their first-person views, and their voice communication. Both ASI agents and human observers' performance was evaluated over 24 trials (18.75% of 128 experimental trials) that were held out for use in testing ASI (thus not available for training ASI).

Table 2. Metrics for ASI agents and human observers.

Metric ID: function	ASI agent & human observer infer/predict	Measure
M1: Prediction of effects of future interventions	Team score (3x per trial at fixed times)	Normalized RMSE, or RMSE divided by the mean of all team scores for each trial 1–NRMSE presented here to match the direction of other measures
M3: Inference of member mental model/knowledge	Given map information (3x)	Mean accuracy. Guessing computed as the conditional probability of correctly guessing the first then second of three map options in each trial, or $1/3 \times 1/2 = 1/6$
M6: Inference of member mental model/knowledge	Given marker block meanings (3x)	Mean accuracy. Guessing computed as conditional probability of correctly guessing the first then second options. Value is 1/3 since one of two labels is twice as frequent
M7: Prediction of action given member beliefs (Sally-Anne)	Room entry in response to another participant's marker block (many per trial)	Mean accuracy. Guessing computed based on random selection of 'did enter' or 'did not enter' room for each occurrence

3 Artificial Social Intelligence

Six program performers were tasked with designing and building ASI created distinctly different agents to process the data from this experiment into inferences and predictions.

The University of Arizona team, led by Adarsh Pyarelal, used dynamic Bayes networks (DBNs) to model individual and team activity states and mental states (ToM), using in-game participant behavior, natural language processing, and speech analysis.

The SIFT team, led by Chris Geib, employed MC Tree Search over learnable action grammars to generate multiple candidate explanations for observed behavior. Explanations included explicit ascriptions of ToM beliefs for each agent. The system then used weighted model counting over the explanations to probabilistically infer the most likely mental states and asymmetric beliefs between team members.

The team from University of Southern California, led by David Pynadath, applied recursive POMDPs as candidate participant models with ToM, constructed by combining a RDDL specification of the domain with perturbations along domain-independent dimensions. The ASI agent performed Bayesian inference to update beliefs over these candidate models based on observed team and individual behavior.

The team from DOLL/MIT, led by Paul Robertson, generated narratives from stories that represent, for each team member, a story of the team. The Narrative provided a rationale for the past and predictions for the future. This ASI agent also used mechanisms for inverse planning, probabilistic ToM, probabilistic conditional preference, story understanding (Genesis), and learned player capability, such as speed.

The team from Carnegie Mellon, led by Katia Sycara, implemented a modular neural network Theory of Mind (ToM) model that infers an individual's beliefs, goals and intentions from observations and environmental context; introspection resolves deviations between predicted and observed behaviors. Combined ToM models of teammates provided reasoning over shared mental models, team processes and produce appropriate individual and team interventions.

The team from Charles River Analytics, led by Bryan Loyall, created a Cognitive Inverter that uses probabilistic programming to recognize goals, behaviors, and mental states from open world observations. A Strategic Coach will select the most effective interventions, based on principles from interactive narrative research.

4   Findings

An evaluation compared inferences and predictions by six ASI agents to a human baseline of three observers for M1, M3, and M6, as well as that of two observers for M7, and to a guessing baseline that assumes a random draw from a known distribution for the possible response options. As summarized in Fig. 5, the human baseline was higher (better) than the performance of all ASI agents on each metric, and when computed both as an average rank (human baseline rank = 1.0, average ASI agent rank = 4.2) and in terms of average performance over median value on each measure (human baseline = 0.12, ASI agents = -0.01). No one ASI agent consistently outperformed the others. The variation between agents is likely due to differences in approach. Variation between humans and ASI agents may be due both to differences in their respective inference and prediction methods, and variations in the data that fed those methods. ASI agents consumed testbed message bus data; humans used mainly video and audio. These data sources differ in representation of information and in the information they represent. Humans and ASI agents performed better than guessing in nearly all cases; average performance over guessing was similar between the human baseline (0.47) and ASI agents (0.35) but varied somewhat by metric (see Fig. 6).

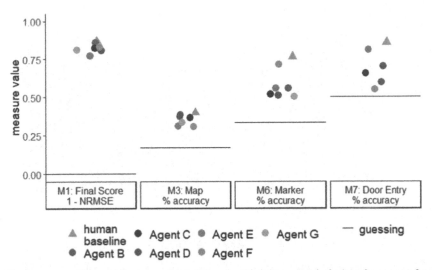

Fig. 5. Accuracy of human observers (triangle) and artificial agents (circles) on four tests of social intelligence.

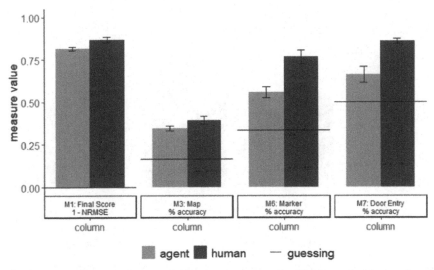

Fig. 6. Accuracy of human observers (yellow) and average of artificial agents (blue) on four tests of social intelligence. Error bars where provided represent ± 1SE.

For those measures on which agents performed most similarly to each other (M1 and M6), agent accuracy tended to improve over time within each trial (see Figs. 7 and 8).

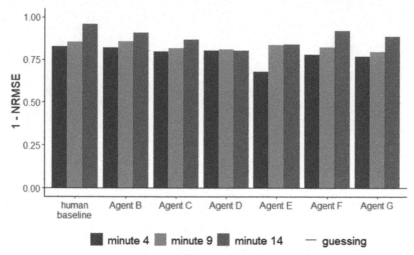

Fig. 7. Accuracy predicting final score (M1) thrice per trial, measured as 1-NRMSE. Guessing would result in a score of zero on this measure.

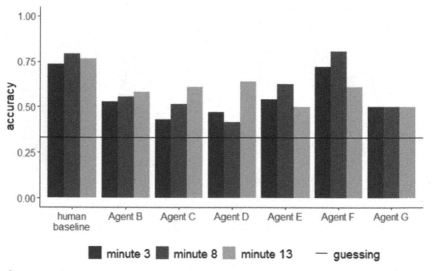

Fig. 8. Percent accuracy for inferring marker block semantics (M6), an indicator of false beliefs.

The results collectively suggest that these ASI agents were able to reliably predict team score (M1) and actions of individual members (M7), infer divergent beliefs (M3), and infer false beliefs (M6). However, the ability of these ASI agents to infer false beliefs (M6) and predict future actions related to false beliefs (M7) lags further behind human capabilities than their ability to predict future performance (M1) and infer divergent beliefs (M3).

ASI agents were also able to take advantage of information within the trial as it progressed. This suggests that these ASI agents learned something about the structure of the task and team coordination that enabled them to assess performance (M1) and false beliefs (M6) more accurately as the trial progressed. In the case of performance scores, ASI may have been able to take advantage of decreasing variance in scores as the trial progressed and the diminishing likelihood of accruing more points by rescuing victims. In the case of M6, ASI agents had additional opportunities to observe participant behavior related to marker block placement and movement given others' placement, and therefore allowed ASI agents the opportunity to update prior beliefs on the likely marker block assignment for each participant. Agents did not reliably increase the accuracy of their inferences concerning divergent map information (M3). Analyses by other program researchers indicate that participants often did not use the information provided by maps. Thus, participant planning, navigation, and communication may have held few of the cues that ASI presumably needed to infer that distribution.

5 Conclusions

This study developed a rich search and rescue simulation that elicits human taskwork and teamwork. ASI agents successfully used data from this environment to make inferences and predictions that often approached the accuracy of those made by human observers, though ASI and humans used somewhat different data sources (e.g., ASI used message bus traffic and humans used video). The qualitative rationales of the human observers, now under study, may provide insights to refine the design of ASI agents. The rich data provide many opportunities to analyze the relationships between the survey-based variables and action-based variables to further develop reliable and generalizable Machine Theory of Mind (MToM) in the urban search and rescue task environment.

The generalizability of these findings will be tested in planned research. In a 2022 experiment, we will introduce significant perturbations in the task, such as deprivation of communications or changes in task structure or rewards. In research after that, we plan to change the task domain. We predict that ASI will generalize if they develop and maintain an accurate MToT, that is if they are focused not on individual USAR tasks, but on teamwork skills such as leadership, backup behavior, and communication.

Future research will also develop ASI agents that advise teams by leveraging the inferential and predictive abilities enabled by a MToT. That research will evaluate the effects of ASI interventions on team performance, team process, and team member perceptions of the utility and trustworthiness of the ASI designed to aid them.

Acknowledgments. This material is based upon work supported by the Defense Advanced Research Projects Agency (DARPA) under Contract No. HR001119C0130. Any opinions, findings and conclusions or recommendations expressed in this material are those of the author(s) and do not necessarily reflect the views of the Defense Advanced Research Projects Agency.

References

1. Baron-Cohen, S., Leslie, A.M., Frith, U.: Does the autistic child have a "theory of mind"? Cognition **21**(1), 37–46 (1985)
2. Brown, T.A., Perry, S.K.B., Braun, M.T., McCormack, R., Orvis, K.L., DeCostanza, A.H.: A dynamic exploration of multiteam system face-to-face boundary spanning. Paper Presented at the 2017 Annual INGroup Conference, Minneapolis, MN, July 2017
3. Corral, C., Tatapudi, K., Buchanan, V., Huang, L., Cooke, N.: Building a synthetic task environment to support artificial social intelligence research. In: Proceedings of the International Human Factors and Ergonomics Society Annual Meeting (in press)
4. Gopnik, A., Wellman, H.: Why the child's theory of mind really is a theory. Mind Lang. **7**, 145–171 (1992)
5. Gordon, R.: Folk psychology as simulation. Mind Lang. **1**, 158–171 (1986)
6. Huang, L., et al.: ASIST Study 2 June 2021 Exercises for Artificial Social Intelligence in Minecraft Search and Rescue for Teams, 7 June 2021. https://doi.org/10.17605/OSF.IO/GXPQ5
7. Kitano, H., Asada, M., Kuniyoshi, Y., Noda, I., Osawa, E., Matsubara, H.: RoboCup: a challenge problem for AI. AI Mag. **18**(1), 73 (1997). https://doi.org/10.1609/aimag.v18i1.1276
8. Lematta, G.J., et al.: Developing human-robot team interdependence in a synthetic task environment. Proc. Hum. Factors Ergon. Soc. Annual Meet. **63**(1), 1503–1507 (2019). https://doi.org/10.1177/1071181319631433
9. MacMillan, J., Paley, M.J., Levchuk, Y.N., Entin, E.E., Serfaty, D., Freeman, J.T.: Designing the best team for the task: optimal organizational structures for military missions. In: McNeese, M., Salas, E., Endsley, M. (eds.) New Trends in Cooperative Activities: System Dynamics in Complex Settings. Human Factors and Ergonomics Society Press, San Diego (2002)
10. McNeese, N.J., Cooke, N.J., Fedele, M.A., Gray, R.: Theoretical and methodical approaches to studying team cognition in sports. Proc. Manuf. **3**, 1211–1218 (2015)
11. Premack, D., Woodruff, G.: Does the chimpanzee have a theory of mind? Behav. Brain Sci. **1**(4), 515–526 (1978)
12. Rabinowitz, N., Perbet, F., Song, F., Zhang, C., Eslami, S.A., Botvinick, M.: Machine theory of mind. In: International Conference on Machine Learning, pp. 4218–4227. PMLR, July 2018
13. Wimmer, H., Perner, J.: Beliefs about beliefs: representation and constraining function of wrong beliefs in young children's understanding of deception. Cognition **13**(1), 103–128 (1983)
14. Yurko, R., et al.: Going deep: models for continuous-time within-play valuation of game outcomes in American football with tracking data. J. Quant. Anal. Sports **16**(2), 163–182 (2020)

Modular Procedural Generation for Voxel Maps

Adarsh Pyarelal$^{(\boxtimes)}$ ⓘ, Aditya Banerjee, and Kobus Barnard ⓘ

University of Arizona, Tucson, AZ 85721, USA
{adarsh,abanerjee,kobus}@email.arizona.edu

Abstract. Task environments developed in Minecraft are becoming increasingly popular for artificial intelligence (AI) research. However, most of these are currently constructed manually, thus failing to take advantage of procedural content generation (PCG), a capability unique to virtual task environments. In this paper, we present mcg, an open-source library to facilitate implementing PCG algorithms for voxel-based environments such as Minecraft. The library is designed with human-machine teaming research in mind, and thus takes a 'top-down' approach to generation, simultaneously generating low and high level machine-readable representations that are suitable for empirical research. These can be consumed by downstream AI applications that consider human spatial cognition. The benefits of this approach include rapid, scalable, and efficient development of virtual environments, the ability to control the statistics of the environment at a semantic level, and the ability to generate novel environments in response to player actions in real time.

Keywords: Artificial social intelligence · Procedural content generation

1 Introduction

Minecraft [3] has recently emerged as an attractive platform for artificial intelligence (AI) research [7,8,10,13,15,16,19,23] owing to its popularity, ease of instrumentation and modification, and its ability to support complex tasks in an open-world environment [31]. A voxel-based game environment such as Minecraft's is well-suited for designing controlled AI experiments, as it enables researchers to access and manipulate precise details of the environment without having to deal with complications such as curvature or deformable objects.

Research was sponsored by the Army Research Office and was accomplished under Grant Number W911NF-20-1-0002. The views and conclusions contained in this document are those of the authors and should not be interpreted as representing the official policies, either expressed or implied, of the Army Research Office or the U.S. Government. The U.S. Government is authorized to reproduce and distribute reprints for Government purposes notwithstanding any copyright notation herein.

© The Author(s), under exclusive license to Springer Nature Switzerland AG 2022
N. Gurney and G. Sukthankar (Eds.): AAAI-FSS 2021, LNCS 13775, pp. 85–101, 2022.
https://doi.org/10.1007/978-3-031-21671-8_6

However, most Minecraft environments currently used in AI research [9,10, 17] are constructed manually, thus failing to fully take advantage of a unique possibility afforded by a virtual environment - namely, the ability to generate environments procedurally.

In this paper, we present mcg, a library for procedurally generating voxel environments for AI research. The library is part of the ToMCAT project [7], which is developing a suite of modular, open-source AI technologies to support human-machine teaming and a Minecraft-based testbed to evaluate them. The design of mcg addresses a number of requirements for AI research that are not sufficiently addressed by existing approaches.

The rest of the paper is organized as follows. In Sect. 2, we discuss why procedural content generation (PCG) is particularly important in the context of controlled experimental research. In Sect. 3, we describe our approach in relation to other existing work on PCG for AI research in Minecraft. In Sect. 4, we describe how mcg integrates higher-level semantics into the PCG workflow to support human-machine teaming research. In Sect. 5, we present the core classes implemented in mcg, and in Sect. 6, we describe existing and potential integrations with downstream AI applications. In Sect. 7, we present a tutorial that illustrates the usage of the library. Finally, we conclude in Sect. 8 by summarizing progress, noting limitations, and describing our plans for future work.

2   PCG for AI Research

There are a number of reasons to favor procedural content generation over manual environment creation in a research context. We discuss the key ones in this section.

2.1   Parametric Generation

When designing an environment for human and artificial agents to perform tasks in, it is desirable to have fine-grained control over certain features of the environment, as they can have significant effects on task performance. For example, in a recent simulated urban search and rescue (USAR) experiment [17], a direct correlation was observed between the size of the number of rooms in the building and the participants' performance on the task. Similarly, other factors that influence their performance include the number of victims, their distribution in the building, and the presence and locations of obstacles that inhibit navigation.

Depending on the objectives of the experiment, some of these features will be control variables and others will be independent variables. In the case of features that serve as control variables, it is likely that the values of these variables are settled upon through a process of iterative experimental design. For example, designers of a synthetic USAR task environment (e.g., [9,17]) will likely need to try a few different values for the number of rooms, the number of victims, the number of blockages, etc. in order to arrive at a configuration that satisfies the experimental requirements. Note that while we use a running example of a

USAR task in this paper, the approach we are proposing is general enough to be applicable to any task environment that requires navigation and human spatial reasoning.

A top-down procedural generation approach allows for rapid iteration over these different configurations, resulting in an accelerated experimental design process. As an example, we can go from a gridworld environment with four cells to one with 400 cells simply by changing a single parameter (see Fig. 1).

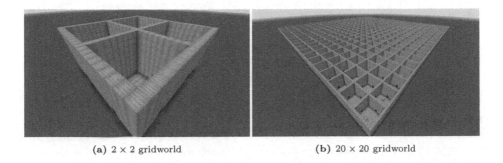

(a) 2 × 2 gridworld   (b) 20 × 20 gridworld

Fig. 1. Gridworlds. Two examples of gridworlds generated using mcg. The size of the gridworld (i.e., the number of rooms) is controlled by a single parameter that is passed as an argument to the generator executable.

Similarly, randomizing the environment is important for certain types of experiments. Indeed, this can be viewed as a special case of parametric generation, with the random seed serving as the parameter to be varied. In Fig. 2, we show four possible dungeon layouts obtained by varying the size and random seed parameters passed to a dungeon world generator implemented using mcg.

2.2 Controlling the Statistics of Generated Scenes

In experiments where environments matter, they should not be limited to what designers intuitively create. For example, simply saying "maybe this complex needs a cul-de-sac" to investigate how that would affect participants' frustration levels in USAR scenarios does not lead to careful science. Instead, one should create a hypothesis such as 'being forced to turn around leads to frustration', and be able to generate various scenes with and without this attribute that are otherwise similar. For example, one might use various world pairs that differ in whether or not there is a passageway. Variation is needed to help establish that differing results are likely due to the manipulation targeted at testing the hypothesis rather than some other attribute of a world created haphazardly because the researcher thought adding a cul-de-sac was an interesting idea.

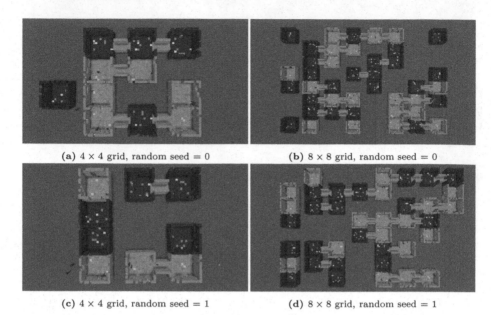

(a) 4 × 4 grid, random seed = 0   (b) 8 × 8 grid, random seed = 0

(c) 4 × 4 grid, random seed = 1   (d) 8 × 8 grid, random seed = 1

Fig. 2. Parametric Dungeon Generation. Dungeons generated with different grid sizes (4 × 4 and 8 × 8) and random seeds (0 and 1), using a simplified variant of the constraint-based algorithm described in [20]. We define an $N \times N$ grid, and then randomly select a number of grid cells to place dungeon rooms on. There are two types of rooms that can be 'spawned' on a grid cell. The stone brick rooms (grey) contain diamond blocks as treasures for the player to gather, and 'wither skeletons' as monsters for the player to battle. The 'nether' brick rooms (brown) contain gold block treasures and 'blaze' monsters, and are more difficult to navigate, as they have randomly placed patches of lava that the player can fall into if they are not careful. The stone brick rooms also contain randomly placed spiderwebs on the walls for aesthetic purposes. Finally, we connect the rooms with stone brick corridors. Notably, we take a modular approach to generation - each type of room is defined using a class that inherits from the AABB class described in Sect. 5.1 - the treasures and monsters are placed when the room is instantiated, rather than after all the rooms have been placed and interconnected. This gives us a lot of flexibility. For example, the class that corresponds to the stone brick rooms could be instantiated for some of the cells in the gridworld environment in Fig. 1 (thus setting up an interesting surprise for players who may not have been expecting to battle skeletons in a USAR scenario!). (Color figure online)

Put differently, features proposed for exploring hypotheses should appear in different contexts with well defined probabilities to guard against confounding effects between the presence of the feature and its possibly unique or statistically biased context. While this could be arranged manually, doing so is tedious and harder to get right. On the other hand, specifying the environments procedurally forces researchers to be more clear about the logic of their experiment, makes development easier as modifications can be studied rapidly, and better supports extensions, scaling, and repeatability.

2.3   Changing the World in Response to Player Action

The ToMCAT project is mandated to support a large range of behavioral psychology studies into team performance. It is easy to construct scenarios where we will need to change the Minecraft environment as a function of what the human players are doing, their affective state, brain activity (using EEG or fNIRS equipment), and where they are in the virtual environment. As such, it is not predictable where, and hence precisely what the needed modification will be. For example, suppose we are interested in how robust a team's performance is to unexpected events such as a room collapse when the team members cannot see each other. To do this, we would need to programmatically collapse a room in the task environment according to a defined stochastic process, but only when they are out of view of each other. Notably, the room that needs to collapse is not known in advance. While we could have a single room collapse model manually specified for each room, the awkwardness of this approach amplifies with each additional changeable feature. For example, a second room collapse entails being ready for any two rooms to change in any order.

Currently, mcg supports this kind of programmatic change in a scalable manner, since the high-level representation it outputs provides semantic 'hooks' that a Minecraft mod can leverage to preserve the desired collapse models across task environments with different numbers of rooms, varied room layouts, and scenarios in which different numbers of rooms will need to be collapsed. While the existing executables built using mcg write files to disk, it is conceivable that the library could be used to provide a 'PCG as a service' program that can generate complex environment specifications on the fly.

2.4   Task Environments as Code

Initially, the task environments for the ToMCAT project were built manually, rather than procedurally. As the experimental design evolved, it became quickly apparent that we would need to keep track of the different versions of the task environment, so that (i) it would be easy to revert back to an older version if necessary, and (ii) the version could be added to the provenance for a given experimental trial.

While source code management (SCM) systems (e.g., git [2]) excel at version management, they are designed for text files rather than binary files such as the ones corresponding to the manually-constructed Minecraft environments. Managing binary files (especially ones that are liable to change frequently, as is the case with an iterative experimental design process) with SCM systems results in the source code repository getting bloated, hindering developer productivity and collaboration.

For these reasons above, we decided to maintain versions of the binary save files on a public server that developers could access. However, we soon realized that this approach had its own share of problems, the most troublesome of which was the fact that every change to the environment required manually uploading the updated binary files to our server, making it easy for the environment to get out of sync with the source code of the ToMCAT Minecraft mod.

Switching to procedurally generated environments addresses all of these issues - taking an 'environment as code' approach allows us to effectively leverage SCM systems to manage environment versions, making tasks like reverting back to a previous version or comparing versions much easier than with manually constructed environments. In addition, we no longer have to worry about manually synchronizing the task environment and the code that interacts with it - the SCM system takes care of this for us.

3 Decoupled PCG for Rapid Iteration

There exists prior work on procedural generation to support AI experiments in Minecraft. Notably, Project Malmo [19] provides a declarative XML-based API to specify 'missions', including the parametric generation and placement of individual blocks, entities, and simple structures such as spheres and cuboids. In addition, it supports implementing custom procedural generation algorithms as Java classes in the Malmo mod and exposing them via the XML API.

However, the procedural generation capabilities in Project Malmo are tightly coupled with Minecraft itself - to view the results of a procedural generation algorithm implemented in a Malmo class, one would need to recompile the Malmo mod and relaunch Minecraft with it loaded. This process is fairly slow and does not fit well into a workflow that involves the need for rapid iteration through environments. Ideally, there should be a way to visualize the outputs of procedural generation without having to launch the full game.

In contrast, our library is *decoupled* from Minecraft - it outputs declarative specifications of an environment that can be consumed by other downstream applications, including a Minecraft mod that can translate the specification into in-game entities, blocks, and structures. The data structures and algorithms in our library are general enough that they could be used for any other voxel-based environment - the only things that would need to be modified are the labels for the block and entity types.

4 Connection to Human Spatial Cognition

One of the primary motivations for developing mcg was to explicitly inject high-level semantic information (labels of relevant locations and structures, layout and topology, etc.) into the generation process. The Malmo API and the Minecraft Forge event bus give us access to low-level information about the positions of the player and individual blocks in the environment. However, humans tend to reason about their environment at a high level of abstraction using spatial reference systems [30]. For example, a human carrying out tasks in a Minecraft environment will tend to think about rooms and the spatial relations between them rather than the individual blocks that the structures are comprised of.

Furthermore, humans rely on high-level spatial representations of their environment for navigation [12]. These representations have been hypothesized to take the form of Euclidean maps [24] or graph-like representations [32], though there is evidence that both representations may be simultaneously maintained and used in different contexts [25].

One way to incorporate high-level semantics is by manually specifying location boundaries, labels, and hierarchies after an environment is built. However, this method is prone to human error and bottlenecked by the time it takes for humans to annotate regions and identify area boundaries in a pre-built map. This method will certainly not scale to large or stochastically generated maps. In contrast, the mcg library takes a 'top-down' approach, producing the following machine-readable representations *simultaneously*, in lockstep with each other.

- **High-Level Representation (HLR):** Also known as a 'semantic map', this is a JSON file that contains information about the labels and locations of areas, their connections with each other, and their hierarchical relationships, as well as the `Entity` and `Object` instances in the environment. This representation supports linking explicitly to human spatial cognition, as the locations and their spatial relations to each other form a machine-readable representation of a global spatial reference system [30].
- **Low-Level Representation (LLR):** This is a JSON file that contains low-level information about all the blocks and entities in the environment. Among other uses, this representation can be consumed by a Minecraft mod to generate an environment procedurally, but with the actual PCG algorithms offloaded to the mcg library.

These specifications can then be used by other programs, some examples of which we describe in greater detail in Sect. 6.

5 Approach

The mcg library provides a set of core components that can be extended and composed to design rich voxel-based task environments. In this section, we briefly describe these components[1] and the design philosophy behind them, followed by a tutorial on how to use the library.

---

[1] The full documentation for the C++ API can be found at https://ml4ai.github.io/tomcat/cpp_api/index.html.

5.1 Core Classes

Pos. This class represents a point in the 3D integer lattice ($\mathbb{Z}^3$) [22] - or in other words, a vector in a 3D Euclidean space with its Cartesian components restricted to integer values, reflecting the voxelated nature of the Minecraft environment.

AABB. An axis-aligned bounding box (AABB) is an elementary cuboidal structure that can be efficiently represented using a pair of 3D coordinates that correspond to vertices on opposite ends of one of its space diagonals. The AABB class instantiates an empty cuboidal space that effectively serves as a blank canvas to implement PCG algorithms in. For example, one could implement Perlin noise generation [26,29] to add water blocks within an AABB made of grass to create a water body, or constrained growth algorithms [14,21]. AABBs of different types can be defined using mcg by subclassing the AABB class, and can be manipulated, nested, and combined to produce complex structures (see Fig. 3).

Block. This class represents a single Minecraft block with a given material and position. It allows for fine-grained placement of individual blocks in the game environment - for example, the diamond and gold treasure blocks in Fig. 2.

Entity. This class represents an entity that is to be placed in the task environment, The constructor for this class takes two required arguments - the type and position (a Pos object[2]) of the entity, and a set of optional arguments corresponding to the different equipment types that a Minecraft entity can have. We use this class to generate and place the wither skeletons and blazes in the dungeons in Fig. 2.

World. This class represents the overall environment, and contains the lists of the AABBs, Blocks, Entitys, Objects and Connections in it as class attributes.

Object. An object represents a Block with some additional semantics. An instance of this class contains information about an id, type, and Block associated with the Object. It is particularly useful in cases where a block holds some semantic meaning, like the victim blocks in [17].

Connection. The Connection class represents a spatial connection between AABBs. It is meant to encompass a variety of structures that can fall under the semantic label of 'connection' - it can be used to represent both 'point-like' connections (e.g., a door between rooms) and 'extended' connections (e.g., a corridor that connects two locations). Some care must be taken with Connection objects. Unlike entities and objects in an AABB that will be automatically moved to the appropriate locations when an AABB undergoes spatial translation, Connection objects will not be so reliably updated. However, since Connection objects can be stored in AABB objects and World objects, a potential workaround for this would be to instantiate connections dynamically when AABBs are moved around.

---

[2] While Minecraft allows for the components of the Cartesian coordinates of Entity objects to be double-precision floating point numbers, we restrict them to be integers in mcg for simplicity.

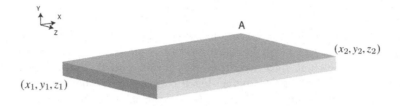

(a) An AABB represented by the pair of coordinates (x_1, y_1, z_1) and (x_2, y_2, z_2) which represent the top left and bottom right corners of the cuboid respectively.

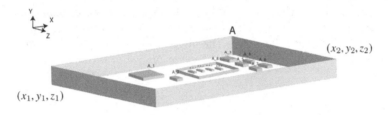

(b) An AABB can itself can contain one or more AABBs inside it, as shown in this example - the AABB in figure 3a contains a number of child AABBs. Grouping AABBs into a hierarchy gives us the benefit of encapsulation. For example, if a set of AABBs is contained within a parent AABB and each child AABB is defined relative to the parent's boundary or to the other child AABDs, one only needs to move the parent AABB to automatically move the child AABBs into the correct relative positions as well.

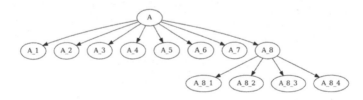

(c) A graph-like representation is automatically created and kept track of by mcg, to facilitate linking with human spatial cognition (section 4). The graph above shows the parent-child relationships between the AABBs in figure 3b.

Fig. 3. Axis Aligned Bounding Boxes (AABBs). We use AABBs as the semantic building blocks of mcg. They can be combined and nested into larger AABBs to form complex structures that are addressable as semantically meaningful components. In this figure, we show an example of a location hierarchy formed by nesting AABBs.

6   Applications

The machine-readable high-level and low-level representations that are simultaneously produced by `mcg` can be consumed by a number of downstream applications. We divide them into two broad categories: *agents* and *non-agents*.

As mentioned earlier, `mcg` is being developed as part of the ToMCAT project [7], which is in turn part of DARPA's Artificial Social Intelligence for Successful Teams (ASIST) program [11]. The testbed developed for the program [9] publishes real-time measurements of each participant's state, environment, and actions in Minecraft to an MQTT message bus [4], along with data from other sources such as physiological sensors and pre and post-task questionnaires.

The term 'agent' is a fairly overloaded one. However, in this paper, we use the term to refer to programs that the various ASIST performer teams are developing that subscribe to topics on the message bus, process it in a streaming manner, and publish their outputs back to the message bus, where they can potentially be used by other, downstream agents.

In contrast, we use the term 'non-agents' to mean software components that are not primarily designed to process streams of information. The potential applications and their relation to the high and low level representations are shown in Fig. 4.

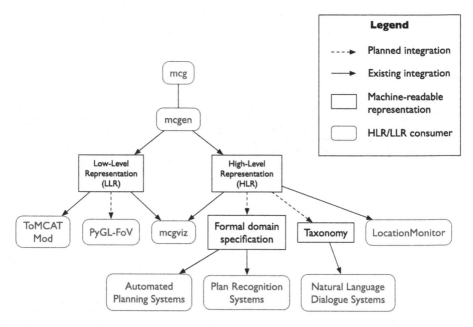

Fig. 4. Applications. In this figure, we show the existing and potential integrations of `mcg`. The agents (the PyGL-FoV and location monitor agents, natural language dialog systems, plan recognition and planning systems) can potentially exchange data with each other, but we do not show those connections in order to focus on how the HLR and LLR are used by the agents.

6.1 Non-agents

mcgen. The mcgen program is being developed for ToMCAT experiments, and is representative of generator executables that can be built using mcg. The environments shown in Fig. 1, Fig. 2, and Fig. 5 are all generated using mcgen.

mcgviz. mcgviz is a Python script included with mcg, that takes the HLR and LLR output by mcg to produce visualizations of the environment. Using the HLR, it can construct either a graph structure (e.g. Fig. 5a) or a 'blueprint' style visualization showing a top-down view of the AABBs in the generated environment (see Fig. 5b). It can also combine the LLR and HLR to provide a more detailed map with individual colored patches corresponding to the different types of blocks in the environment.

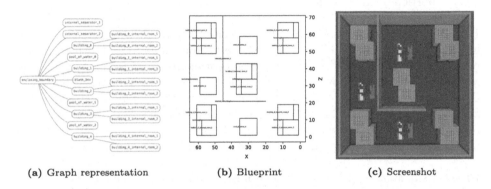

(a) Graph representation   (b) Blueprint   (c) Screenshot

Fig. 5. Three different views of the same **ZombieWorld** environment. To construct this environment, we define an enclosing boundary AABB to which we add two main components, a ZombieWorldGroup and a ZombieWorldPit. The ZombieWorldGroup is a building with two rooms, internal doors and a zombie and villager, while the ZombieWorldPit is a pool of lava or water, depending on how it is initialized. We place these structures in a 3 × 3 grid such that when it is time to place a ZombieWorldPit, we randomly choose whether to fill it lava or water or skip placing the pit entirely. We also add two internal walls within the enclosing boundary.

ToMCAT Mod. The ToMCAT mod is a Minecraft mod that builds upon the Malmo Mod [19] with additional functionality for human-machine teaming research. Currently, the LLR produced by mcg is consumed by the ToMCAT mod to construct the in-game environment (see Fig. 5c).

6.2 Agents

LocationMonitor. The LocationMonitor agent developed by IHMC [1] for the ASIST program uses a 'semantic map' - that is, the HLR output by mcg - to construct an internal representation of named locations (e.g. rooms, hallways) with their boundaries and connections to other named locations. Using this internal representation, it monitors the player's position (in Cartesian coordinates) and publishes a message to the message bus whenever a player goes from one named location to another.

PyGL-FoV. PyGL-FoV [5] is an agent that uses observations of the Cartesian coordinates of the player, the pitch and yaw of the gaze vector of their Minecraft avatar, and a low-level representation of the environment to compute whether certain blocks of interest are visible on the player's screen at any given time.

Dialog Systems. There is growing interest in using Minecraft as an environment to develop dialog-enabled artficial agents [7,13,18]. Dialog systems such as the ToMCAT DialogAgent[3] rely on a taxonomy of concepts to ground natural language extractions to. In order to ground to specific locations that are referred to by participants (especially if they have been provided a blueprint with the location labels beforehand), the taxonomy will need to incorporate location names - the HLR produced by `mcg` can be used to automate the construction of the spatial portion of the taxonomy.

Planning and Plan Recognition Systems. The HLR produced by `mcg` contains information about named locations and their connections to each other - it can be used to automatically construct portions of planning problem specifications related to spatial information. For example, the connectivity information in the HLR can be used to automatically generate a number of predicates such as `connected(L1, L2)` (i.e., AABBs L1 and L2 are connected), and the hierarchical relations in the HLR can be used to construct predicates such as `contains(L1, L2)` (i.e. the AABB named L1 contains the AABB named L2), etc.

Probabilistic Modeling Systems. Probabilistic models of participants performing tasks in Minecraft (e.g., [27]) can also make use of the HLR produced by `mcg` to construct initial concise internal representations of the task environment.

In general, developing AI agents with machine social intelligence will require some kind of explicit high-level environment representation to reason about the beliefs, desires, and intentions of their human partners. `mcg` treats this high-level representation as a first-class citizen in its generation framework.

7   Tutorial

In this tutorial, we showcase some of `mcg`'s capabilities and demonstrate how to use the classes described in Sect. 5. The goal of this tutorial is to create a house with two rooms and a zombie in a purely programmatic manner.

7.1   World Setup

We start by creating an empty world. In a file named `mcg_tutorial.cpp`, we add the following:

---

[3] https://github.com/clulab/tomcat-text.

```
#include "mcg/World.h"
using namespace std;

class TutorialWorld : public World {
  public:
    TutorialWorld() {};
    ~TutorialWorld(){};
};

// Create the world and write the JSON output to file.
int main(int argc, char* argv[]) {
  TutorialWorld world;
  world.writeToFile("semantic_map.json", "low_level_map.json");
  return EXIT_SUCCESS;
}
```

This minimal program will produce two files, semantic_map.json and
low_level_map.json that correspond to the HLR and LLR respectively. The
LLR is used by the WorldBuilder class in the ToMCAT Minecraft mod to construct the environment. At this point, the generated world will be empty[4].

7.2   Creating a Room

We now add a single room to this world. To do so, we define a class Room that
extends AABB, and whose constructor takes a string identifier and a Pos object
representing the top left corner of the room[5].

```
...
#include "mcg/AABB.h"

class Room : public AABB {
  public:
    Room(string id, Pos& topLeft) : AABB(id) {}
    ~Room(){};
};
...
```

Note that we invoke the superclass constructor, which sets all instances of
Room to have a material type of blank and the coordinates of the top left and
bottom right corner set to $(0, 0, 0)$. To turn this blank Room into an actual room,
modify the constructor as shown below.

```
...
Room(string id, Pos& topLeft) : AABB(id) {
  // Set the base material to be 'log'
  this->setMaterial("log");

  // Define the object's boundaries
  Pos bottomRight(topLeft);
  bottomRight.shift(5, 4, 5);
  this->setTopLeft(topLeft);
  this->setBottomRight(bottomRight);
}
...
```

---

[4] To actually view the generated environment in Minecraft, you can use the script
   tools/run_mcg_tutorial that is included in the repository.
[5] By the 'top left' corner of an AABB, we mean the corner with the lowest values of
   the X, Y and Z coordinates.

This gives us a room made of logs with a 6×6 block base and a height of five blocks. Finally, modify the `TutorialWorld` constructor to place a `Room` instance at $(1, 3, 1)$[6]. The constructor should now look as follows:

```
...
TutorialWorld() {
  Pos topLeft(1, 3, 1);
  auto room1 = make_unique<Room>("room_1", topLeft);
  this->addAABB(move(room1));
};
...
```

7.3   Adding Details

We now add some details to this room - namely, a floor, roof, windows, and a zombie (see Fig. 6a) - by adding the following to the `Room` constructor.

```
...
// The floor should be made of planks
this->generateBox("planks", 1, 1, 0, 4, 1, 1);

// Add windows made of glass
this->generateBox("glass", 0, 5, 1, 1, 1, 1);
this->generateBox("glass", 5, 0, 1, 1, 1, 1);
this->generateBox("glass", 1, 1, 1, 1, 0, 5);

// Add a roof (will be made of logs)
this->hasRoof = true;

// Add a zombie
mt19937_64 gen; // Random number generator engine
Pos randomPos = this->getRandomPos(gen, 1, 1, 1, 2, 1, 1);
auto zombie = make_unique<Entity>("zombie", randomPos);
this->addEntity(move(zombie));
...
```

Note that the coordinates passed to the `generateBox` method are relative to the `AABB` itself, so we do not need to respecify them when placing a second room.

7.4   Multiple Rooms

Finally, we combine two `Room` instances to create a house. To do so, we create a second `Room` instance and add both rooms to an enclosing `AABB`. This is done by adding the following code to the `TutorialWorld` constructor:

```
...
Pos topLeft(1, 3, 1);
auto room1 = make_unique<Room>("room_1", topLeft);
auto room2 = make_unique<Room>("room_2", topLeft);
room2->shiftX(5);

auto house = make_unique<AABB>("house");
house->addAABB(move(room1));
house->addAABB(move(room2));
this->addAABB(move(house));
...
```

---

[6] We set the y-coordinate equal to 3 to match the level of the ground in the Minecraft world.

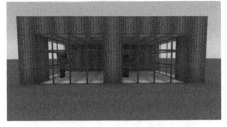

(a) The `TutorialWorld` `Room` with all the details added in §7.3. It now has a floor made of planks, windows on three sides, a roof, and a zombie.

(b) The completed `TutorialWorld` house. It has two rooms, each with the details added in §7.4.

Fig. 6. The `TutorialWorld` house - partial and completed versions.

Figure 6b shows the completed `TutorialWorld` with a house that has two rooms. The code for this tutorial along with instructions on how to compile and run it can be found in the `libs/mcg/examples/mcg_tutorial` folder[7].

8 Conclusion

In this paper, we laid out the motivations for incorporating procedural content generation into human-machine teaming experiments, and presented our open-source C++ library, `mcg`, which integrates low-level content generation with high-level semantics in order to support human-machine teaming research. The library provides a set of core components that can be extended and composed to construct detailed voxel maps while simultaneously generating machine-readable representations of the environment that can be used by downstream programs.

8.1 Limitations

Aesthetic Concerns. It is worth noting that generating a structure with non-rectilinear geometry - for example, something like the Sydney Opera House [6] - will be more difficult to do procedurally than manually. In general, if aesthetic appeal is a significant concern (like it is in the GDMC settlement generation competition [28]), an AABB-based procedural generation approach is likely not an ideal one. However, in the context of controlled human-machine teaming experiments, we expect that the fine-grained control, reproducibility, and scalability afforded by `mcg` will outweigh the aesthetic benefits of manual environment generation.

Programming Overhead. Another potential concern with a procedural generation approach to Minecraft task environment creation is that it is easier to train people to manually modify Minecraft environments than to write programs to

---

[7] All folder names are given relative to the root of the version of the ToMCAT repository corresponding to the 2021_IEEE_CoG tag.

generate the environments procedurally. This is not an insignificant concern, especially when considering that human-machine teaming experiments are often designed in collaboration with researchers who are not used to writing C++ programs. However, our stance is that the benefits of using a PCG approach (and the downsides of manual environment creation) are significant enough to warrant investing in procedural generation.

8.2   Future Work

We intend to continue to develop mcg as a part of the ToMCAT project, and hope to pilot it with human subjects in our experiments in the near future. Along with making it easier to use and better documented, we will also implement additional AABB-based algorithms to enable researchers to create rich, yet controlled voxel-based virtual task environments for human-machine teaming research.

References

1. Florida Institute for Human & Machine Cognition (2021). https://www.ihmc.us
2. git-scm.com (2021). https://git-scm.com
3. Minecraft Official Site. https://www.minecraft.net (2021)
4. MQTT: The Standard for IoT Messaging (2021). https://mqtt.org
5. PyGL Field of View. https://gitlab.com/cmu_asist/pygl_fov (2021)
6. Sydney Opera House: Official Website (2021). https://www.sydneyoperahouse.com
7. ToMCAT: Theory of Mind-based Cognitive Architecture for Teams. https://ml4ai. github.io/tomcat (2021)
8. Bartlett, C.E., Cooke, N.J.: Human-robot teaming in urban search and rescue. Proc. Hum. Factors Ergon. Soc. Annu. Meet. **59**(1), 250–254 (2015). https://doi. org/10.1177/1541931215591051
9. Corral, C.R., Tatapudi, K.S., Buchanan, V., Huang, L., Cooke, N.J.: Building a synthetic environment to support artificial intelligence research. In: Proceedings of the 65th Annual Meeting of the Human Factors and Ergonomic Society (2021). (under review)
10. Demir, M., McNeese, N.J., Cooke, N.J.: Dyadic team interaction and shared cognition to inform human-robot teaming. Proc. Hum. Factors Ergon. Soc. Annu. Meet. **62**(1), 124–124 (2018). https://doi.org/10.1177/1541931218621028
11. Elliott, J.: Artificial Social Intelligence for Successful Teams (ASIST) (2019). https://www.darpa.mil/program/artificial-social-intelligence-for-successful-teams
12. Gallistel, C.R.: The organization of learning. MIT Press, Cambridge (1990)
13. Gray, J., et al.: CraftAssist: A Framework for Dialogue-enabled Interactive Agents. CoRR abs/1907.08584 (2019). http://arxiv.org/abs/1907.08584
14. Green, M.C., Salge, C., Togelius, J.: Organic Building Generation in Minecraft. CoRR abs/1906.05094 (2019). http://arxiv.org/abs/1906.05094
15. Guss, W.H., et al.: The MineRL 2020 Competition on Sample Efficient Reinforcement Learning using Human Priors. CoRR abs/2101.11071 (2021). https://arxiv. org/abs/2101.11071
16. Guss, W.H., et al.: MineRL: a large-scale dataset of minecraft demonstrations. In: Kraus, S. (ed.) Proceedings of the Twenty-Eighth International Joint Conference on Artificial Intelligence, IJCAI 2019, Macao, China, 10–16 August 2019, pp. 2442–2448 (2019). https://doi.org/10.24963/ijcai.2019/339

17. Huang, L., et al.: ASIST Experiment 1 Study Preregistration (2020). https://doi.org/10.17605/OSF.IO/ZWAU9
18. Jayannavar, P., Narayan-Chen, A., Hockenmaier, J.: Learning to execute instructions in a Minecraft dialogue. In: Jurafsky, D., Chai, J., Schluter, N., Tetreault, J.R. (eds.) Proceedings of the 58th Annual Meeting of the Association for Computational Linguistics, ACL 2020, Online, 5–10 July 2020, pp. 2589–2602. Association for Computational Linguistics (2020). https://doi.org/10.18653/v1/2020.acl-main.232
19. Johnson, M., Hofmann, K., Hutton, T., Bignell, D.: The malmo platform for artificial intelligence experimentation. In: Kambhampati, S. (ed.) Proceedings of the Twenty-Fifth International Joint Conference on Artificial Intelligence, IJCAI 2016, New York, NY, USA, 9–15 July 2016, pp. 4246–4247. IJCAI/AAAI Press (2016). http://www.ijcai.org/Abstract/16/643
20. van der Linden, R., Lopes, R., Bidarra, R.: Procedural generation of dungeons. IEEE Trans. Comput. Intell. AI Games 6(1), 78–89 (2014). https://doi.org/10.1109/TCIAIG.2013.2290371
21. Lopes, R., Tutenel, T., Smelik, R.M., De Kraker, K.J., Bidarra, R.: A constrained growth method for procedural floor plan generation. In: Proceedings 11th International Conference Intelligence Games Simulution, pp. 13–20. Citeseer (2010)
22. Maehara, H., Martini, H.: Elementary geometry on the integer lattice. Aequationes Math. 92(4), 763–800 (2018). https://doi.org/10.1007/s00010-018-0557-4
23. Nguyen, C., Reifsnyder, N., Gopalakrishnan, S., Muñoz-Avila, H.: Automated learning of hierarchical task networks for controlling minecraft agents. In: IEEE Conference on Computational Intelligence and Games, CIG 2017, New York, NY, USA, 22–25 August 2017, pp. 226–231. IEEE (2017). https://doi.org/10.1109/CIG.2017.8080440
24. O'Keefe, J., Nadel, L.: The Hippocampus as a Cognitive Map. Clarendon Press, Oxford (2016)
25. Peer, M., Brunec, I.K., Newcombe, N.S., Epstein, R.A.: Structuring knowledge with cognitive maps and cognitive graphs. Trends in Cogn. Sci. 25(1), 37–54 (2021). https://doi.org/10.1016/j.tics.2020.10.004
26. Perlin, K.: An image synthesizer. In: Cole, P., Heilman, R., Barsky, B.A. (eds.) Proceedings of the 12th Annual Conference on Computer Graphics and Interactive Techniques, SIGGRAPH 1985, San Francisco, California, USA, 22–26 July 1985, pp. 287–296. ACM (1985). https://doi.org/10.1145/325334.325247
27. Pyarelal, A.: UArizona ASIST Experiment 1 Preregistration (2021)
28. Salge, C., Green, M.C., Canaan, R., Togelius, J.: Generative design in minecraft (GDMC): settlement generation competition. In: Dahlskog, S., et al. (eds.) Proceedings of the 13th International Conference on the Foundations of Digital Games, FDG 2018, Malmö, Sweden, 07–10 August 2018, pp. 49:1–49:10. ACM (2018). https://doi.org/10.1145/3235765.3235814
29. Santamaría-Ibirika, A., et al.: Procedural approach to volumetric terrain generation. Visual Comput. 30(9), 997–1007 (2014)
30. Shelton, A.L., McNamara, T.P.: Systems of spatial reference in human memory. Cogn. Psychol. 43(4), 274–310 (2001). https://doi.org/10.1006/cogp.2001.0758
31. Szlam, A., et al.: Why Build an Assistant in Minecraft? CoRR abs/1907.09273 (2019). http://arxiv.org/abs/1907.09273
32. Warren, W.H.: Non-Euclidean navigation. J. Exp. Biol. 222(Pt Suppl 1), jeb187971 (2019). https://doi.org/10.1242/jeb.187971

Task Complexity and Performance in Individuals and Groups Without Communication

Aditya Gulati$^{(\boxtimes)}$, Thuy Ngoc Nguyen, and Cleotilde Gonzalez

Dynamic Decision Making Laboratory, Carnegie Mellon University,
5000 Forbes Ave, Pittsburgh, PA 15213, USA
aditya@ellisalicante.org, {ngocnt,coty}@cmu.edu

Abstract. While groups where members communicate with each other may perform better than groups without communication, there are multiple scenarios where communication between group members is not possible. Our work analyses the impact of task complexity on individuals and groups of different sizes while solving a goal-seeking navigation task without communication. Our major goal is to determine the effect of task complexity on performance and whether agents in a group are able to coordinate to perform the task effectively despite the lack of communication. We developed a cognitive model of each individual agent that performs the task. We compare the performance of this agent with individual human performance, who worked on the same task. We observe that the cognitive agent is able to replicate the general behavioral trends observed in humans. Using this cognitive model, we generate groups of different sizes where individual agents work in the same goal-seeking task independently and without communication. First, we observe that increasing task complexity by design does not necessarily lead to worse performance in individuals and groups. We also observe that larger groups perform better than smaller groups and individuals alone. However, individual agents within a group perform worse than an agent working on the task alone. This effect is not the result of agents within a group covering less ground in the task compared to individuals alone. Rather, it is an effect resulting from the overlap of the agents within a group. Importantly, agents learn to reduce their overlap and improve their performance without explicit communication. These results can inform the design of AI agents in human-machine teams.

Keywords: Cognitive model · Instance-based learning theory · Group size · Task complexity

1 Introduction

While many people prefer working alone, some tasks are either too large or complicated to be taken on alone. Having a team of people is often crucial for

---

A. Gulati–Currently at the ELLIS Unit Alicante Foundation.

N. Gurney and G. Sukthankar (Eds.): AAAI-FSS 2021, LNCS 13775, pp. 102–117, 2022.
https://doi.org/10.1007/978-3-031-21671-8_7

success. However, a group is usually only effective if members in the group can work together towards their shared objectives. Communication is often seen as a vital tool for coordination between members of groups. Indeed, past studies have shown that groups where members can communicate with each other do better than those groups where such communication channels do not exist [15,21,25].

It is evident that communication is useful, and even though our tools for communication are better than they have ever been, there can be situations where members of a group cannot communicate with each other. Such situations can arise when people do not want to communicate to avoid being spotted (for example, a group of Navy SEALS raiding a building) or when people simply do not have access to communication systems (for example, a group of explorers split up in a network of underground caves). Thus, our work focuses on studying groups where members cannot communicate with each other. For this study, we use a search and rescue task in a simulated scenario called the Minimap [20], which is explained in detail in the following section.

There are multiple algorithms that focus on optimally solving search and rescue tasks [3,14]. However, an important goal in human-machine teaming is to create systems that can work well with humans and not just perform tasks optimally [2]. For this, it is important to understand how humans behave. While Reinforcement Learning (RL) [8,26] has been shown to capture some trends in human behaviour [13,24] and is widely used, it is focused on finding optimal solutions and not on understanding how humans make decisions [4]. Thus, we focus on using cognitive models to predict how a group of humans will behave on the Minimap.

To do this, we analyse data from simulations run with Instance-Based Learning Agents (IBL Agents), built based on Instance-Based Learning Theory (IBLT) [12]. IBL models have been shown to model the human decision making process accurately, and they are useful tools to understand and predict human behaviour [5–7,10,11]. Our goal is to create IBL models of teams that do not communicate and use them to understand the advantages of working in a group and its impact on individual members in the group. In particular, we focus on how the complexity of the task plays a role in the performance of individuals and groups of different sizes.

We produce data for individual IBL agents performing the task, and for individuals and groups of sizes 3 and 6, where each group of agents performs the Minimap task in three different scenarios which vary in their degree of difficulty. In scenarios where agents cannot share information with each other, it becomes important for them to infer each others intentions based on each others actions. Theory of Mind refers to the ability of humans to understand and infer the beliefs, desires and intentions of others [22]. Since IBL agents have already been shown to develop a theory of mind in the past [18], here we analyse the performance of human participants with individual agents, and the performance of agents within groups to determine how agents learn to coordinate and become more effective in solving the task without communication.

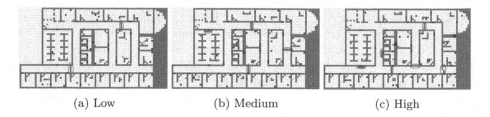

(a) Low   (b) Medium   (c) High

Fig. 1. The three levels of the Minimap task. The light grey cells represent empty cells a participant can walk over. The dark grey cells are walls and the victims are represented by green and yellow cells. The obstacles have been encircled in red. (Color figure online)

2   The Minimap Task

Gridworld tasks are often used in the study of AI as they provide a simple environment for agents to perform multiple tasks in a wide range of applications like navigation or search and rescue tasks. The simplicity of these tasks also makes them suitable for studies on various aspects of human behaviour and decision making [18,19,23]. While the simplicity of these tasks makes experiments easier to conduct and makes data collection easier, it is also important to understand if the behaviour we observe here scales up to more complex richer domains. Thus, building on past work that has created IBL models on gridworld tasks [17–19], our focus here is on scaling up this work, using a more complex richer environment, that we call the Minimap [20].

The Minimap is a 50×100 grid which represents one floor of a building with multiple rooms which have caught fire. Potential victims are spread across the building and their injuries have different degrees of severity with some needing more urgent care than others. The goal of a participant is to rescue as many victims as possible in a stipulated time frame. Each cell on the Minimap can contain a wall, a victim or can be empty. During one run of the game, participants start from a predefined position and move around the empty slots on the grid in an attempt to find victims. The participants at any time have four possible actions - moving up, down, left, or right to the corresponding neighbouring cell.

Figure 1 presents the representations of the three search and rescue scenarios in the Minimap used in this study. Each scenario has two kinds of victims - the more severely injured *yellow* victims and the less severely injured *green* victims. All three scenarios have 24 green and 10 yellow victims. A participant walks around the empty cells (light grey) to search for these victims, but cannot walk through the walls which are represented by the dark grey cells in Fig. 1. The scenarios differ in the placement of victims and the number of obstacles on the map. These obstacles (encircled in red in Fig. 1) are walls which are placed in the middle of a path. These obstacles restrict a participant from taking the path they block, thereby forcing participants to search for longer paths to get around the obstacle. Thus, when there are more obstacles, the structural complexity of the task increases. Since each scenario has a different number of obstacles, they have been assigned 3 levels of complexity - *low* (2 obstacles), *medium* (4 obstacles) and *high* (6 obstacles).

3   IBL Models

IBL models are theoretically grounded cognitive models used to model human decisions from experience based on IBL theory [5–7,10,11].

A key component of an IBL agent is its memory, where an agent stores its experiences. An agent gains experience in two ways: 1) Experiences can be *pre-populated* i.e., these are experiences the agent had before the task started. These are used to simulate prior knowledge that an agent has about the task. 2) Experiences can be *experienced in real time* i.e., the agent experiences new situations which add to its bank of knowledge while performing a particular task.

An experience in the memory is represented as an instance. An instance has three main parts: the situation, decision and utility. The situation is typically a set of attributes used to represent the current state of the environment. The attributes used to define the situation are typically observable features of the environment. The decision is the action the agent took when it was faced with the situation and the utility is the reward it received for taking that decision.

When an agent performing a task needs to make a decision, it looks for instances in its memory which are similar to the current situation and computes an activation function on each of them. The activation function represents how readily available an instance is in the memory [1]. While each attribute can have a different importance, our work here is based on the idea that every attribute that represents the situation is equally important. Thus, the following simplified version of the activation A_i is used for an instance i:

$$A_i = \ln \left(\sum_{t' \in \{1,\dots,t-1\}} (t - t')^{-d} \right) + \sigma \ln \left(\frac{1 - \gamma_i}{\gamma_i} \right) \tag{1}$$

where d is the decay and σ is the noise parameter. t' corresponds to every time step where the situation matched the current situation the agent is faced with and t is the current time step (this is used to capture the idea that it is harder to retrieve instances as they get older). The second part of the equation represents the noise and γ_i is a random number sampled from a uniform distribution $U(0, 1)$.

Based on this activation function, the agent computes the expected utility for every possible action in the current situation. To do this, the agent uses a mechanism called *Blending* which combines the utility associated with all instances corresponding to situation s and action a. For this, it first calculates the retrieval probability of an instance as:

$$p_i = \frac{e^{A_i/\tau}}{\sum_{i=1}^{|l|} e^{A_i/\tau}} \tag{2}$$

where l is the set of all instances with situation s where action a was taken. τ is the temperature defined as $\sigma\sqrt{2}$. If the utility associated with the action a for instance i is u_i, then the blended value is computed as:

$$V(s,a) = \sum_{i=1}^{|l|} p_i u_i \tag{3}$$

The final action taken by the agent is the one with the highest blended value in the given situation.

3.1 IBL Agent for the Minimap Task

An IBL agent $\mathcal{A}_k$ makes decisions based on past experiences which are stored in memory in the form of triplets of the situation (s), the decision (d) and the utility (u). While our work builds upon the work of Nguyen and Gonzalez on the gridworld task [18,19], the representation of an instance in memory was updated in order to deal with the additional complexities of the Minimap task.

The situation s represents the state of the agent in the environment and has two parts - 1) the location of the agent in the grid (the x-y coordinates) and 2) a bit vector to represent the victims rescued by $\mathcal{A}_k$ in the current episode. Each bit represents a victim and is set to 1 if the victim has been rescued in the current episode and 0 if it has not been rescued. The length of the bit vector is equal to the number of goals discovered by $\mathcal{A}_k$ across episodes i.e., a bit is added every time a victim is discovered by $\mathcal{A}_k$. Thus, at the start of every episode, all the bits are set to 0 and are set to 1 as and when the corresponding victim is rescued by $\mathcal{A}_k$.

In every situation, the agent needs to choose an action. For the Minimap task the agent has four possible actions - moving *up, down, left or right*. To make a decision in situation s at time t, the agent $\mathcal{A}_k$ computes the blended value of every possible action (Eq. 3) and picks the action with the highest utility. Thus, for every agent $\mathcal{A}_k$, in every episode, we can define a trajectory $\mathcal{T}_i = \{(s_t, d_t)\}_{t=0}^{T}$.

Each step in $\mathcal{T}_i$ is a part of $\mathcal{A}_k$'s experience on the task. However, to be stored as an instance it needs an associated utility. Since rewards are available only upon rescuing a victim, steps in $\mathcal{T}_i$ are stored with a default utility temporarily. Once a victim is rescued by $\mathcal{A}_k$, the utility of all the instances corresponding to the steps in $\mathcal{T}_i$ which led to the victim are updated with the reward associated with rescuing the victim.

3.2 IBL Models for Group Behaviour

IBL has also been used to model the behaviour of groups of humans [9,16,17]. These studies have been performed on both static and dynamic environments but are performed often in simple choice tasks. This work expands on the past studies of IBL models for groups by testing the impact of group size and task complexity in the Minimap, a task with a large state space.

A group is modelled as multiple IBL Agents performing the task simultaneously without communicating with each other. While the environment is static for a single agent, performing the task with multiple agents makes the environment dynamic for each agent involved. For example, a victim $\mathcal{V}_j$ found by agent $\mathcal{A}_k$ in one episode can be rescued by agent $\mathcal{A}_{k'}$ in a subsequent episode before agent $\mathcal{A}_k$ reaches $\mathcal{V}_j$. Thus, for agent $\mathcal{A}_k$ the environment is dynamic making the task harder for agents in a group.

4   Experiment

We manipulated two factors to understand their impact on the performance of groups - the size of the group and the complexity of the task. The size of the group varied between 1, 3, and 6 agents; the task has three levels of complexity - low, medium, and high. Thus, in total we ran nine scenarios - one for each group size on every level of task complexity.

Each scenario was run for 50 identical trials and all the results presented here have been averaged over these 50 trials. In each trial, the group of agents ran for 50 episodes. Each agent started the first episode with no instances in its memory. As an agent moved around the map, it kept adding instances to its memory which were carried forward across episodes. Thus, an agent started with no prior knowledge and learnt how to perform the task over the 50 episodes it ran.

Each episode was set up in the same way and had at most 2500 steps for each agent. An episode ended if the group rescued every victim or the limit of 2500 steps was reached. A victim could be rescued at most once in each episode. Once a victim was rescued, it "dissappeared" from the map until the start of the next episode. Rescuing a green victim gave the agent 0.25 points (r_{green}) while rescuing a yellow victim gave the agent 0.75 points (r_{yellow}) since the yellow victims have more serious injuries. If an agent tried to walk over a wall, it would stay in the same cell and receive a penalty of -0.05 points.

Agents performing the task were not aware of each others positions or actions at any time during an episode. However, if multiple agents tried to move to the same cell, one of them was chosen uniformly randomly and allowed to move while the others received a penalty of -0.01 points. The simulations were run on a machine with a 3.4 GHz Intel(R) Core(TM) i7-4770 processor.

For every group, we measured the following parameters to analyse their behaviour:

- **Performance:** The performance (P) of an agent $\mathcal{A}_k$ is measured by the total reward collected for rescuing victims across N episodes i.e., if r_n is the reward collected by $\mathcal{A}_k$ in the nth episode, then P is defined as:

$$P = \frac{\sum\limits_{n=1}^{N} r_n}{\sum\limits_{n=1}^{N}(N_{green} \times r_{green} + N_{yellow} \times r_{yellow})} \qquad (4)$$

The performance of a group is measured as the sum of the performances of every individual in the group.

- **Coverage:** The coverage is used to measure the ability of a group to explore the map in an episode. If L_k is the set of locations on the map visited by agent $\mathcal{A}_k$ and L_{map} is the set of all locations that an agent can visit, then the coverage of a group of size M is defined as:

$$\text{Coverage} = \frac{|\bigcup_{k=1}^{M} L_k|}{|L_{map}|} \tag{5}$$

- **Overlap:** The overlap measures in every episode the amount of common area explored by an agent $\mathcal{A}_k$ and the other agents in its group. It is defined as

$$\text{Overlap} = \frac{|L_k \cap (\bigcup_{k' \neq k} L_{k'})|}{|L_k|} \tag{6}$$

- **Discovery Time:** This metric helps us understand how easy it is for a group to find victims. If V is the set of all victims rescued across all episodes, then the discovery time for a victim $v \in V$ is the first episode where the victim was rescued by any agent in the group. For a group of agents, the discovery time measured is the average discovery time of each of the rescued victims and ranges between 1 and 50.

5   Results

To understand the impact of group size and task complexity on the behaviour of groups, we start by looking at the performance of individual agents in relation to the performance of human participants in a data set in which individuals aim to do the Minimap task in an interactive experimental tool.

We compare the performance of independent IBL agents to human participants performing the Minimap task alone. This helps us establish whether the trends noted in the performance of individual IBL agents on the Minimap task are similar to those of human participants. This would support the expectation that predictions made in groups of IBL models may be observed in groups of humans as well.

5.1   Humans and Individual IBL Agents

An experiment with an interactive version of the Minimap was conducted with human participants by Nguyen and Gonzalez and the data set has been made available publicly[1].

The data was collected from 297 participants performing the Minimap task under six different conditions. Out of these six conditions, three matched the

---

[1] https://osf.io/5gmsc/?view_only=b7b13bcae1da448e8c3a5d58ad976e34.

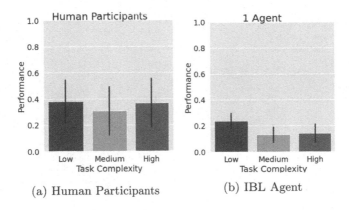

(a) Human Participants   (b) IBL Agent

Fig. 2. Performance of humans and agents on the Minimap task

situation of the Minimap task for the IBL agents in each of the three levels of complexity as described earlier. This resulted in a dataset of 149 participants distributed roughly equally between the three levels of structural complexity. Although not exactly equivalent to the task done by the IBL agents, human participants can be roughly compared to individual IBL agents as shown in Fig. 2.

Figure 2a shows the average performance of the human participants and Fig. 2b shows the performance of IBL agents performing the task independently. For each level of complexity, 50 IBL agents were used to estimate performance. It is important to observe that the IBL agents were not fit to human data. The results presented here are pure predictions, based on the IBL theory. The IBL agents reflect how different complexity levels impact the performance of individual agents.

Figure 2 shows that humans as well as IBL agents perform worse on the medium structural complexity task compared to the other two levels of complexity. This contradicts the intuitive expected linear relation between complexity level and performance, suggesting that the design of task complexity that relies only on structural characteristics (i.e., the number of obstacles), does not necessarily result in a more complex task in terms of performance and decisions that humans or agents make.

To understand these trends better, we look at how human participants and IBL agents perform across episodes (Figs. 3a and 3b) and the coverage of human participants and IBL agents (Figs. 3c and 3d). It is clear that human participants outperform independent IBL agents. This is largely due to the fact that human participants are able to explore a larger portion of the grid. Additionally, we see that the complexity of the task has negligible impact on the ability of human participants to explore the map and similar trends can be seen for independent IBL agents.

The data from human participants was available only for individual participants and not for groups. The similarity in trends for individual human

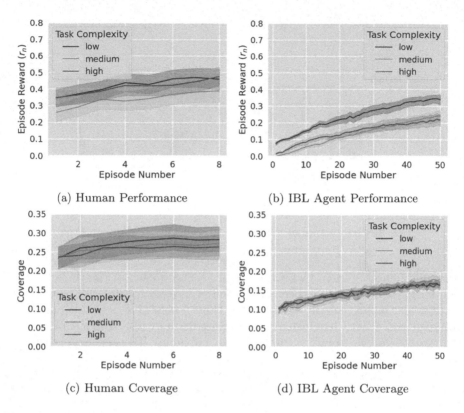

Fig. 3. Performance and coverage of human participants and a single IBL agent across episodes on the Minimap task

participants and independent IBL agents is encouraging. In the following sections, we focus on the performance of a group of IBL agents that do not communicate with each other and on the behaviour of individual agents within each group. The predictions of groups of IBL agents can be used as predictions about the possible behaviour of similarly structured groups of human participants.

5.2   Group Performance

Figure 4 shows the average performance with structural complexity for groups of 3 and 6 agents across three levels of structural complexity. Again, we observe that groups perform worse on the medium structural complexity compared to the other two levels of complexity, regardless of the group size. There appears to be a small advantage in larger groups, where the performance is slightly better in the groups of 6 agents compared to groups of 3 agents. Additionally, the difference in performance between the medium and high complexity tasks also appears to be larger in groups of larger size. To better understand these trends, we look at how the performance and coverage of groups changes across episodes.

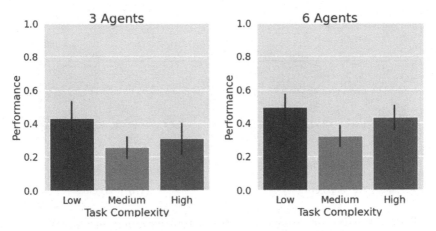

Fig. 4. Relation between performance and task complexity for groups of size 3 and 6

Performance Across Episodes. Fig. 5 shows the variation in performance across episodes for groups of sizes 3 and 6, and for individual agents for all three levels of structural complexity. The x-axis represents the episode number and the y-axis represents the reward the group collected in the corresponding episode i.e., r_n from Eq. 4.

Figure 5a shows the reward collected over time for groups of three agents. Here again, the group is initially performing worse on the medium structural complexity task. However, as time passes, the agents learn to find victims on the medium structural complexity task. Thus, their performance starts picking up and comes close to the performance on the high structural complexity task. In groups, because there are more agents the effects seen with one agent are more pronounced i.e., the difference between performance on the medium structural complexity task and the other complexity levels is significantly higher. This effect is even more pronounced for larger groups as seen in Figure 5b. This indicates that it is not the number of obstacles that truly impact performance but rather how hard it is to find victims.

In line with these ideas, we computed the average time taken to find each victim in the different Minimap scenarios. We noted that on average, a victim was rescued for the first time around the 20th episode by groups solving the medium structural complexity task in contrast to the low and high structural complexity task where victims were rescued for the first time around the 10th episode. The average discovery time for victims stayed the same regardless of the size of the group. This independence of discovery time from group size coupled with the fact that the dip in performance on the medium complexity task was noted in human participants and independent IBL agents makes it likely that groups of humans will take longer to find victims on the medium structural complexity Minimap task compared to the low and high structural complexity task. This again, suggests that the structural complexity alone does not determine how complex the task can be for a group of agents.

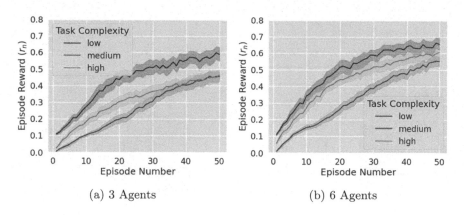

Fig. 5. Trends of reward collected per episode for groups of size 3 and 6

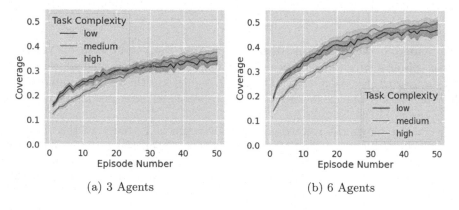

Fig. 6. The area covered by a group over time for groups of size 3 and 6

Coverage. On the Minimap task, the more ground a group can cover, the more likely the members of the group are to find victims. Intuitively, a larger group should be able to cover more ground, thereby allowing the group to rescue more victims.

Figure 6 shows the change in coverage over time for groups of size 3 and 6. The x-axis represents the episode number and the y-axis represents the coverage of a group in an episode as defined in Eq. 5. As time passes, the groups are able to cover more ground in each episode. Additionally, larger groups cover more ground than smaller ones, which indicates that larger groups will perform better.

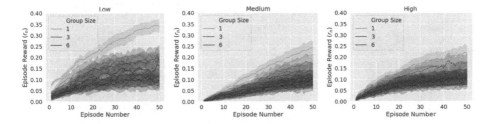

Fig. 7. Performance of different agents in groups of size 3 and 6 for three levels of structural complexity. (Color figure online)

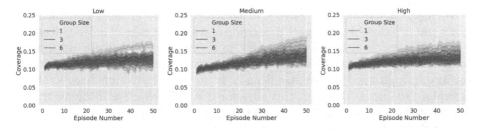

Fig. 8. The area covered by every member of a group over time for groups of size 3 and 6

5.3 Individual Performance Within Groups

While it is clear that larger groups perform better because they are able to cover more ground, it is also important to understand how individual agents in the group perform. Does the performance of a group increase because each agent performs better? Or does the performance of each agent stay the same and it is just more agents that allow groups to perform better? We answer these questions in this section.

Figure 7 shows the performance of individual agents in groups of 3 and 6 compared to when individual agents perform the task alone. For each plot, the x-axis represents the episode number and the y-axis represents the reward per episode i.e., r_n as used in Eq. 4. Each curve represents a single agent and the group size is indicated by the color.

The major observation is that individuals within a group perform worse than individuals that work in the task alone, regardless of the complexity of the task. Furthermore, the larger the group is, the worse the individual performance within a group is. To explain this effect, we look at how individuals within a group cover the task space (i.e., coverage) and how much they overlap with each other while doing the task.

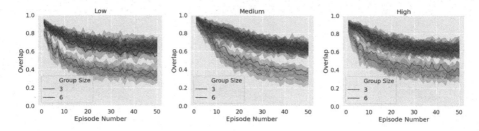

Fig. 9. The overlap for every member of a group over time for groups of size 3 and 6

Coverage. While Fig. 6 revealed that larger groups cover more ground, Fig. 8 shows the coverage of each agent in a group and the coverage of independent IBL agents. While it is clear that each agent in a group covers less ground than an agent working alone, the difference in coverage is minor. This makes it clear that working in a group does not significantly hamper an individual agents' ability to explore the map. However, this advantage is only effective if the agents are able to split up over different parts of the map effectively.

If individual agents are unable to split up effectively, larger groups may not be effective since some agents in these larger groups will just be repeating the work done by other agents. Splitting up may be easier for groups where agents can communicate (since they can plan out strategies to pick different areas) compared to groups like the ones studied here. Thus, we look at how effectively agents in groups are able to split up by looking at the overlap in coverage by agents in groups.

Overlap. Figure 9 shows the overlap in every episode for every agent in a group of size 3 or 6 for all three levels of structural complexity. The x-axis indicates the episode number and the y-axis indicates the overlap measured in the corresponding episode as defined in Eq. 6.

While the overlap is understandably higher for agents in larger groups, it reduces over time regardless of task complexity. This indicates that the agents learn to find specific areas of the map and focus on them without getting in the way of their teammates - even without explicitly communicating with each other. The overlap for every agent decreases over time, but never goes down to 0 indicating that there is always some overlap between all members of a group. These trends explain how groups are able to cover a larger area over time and why the performance of an individual in a group stays below the performance of an agent acting alone.

Thus, each agent working in a group performs worse than an agent working alone, but groups as a whole still perform better than individuals and larger groups perform better than smaller ones.

6   Conclusion

Working in groups is crucial and is something humans do often. To design AI that is able to work along with humans in groups, it is important to design models that emulate the way humans work in groups. Towards this end, we have worked on predicting the behaviour of humans in groups where members cannot communicate with each other. Particularly, we investigate how these groups of different sizes are impacted by task complexity. We created individual agents based on a cognitive theory of decisions from experience [12].

We saw that the trends for the performance of a single IBL agent are similar to those seen for human participants working on the task alone. We find that human participants as well as individual agents perform worse in the task of medium structural complexity than in the task of high structural complexity. This same effect is also observed on the average group performance regardless of the size of the group. This provides a lesson regarding how to design tasks of various complexities: defining complexity of a task based only on structural factors may not be enough to determine how complex a task will be in practice. We note that the reason the medium complexity map is harder, even though it has less obstacles than the high complexity map, is because it is harder to reach victims in this map.

In addition, we found that larger groups perform better, but the individual agents within a group perform worse than an agent attempting the same task alone. Moreover, the larger the group is, the worse individual agents within a group will perform. This effect does not seem to be due to the area that individual agents within a group cover compared to individual agents working alone. Rather, it seems that this is due to the overlap among agents. The overlap is greater in larger groups, but all agents within each group learn to improve their performance across episodes by reducing the amount of overlap between them - even without explicitly communicating.

Overall, we expect that these results will also hold for groups of human participants that do not communicate with each other and are important to consider while designing new AI for human-machine teams.

Acknowledgements. This research was sponsored by the Defense Advanced Research Projects Agency and was accomplished under Grant Number W911NF-20-1-0006.

References

1. Anderson, J.R., Lebiere, C.J.: The Atomic Components of Thought. Psychology Press (2014)
2. Bansal, G., Nushi, B., Kamar, E., Lasecki, W., Weld, D., Horvitz, E.: Beyond accuracy: the role of mental models in human-AI team performance. In: HCOMP. AAAI, October 2019. https://www.microsoft.com/en-us/research/publication/beyond-accuracy-the-role-of-mental-models-in-human-ai-team-performance/

3. Becker, M., Blatt, F., Szczerbicka, H.: A multi-agent flooding algorithm for search and rescue operations in unknown terrain. In: Klusch, M., Thimm, M., Paprzycki, M. (eds.) MATES 2013. LNCS (LNAI), vol. 8076, pp. 19–28. Springer, Heidelberg (2013). https://doi.org/10.1007/978-3-642-40776-5_5

4. Botvinick, M., Ritter, S., Wang, J.X., Kurth-Nelson, Z., Blundell, C., Hassabis, D.: Reinforcement learning, fast and slow. Trends Cogn. Sci. **23**(5), 408–422 (2019). https://doi.org/10.1016/j.tics.2019.02.006

5. Dutt, V., Ahn, Y.-S., Gonzalez, C.: Cyber situation awareness: modeling the security analyst in a cyber-attack scenario through instance-based learning. In: Li, Y. (ed.) DBSec 2011. LNCS, vol. 6818, pp. 280–292. Springer, Heidelberg (2011). https://doi.org/10.1007/978-3-642-22348-8_24

6. Dutt, V., Gonzalez, C.: The role of inertia in modeling decisions from experience with instance-based learning. Front. Psychol. **3**, 177 (2012). https://doi.org/10.3389/fpsyg.2012.00177. https://www.frontiersin.org/article/10.3389/fpsyg.2012.00177

7. Dutt, V., Gonzalez, C.: Accounting for outcome and process measures in dynamic decision-making tasks through model calibration. Technical report, Carnegie Mellon University, Pittsburgh, United States (2015)

8. Gershman, S.J., Daw, N.D.: Reinforcement learning and episodic memory in humans and animals: an integrative framework. Ann. Rev. Psychol. **68**(1), 101–128 (2017). https://doi.org/10.1146/annurev-psych-122414-033625

9. Gonzalez, C., Ben-Asher, N., Martin, J.M., Dutt, V.: A cognitive model of dynamic cooperation with varied interdependency information. Cogn. Sci. **39**(3), 457–495 (2015)

10. Gonzalez, C., Dutt, V.: Instance-based learning: integrating sampling and repeated decisions from experience. Psychol. Rev. **118**(4), 523 (2011)

11. Gonzalez, C., Dutt, V.: Refuting data aggregation arguments and how the instance-based learning model stands criticism: a reply to Hills and Hertwig. Psychol. Rev. **119**(4), 893–898 (2012). https://doi.org/10.1037/a0029445

12. Gonzalez, C., Lerch, J.F., Lebiere, C.: Instance-based learning in dynamic decision making. Cogn. Sci. **27**(4), 591–635 (2003). https://doi.org/10.1207/s15516709cog2704_2. https://onlinelibrary.wiley.com/doi/abs/10.1207/s15516709cog2704_2

13. Gureckis, T.M., Love, B.C.: Short-term gains, long-term pains: how cues about state aid learning in dynamic environments. Cognition **113**(3), 293–313 (2009). https://doi.org/10.1016/j.cognition.2009.03.013

14. Jensen, E.A.: Dispersion and exploration for robot teams. In: Proceedings of the 2013 International Conference on Autonomous Agents and Multi-Agent Systems, pp. 1437–1438 (2013)

15. King, A.J., Narraway, C., Hodgson, L., Weatherill, A., Sommer, V., Sumner, S.: Performance of human groups in social foraging: the role of communication in consensus decision making. Biol. Lett. **7**(2), 237–240 (2011). https://doi.org/10.1098/rsbl.2010.0808. https://royalsocietypublishing.org/doi/abs/10.1098/rsbl.2010.0808

16. Lejarraga, T., Lejarraga, J., Gonzalez, C.: Decisions from experience: how groups and individuals adapt to change. Mem. Cogn. **42**(8), 1384–1397 (2014). https://doi.org/10.3758/s13421-014-0445-7

17. McDonald, C., Nguyen, T.N., Gonzalez, C.: Multi-agent specialization and coordination without communication in a gridworld task. In: ACM Collective Intelligence Conference (2021)

18. Nguyen, T.N., Gonzalez, C.: Cognitive machine theory of mind. In: CogSci (2020)
19. Nguyen, T.N., Gonzalez, C.: Effects of decision complexity in goal seeking grid-worlds: a comparison of instance based learning and reinforcement learning agents. Technical report, Carnegie Mellon University (2020)
20. Nguyen, T.N., Gonzalez, C.: Minimap: a dynamic decision making interactive tool for search and rescue missions. Technical report, Carnegie Mellon University (2021)
21. Oesch, N., Dunbar, R.I.M.: Group size, communication, and familiarity effects in foraging human teams. Ethology **124**(7), 483–495 (2018). https://doi.org/10.1111/eth.12756. https://onlinelibrary.wiley.com/doi/abs/10.1111/eth.12756
22. Premack, D., Woodruff, G.: Does the chimpanzee have a theory of mind? Behav. Brain Sci. **1**(4), 515–526 (1978). https://doi.org/10.1017/S0140525X00076512
23. Rabinowitz, N.C., Perbet, F., Song, H.F., Zhang, C., Eslami, S., Botvinick, M.: Machine theory of mind. arXiv preprint arXiv:1802.07740 (2018)
24. Simon, D., Daw, N.: Environmental statistics and the trade-off between model-based and td learning in humans. In: Shawe-Taylor, J., Zemel, R., Bartlett, P., Pereira, F., Weinberger, K.Q. (eds.) Advances in Neural Information Processing Systems. vol. 24. Curran Associates, Inc. (2011). https://proceedings.neurips.cc/paper/2011/file/c9e1074f5b3f9fc8ea15d152add07294-Paper.pdf
25. Sumner, S., King, A.J.: Actions speak louder than words in socially foraging human groups. Commun. Integr. Biol. **4**(6), 755–757 (2011). https://doi.org/10.4161/cib.17701. pMID: 22446547
26. Sutton, R.S., Barto, A.G.: Reinforcement Learning: An Introduction. MIT Press (2018)

Development of Emergent Leadership Measurement: Implications for Human-Machine Teams

Ellyn Maese[1]([✉]), Pablo Diego-Rosell[2], Les Debusk-Lane[3], and Nathan Kress[4]

[1] Gallup Inc., Omaha, NE 68154, USA
Ellyn_Maese@Gallup.com
[2] Gallup Inc., 46006 Valencia, Spain
[3] Gallup Inc., Richmond, VA 23120, USA
[4] Gallup Inc., Omaha, NE 68135, USA

Abstract. Emergent leadership refers to the dynamic by which, when there is no appointed leader in a group, one or more members assume leadership behaviors. Understanding emergent leadership in task-oriented human-machine teams is critical to optimize the role and input of machine agents. We find, however, a dearth of measures of emergent leadership to guide the development of machine agents. Here we describe the initial development of peer-report and natural language processing (NLP) -derived measurement techniques for indexing emergent leadership in a team context, rooted in the leaderplex model (Denison et al. 1995; Quinn 1984); we take a behavioral approach to indexing emergent leadership which emphasizes the diverse functions of leaders in the team context. We describe initial evidence of validity, areas of further exploration, and implications for human-machine teams. Overall, we find good concordance between peer-report measures of leadership behaviors and peer-report identification of emergent leaders, as well as with initial NLP behavioral marker extractions. Our mixed-method approach presents a first step in developing language-derived computational methods to enhance machine agent artificial social intelligence and theory of mind, ultimately improving their effectiveness in human-machine teams.

Keywords: Emergent leadership · Human-machine teams · Artificial social intelligence

1 Emergent Leadership in Teams

1.1 The Functions of Leadership

From the standpoint of team effectiveness, leadership is important for orchestrating behavior towards a common goal (e.g., Hoyt and Blascovich 2003). Although many task-oriented teams have a predefined leadership structure or status hierarchy (e.g., command units, business units), many teams are formed to carry out tasks with no appointed leadership and no clear status hierarchy. Such teams are often comprised by individuals with complementary functions working towards a common goal. In such self-managed

N. Gurney and G. Sukthankar (Eds.): AAAI-FSS 2021, LNCS 13775, pp. 118–145, 2022.
https://doi.org/10.1007/978-3-031-21671-8_8

teams, overall team effectiveness and task effectiveness depend on individual members assuming responsibility for the quality of their own contributions to both process and outcome, and sometimes also entail members adopting leadership functions (Carte and Becker 2006; Carte et al. 2006; O'Connell et al. 2002).

Emergent leadership is the dynamic by which one or more group members assume leadership behaviors in the absence of a formal leader (Carte et al. 2006). Emergent leadership is recognized as an emergent team characteristic in virtual teams (i.e., in which members interact virtually rather than in person) as well as traditional teams (Carte et al. 2006; Hoch and Dulebon 2017; Yoo and Alavi 2004).

Leadership is comprised of multiple roles and activities that support team members in producing quality contributions and working effectively with other team members towards a common goal. We apply the leaderplex framework (Denison et al. 1995; Quinn 1984; see Table 1) which categorizes eight such functions. This framework has been widely applied in leadership research, and has been used to demonstrate that these behaviors emerge organically within self-managed teams, including within a virtual environment (Cart et al. 2006; Carte and Becker 2006).

Table 1. Leadership behaviors as outlined by the Leaderplex model

Dimension	Description
Innovator	Envisions, encourages, and facilitates change
Broker	Acquires resources and maintains units' external legitimacy through development, scanning, and maintenance of a network of external contacts
Producer	Seeks closure, and motivates those behaviors that will result in completion of the group's task
Director	Engages in goal setting and role clarification, sets objectives, and establishes clear expectations
Coordinator	Maintains structure, does the scheduling, coordinating, and problem solving, and sees that rules and standards are set
Monitor	Collects and distributes information, checks on performance, and provides a sense of continuity and stability
Facilitator	Encourages the expression of opinions, seeks consensus, and negotiates compromise
Mentor	Listens actively, is fair, supports legitimate requests, and attempts to facilitate development of individuals

Team members may exhibit a constellation of these behaviors as they work towards a collective shared goal. Therefore, self-managed teams may develop a variety of leadership structures. In some teams, a single member may take on all or most of these functions and emerge as a clear solitary leader. In others, two or more members of the team may assume leadership behaviors, such that a pattern of shared or distributed leadership emerges, which can also be highly effective for team performance (Carson et al. 2007; Day et al. 2004). Conversely, these behaviors may also be largely absent, with no clear emergent leadership. Here, we develop measures of emergent leadership which can encompass all variations in structure.

1.2 Implications of Emergent Leadership for Human-Machine Teams

Human-machine teams consist of integrated task- or goal-oriented units composed of both humans and machines, wherein "machines" may span automated (unintelligent) systems to the most advanced artificial intelligence. Previous research and applications have demonstrated that human-machine teams can be highly effective – even more so than either in isolation – but their effectiveness as a unit depends on careful integration of complementary roles and tasks, team structure, and team-building (Walliser et al. 2019); leadership is critical in all of these respects. In particular, when it comes to developing intelligent agents capable of effectively assimilating in human teams, an understanding of team processes and dynamics like leadership is critical to a machine theory of mind and artificial social intelligence.

The importance of leadership in facilitating team effectiveness has been detailed for many decades (e.g., Cohen and Bailey 1997; Kozlowski et al. 1996; Zaccaro et al. 2001), including in self-managed and virtual teams (Yoo and Alavi 2004; Carte et al. 2006; Carte and Becker 2006; Hoch and Dulebon 2017). From this perspective alone, understanding leadership structures and behaviors is critical for machine agents in successfully integrating into human teams.

At the most basic level, in order to be effective in human-machine teams, machine agents must possess some knowledge of human leadership, including the behaviors that constitute leadership and the functions of those behaviors, as well as the leadership structure of the team. A more advanced utilization would entail a machine agent assuming leadership roles or behaviors to improve team effectiveness. This would require recognition of the leadership structure and types of behaviors that relate to successful outcomes.

Using the same capabilities, a machine agent could help teams improve their effectiveness by alerting teams when there is suboptimal leadership and/or advising teams to identify leaders, change their leadership structure, or engage in certain leadership behaviors. Finally, given the influence of leaders on team processes, an agent capable of recognizing emergent leaders could target emergent leaders for advice or interventions, as a conduit to improving group outcomes.

1.3 Measuring Emergent Leadership

Currently, we find that most measurement of emergent leadership concerns pre-existing teams and is measured outside of task-performance; there is a lack of validated integration with real-time activities, particularly for teams in completely virtual settings. The few studies that have assessed behavioral markers of emergent leadership (e.g., Carlson et al. 2017) are not well grounded in conceptual models and are thus difficult to validate or generalize.

To meet this need, we employ a multimethod approach to develop a behavioral peer-report measure of emergent leadership for validating additional behavioral markers. Herein, we describe the initial instrument development and psychometric evaluation and provide an initial baseline to capturing team language markers via natural language processing (NLP).

2   Methodology

2.1   Participants

Participants were 201 adults aged 18–49 (M = 22.06, SD = 5.17; 85% between 18–24), recruited from a university student and community sample located in the southwest United States. The sample was majority male (74%) and most were current college students (58%). Participants were diverse in race/ethnicity, with 53% White/Caucasian, 3% Black African American, 13% Hispanic/Latino, 27% Asian, and 2% Middle Eastern. All participants were English speakers, either native (78%) or at least working proficiency, and were screened for familiarity playing computer games. Participants were grouped in 67 team units, with three members per group. Group members had no contact prior to training.

2.2   Procedures

Participants participated in a virtual gamification experiment in a Minecraft environment simulating an urban search and rescue (USAR) task. Participants engaged in two sessions, both conducted virtually. The first session (one hour) consisted of program installation and survey completion. The second session (two and a half hours) consisted of introduction to the task, training, and two 15-min USAR missions.

In each of these missions, teams navigated a collapsed building in the Minecraft environment, and worked together to find and rescue victims that varied in point value. The participants could choose from one of three roles: a medical specialist (medic), a search specialist (searcher), or a heavy equipment specialist (engineer); roles could be changed during the mission.

Teams were randomly assigned to take part in a three-minute planning session with their team members prior to the mission (team planning) or were only allotted time to plan individually (no team planning). Teams were instructed that their goal was to maximize their score by saving victims. This research is part of a multistage research pro-gram funded by DARPA.

2.3   Measures

Emergent Leadership: Peer Report. Respondents provided input on the degree to which their teammates engaged in eight different leadership behaviors adapted from the functions defined by the leaderplex model (Denison et al. 1995; Quinn 1984, see Table 2); an initial qualitative coding of verbal transcripts from pilot testing served to corroborate the relevance of these dimensions and behavioral representations. These items are answered on a 7-point scale of frequency.

Responses from team members were aggregated across respondents (mean rating) to index the degree to which each participant exhibited each leadership behavior. A

Table 2. Emergent leadership behavioral peer-report items

Item	Leaderplex dimension
Suggested new ideas or strategies	Innovator
Kept other team members focused or on task	Monitor/Director
Helped coordinate the actions of team members	Coordinator/Director
Talked about the group's progress during the mission	Monitor
Asked other players to share information during the mission	Facilitator/Monitor
Initiated conversations about the plan or strategy	Director/Producer
Helped the team come to an agreement about what to do next	Producer/Facilitator
Helped other team members figure out what to do or where to go	Mentor

composite for emergent leadership behavior was created by averaging across the eight leadership behavior items.

In addition, respondents were asked to identify the degree to which each team member was a leader during the mission. This item was answered on an 11-point scale in which 0 denotes not a leader at all and 10 denotes always a leader, and also aggregated across respondents (mean rating) to index the degree to which each participant was viewed as a leader by their teammates.

Emergent Leadership: NLP Behavioral Markers. NLP was used to derive potential behavioral markers of leadership, including the number of times each participant initiates communicate with their team members, the number of times each participant has the last word in a conversation with teammates, and the number of times each participant took responsibility. Both the initiation of communication and the last word metrics were extracted from team transcripts across all team sessions.

Participant responsibility was captured with Odin, a computational NLP processor that leverages lexical dependencies, parts-of-speech, and abstractions to detect relevant language (Valenzuela-Escarcega et al. 2015). In this case, language focused on taking responsibility was captured through a series of tokenized word relationships that suggest the participant was taking responsibility.

Additional Self-report Measures. Participants also completed self-report measures of sociable dominance (see Kalma et al. 1993), five-factor personality (Gosling et al. 2003), collective efficacy (measure adapted from a measure previously developed and validated in another government research program), team satisfaction, team viability, and team potency.

Additional Behavioral Measures. Measures of explicit coordination, the three dimensions of plan quality (clarifying roles, clarifying information to be traded, and clarifying sequencing and timing; Stout et al. 1999), compensatory helping, transactive memory, and motivating and confidence building behaviors were derived from qualitative coding of verbatim transcripts of the missions using multiple raters. Team performance was measured as the team's final score on each of the two missions.

In addition, the following behavioral markers were de-rived via NLP (Odin): the number of times each participant spoke about other specific players, spoke about the actions of team members, or spoke about the roles of team members; the number of times each participant agreed with the utterance of another team member; and the number of times each participant spoke about plans, either deliberate (general pre-planning) or contingent (plan based on a condition). For further Odin rule explanations, see Appendix.

3   Results

3.1   Peer-Report Emergent Leadership

Overall, evaluation of item statistics demonstrated that all eight behavioral items of the peer-report measure of emergent leadership were statistically good items. All items displayed reasonable levels of variance, with means and medians close to scale midpoints, all possible response options used, and no evidence of problematic skew or kurtosis (Table 3).

Table 3. Scale and item level descriptive statistics

Item	M	SD	Median	Skew	Kurtosis	Min.	Max.
Overall leadership rating	6.05	1.62	6.00	−0.53	0.38	1.00	9.50
Emergent leadership behavioral composite	4.27	1.03	4.25	−0.17	−0.06	1.19	6.94
Suggested new ideas	4.00	1.28	4.00	−0.24	−0.39	1.00	7.00
Kept team focused	4.17	1.32	4.00	−0.07	−0.34	1.00	7.00
Coordinated other team members	4.63	1.13	4.50	−0.36	0.15	1.00	7.00
Monitored team progress	3.85	1.36	4.00	−0.01	−0.41	1.00	7.00
Prompted info sharing	4.29	1.27	4.50	−0.09	−0.40	1.50	7.00
Initiated conversation about plan	4.08	1.28	4.00	−0.29	−0.29	1.00	7.00
Facilitated team agreement	4.37	1.21	4.50	−0.33	−0.24	1.00	7.00
Helped team members	4.79	1.17	5.00	−0.38	0.23	1.00	7.00

Note. Overall leadership scale possible range 1–10, all other 1–7.

Inter-item correlations were all strong, significant, and positive, but not high enough to indicate redundancies (all $r = .48–.74$, $p < .001$; Table 4).

Table 4. Inter-item correlations

Item	Ideas	Focus	Coordinated	Monitor	Share	Plan	Agree
Kept team focused	.74						
Coordinated other team members	.64	.67					
Monitored team progress	.62	.59	.54				
Prompted info sharing	.63	.66	.62	.62			
Initiated conversation about plan	.73	.64	.66	.62	.64		
Facilitated team agreement	.66	.64	.59	.59	.69	.73	
Helped team members	.59	.64	.71	.48	.56	.62	.65

Note. All $p < .001$. Ideas = suggests new ideas or strategies.

Together, the eight behavioral items demonstrated strong internal consistency (Cronbach's alpha = .931), with strong item-to-total correlations, and no items were identified for deletion to improve the scale (Table 5).

Table 5. Item-total statistic and alpha-if-deleted

Item	Scale mean if items deleted	Scale variance if item deleted	Corrected item-total correlation	Squared multiple correlation	Alpha if item deleted
Suggests new ideas	30.18	51.59	.80	.68	.919
Kept team focused	30.01	51.19	.80	.66	.919
Coordinated other team members	29.55	54.08	.76	.62	.922
Monitored team progress	30.32	52.46	.70	.51	.927
Prompted info sharing	29.89	52.62	.75	.57	.923
Initiated conversation about plan	30.10	51.58	.81	.68	.919
Facilitated team agreement	29.81	52.87	.77	.63	.921

(*continued*)

Table 5. (*continued*)

Item	Scale mean if items deleted	Scale variance if item deleted	Corrected item-total correlation	Squared multiple correlation	Alpha if item deleted
Helped team members	29.39	54.16	.73	.60	.925

Note. Cronbach's alpha = .931.

Exploratory and confirmatory factor analyses indicated that the best solution was a one factor solution, such that the eight indicator items together represent the latent construct of emergent leadership; this model displayed good fit overall ($\chi^2(20) = 56.64$, $p < .001$, RMSEA = .097, CFI = .967, TLI = .953, SRMR = .029). All items loaded strongly and consistently on the latent factor (Table 6).

Table 6. Confirmatory factor analysis

Item	Factor loading	Intercept	Residual variance	R^2
Suggests new ideas	.84	3.14	.30	.71
Kept team focused	.83	3.14	.31	.70
Coordinated other team members	.79	4.07	.37	.63
Monitored team progress	.73	2.83	.47	.53
Prompted info sharing	.77	3.37	.40	.60
Initiated conversation about plan	.84	3.22	.30	.70
Facilitated team agreement	.81	3.64	.35	.65
Helped team members	.77	4.10	.41	.59

Note. $\chi^2(20) = 56.64$, $p < .001$, RMSEA = .097, CFI = .967, TLI = .953, SRMR = .029. Standardized estimates presented.

Item response theory (IRT) evaluations also corroborated that all items have relatively good response properties and clearly distinguish people of different levels of emergent leadership and provide good amount of information at high, low, and average levels (with variation across items), based on item characteristic curves (ICCs) and item information functions (IIFs).

Goodness of fit statistics support the integrity of the items (e.g., all Chi square p > .100, all RMSEA < .04); standardized infit and outfit indicate that all items show reasonable predictability, and six of the eight are highly productive for measurement (Linacre 2002). The test information function also indicates that the scale (all eight items together) provides good information at all levels, but distinguishes best at lower levels (see Tables 7 and 8).

Table 7. Item response theory analysis parameters

Item parameters	a	b1	b2	b3	b4	b5	b6
Suggests new ideas	2.10	−1.88	−1.00	−0.22	0.72	1.59	3.53
Kept team focused	1.98	−2.14	−1.22	−0.27	0.33	1.33	2.41
Coordinated other team members	1.71	−2.26	−2.04	−1.05	0.09	1.01	2.80
Monitored team progress	1.07	−1.57	−1.22	−0.05	0.77	1.67	3.21
Prompted info sharing	1.39	−1.99	−1.55	−0.60	0.44	1.31	2.86
Initiated conversation about plan	1.71	−1.62	−1.34	−0.37	0.50	1.89	3.08
Facilitated team agreement	1.65	−2.32	−1.23	−0.90	0.39	1.28	2.98
Helped team members	1.46	−2.44	−2.45	−1.08	−0.15	1.07	2.29

Table 8. Item response theory analysis fit statistics

Item fit statistics	$\chi 2$	RMSEA	Z-Infit	Z-outfit
Suggests new ideas	22.65	<0.01	−1.68	−1.76
Kept team focused	22.26	<0.01	−1.67	−.174
Coordinated other team members	33.30	0.02	−1.13	−1.31
Monitored team progress	45.87	0.02	−0.65	−0.76
Prompted info sharing	27.67	<0.01	−0.85	−0.97
Initiated conversation about plan	30.44	0.01	−1.45	−1.47
Facilitated team agreement	39.28	0.03	−1.31	−1.51
Helped team members	32.80	0.03	−1.15	−0.94

Note. Infit and outfit presented in standardized format (z-scores). For all $\chi^2\ p > .100$.

The overall peer report of leadership was strongly positively correlated with all behavioral indicators, all $r = .50$–$.70$, all $p < .001$, and the composite of emergent leadership behaviors, $r = .73$, $p < .001$ (Table 9).

Table 9. Correlation of emergent leadership behaviors with leadership ratings

Item fit statistics	Overall leadership ratings
Composite	.73
Suggests new ideas	.68
Kept team focused	.60
Coordinated other team members	.66
Monitored team progress	.50
Prompted info sharing	.52
Initiated conversation about plan	.70
Facilitated team agreement	.55
Helped team members	.58

Note. All $p < .001$.

In further support, participants who were recognized as leaders according to team members' ratings on overall leadership during the mission (i.e., rated above the median) displayed higher levels of all eight leadership behaviors (Table 10).

Table 10. Emergent leaders: mean difference on emergent leadership behaviors

Item parameters	t	df	SE	95%CI lower	95%CI upper	Mean difference	Below median	Above median
Suggests new ideas	−7.30	198	0.16	−1.64	−1.02	−1.33	3.38	4.71
Kept team focused	−7.99	198	0.17	−1.55	−0.89	−1.22	3.61	4.83
Coordinated other team members	−5.38	198	0.14	−1.39	−0.84	−1.12	4.12	5.23
Monitored team progress	−6.55	180	0.18	−1.34	−0.62	−0.98	3.40	4.38
Prompted info sharing	−9.17	198	0.16	−1.40	−0.75	−1.07	3.80	4.87
Initiated conversation about plan	−5.63	198	0.15	−1.70	−1.10	−1.40	3.44	4.84

(continued)

Table 10. (*continued*)

Item parameters	t	df	SE	95%CI lower	95%CI upper	Mean difference	Below median	Above median
Facilitated team agreement	−6.00	198	0.16	−1.22	−0.59	−0.90	3.95	4.86
Helped team members	−7.30	198	0.15	−1.21	−0.61	−0.91	4.37	5.28

Note. All $p < .001$. Below median and above median refer to the median split on overall leadership ratings.

None of the leadership items were significantly correlated with the Five Factor personality traits (agreeableness, extroversion, conscientiousness, emotional stability, openness to experience), nor did these personality traits differentiate those rated as leaders by their peers.

Sociable dominance was not significantly correlated with overall ratings of leadership or the composite of emergent leadership behaviors, however there were several significant item-level correlations. Leadership ratings and several behaviors were negatively correlated with aggressive or domineering attitudes (Table 11).

Table 11. Emergent leadership and key sociable dominance traits

Item parameters	I find it important to get my way	I find it important to get my way even if this causes a row	I quickly feel aggressive with people	I'd rather be disliked (for being unkind) than that people look down on me (for not achieving my aims)
Overall leadership ratings	−.22	−.22		−.17
Behavioral composite	−.20	−.24	−.16	−.20
Suggests new ideas	−.22	−.21		−.20
Kept team focused				−.14
Coordinated other team members	−.22	−.23	−.14	−.18

(continued)

Table 11. (*continued*)

Item parameters	I find it important to get my way	I find it important to get my way even if this causes a row	I quickly feel aggressive with people	I'd rather be disliked (for being unkind) than that people look down on me (for not achieving my aims)
Monitored team progress	−.16	−.15		
Prompted info sharing		−.18	−.15	−.14
Initiated conversation about plan	−.26	−.26	−.19	−.24
Facilitated team agreement	−.15	−.18		−.20
Helped team members		−.20		−.15

Note. Only significant (*p* < .05) correlations presented.

Similarly, those who were distinguished as emergent leaders, when indexed as those who scored above median on the composite of emergent leadership behavior, scored significantly lower on these traits (Table 12).

Table 12. Emergent leaders: mean difference on key sociable dominance traits

Item parameters	*t*	df	SE	95%CI lower	95%CI upper	Mean diff	Below median	Above median
I find it important to get my way	2.63	196	0.14	0.09	0.64	0.37	2.04	1.67
I'd rather be disliked (for being unkind) than that people look down on me (for not achieving my aims)	2.22	196	0.15	0.04	0.64	0.34	2.02	1.68

Note. All *p* < .05. Only significant (*p* < .05) differences presented. Below median and above median refer to the median split on overall leadership ratings.

Leadership ratings, overall leadership behaviors (composite), and several leadership behaviors were also significantly correlated with competency in the mechanics of the task, specifically walking speed (Table 13). Emergent leaders (above the median on composite scale) displayed significantly faster walking speed ($M = 0.45$ vs. $M = 0.49$), $t(190) = 2.19, p = .030$.

Table 13. Emergent leadership and walking speed

Item fit statistics	Walking speed
Overall leadership ratings	−.26
Behavioral composite	−.24
Suggests new ideas	−.19
Kept team focused	−.16
Coordinated other team members	−.20
Monitored team progress	−.15
Prompted info sharing	
Initiated conversation about plan	−.29
Facilitated team agreement	−.22
Helped team members	−.22

Note. All $p < .05$. Only significant correlations presented.

Emergent leaders, as defined by those who scored above the median on the composite scale of emergent leadership displayed more explicit coordination, more compensatory helping, more motivating and confidence building behaviors, more role clarifying behaviors, and more timing and sequencing clarification behaviors during the trial. Emergent leaders were also characterized by speaking more about other specific team members, team members' actions, and team member roles, and engaging in higher levels of planning, particularly deliberate planning (see Tables 14, 15, 16 and 17).

Table 14. Emergent leadership and real-time task behaviors

Item parameters	Explicit coord.	Clarify roles	Clarify info	Clarify timing	Helping	Transactive memory	Motivating confidence building
Behavioral composite	.24	.17		.20	.18		.17
Suggests new ideas	.18		.17				.18

(*continued*)

Table 14. (*continued*)

Item parameters	Explicit coord.	Clarify roles	Clarify info	Clarify timing	Helping	Transactive memory	Motivating confidence building
Kept team focused	.18						
Coordinated other team members							
Monitored team progress	.25	.21				.21	
Prompted info sharing	.21				.21		
Initiated conversation about plan	.29	.23		.28	.16		.18
Facilitated team agreement	.19			.17			
Helped team members				.18			

Note. All $p < .05$. Only significant correlations presented.

Table 15. Emergent leaders and real-time task behaviors

Item parameters	t	df	SE	95%CI lower	95%CI upper	Mean diff	Below median	Above median
Explicit Coordination	−3.29	132	4.55	−23.96	−5.96	− 14.96	37.95	52.90
Clarifying Roles	−2.55	124	0.67	−3.04	−0.38	−1.71	3.05	4.76
Clarifying Timing	−3.05	90	0.59	−2.95	−0.62	−1.79	1.25	3.04
Compensatory Helping	−2.66	112	0.27	−1.25	−0.18	−0.72	0.87	1.58
Motivating & Confidence Building	−2.25	134	0.56	− 2.38	−0.16	−1.27	1.74	3.01

Note. All $p < .05$. Only significant ($p < .05$) differences presented. Below median and above median refer to the median split on overall leadership ratings.

Table 16. Emergent leadership and real-time communication behaviors

Item parameters	Talk about people	Talk about actions	Talk about roles	Giving approval	Talk about plans	Talk deliberate plan	Talk contingent plan
Behavioral composite	.32	.33	.23	.21	.38		
Suggests new ideas	.34	.35	.22	.26	.37		.18
Kept team focused	.27	.27		.18	.33		
Coordinated other team members	.18	.19			.24		
Monitored team progress	.30	.29	.27	.23	.30		
Prompted info sharing	.28	.29	.25	.19	.31	.24	.17
Initiated conversation about plan	.31	.32		.21	.35		
Facilitated team agreement	.19	.21			.26		
Helped team members	.16	.16			.22		

Note. All $p < .05$. Only significant correlations presented.

Table 17. Emergent leaders and real-time communication behaviors

Item parameters	t	df	SE	95%CI lower	95%CI upper	Mean diff	Below median	Above median
Talking about people	−4.23	126	29.46	−187.18	−68.03	−127.61	276.10	403.70
Talking about actions	−4.48	155	21.87	−141.15	−54.74	−97.95	194.89	292.84
Talking about roles	−2.78	123	1.07	−5.10	−0.85	−3.00	6.46	9.43

(continued)

Table 17. (*continued*)

Item parameters	*t*	df	SE	95%CI lower	95%CI upper	Mean diff	Below median	Above median
Giving approval	−2.53	155	2.78	−12.50	−1.54	−8.02	22.06	29.08
Talking about plans	−5.00	117	9.70	−67.73	−29.30	−48.52	77.01	125.53
Talking about deliberate plan	−2.40	155	0.42	−1.82	−0.17	−0.99	1.28	2.27

Note. All $p < .05$. Only significant ($p < .05$) differences presented. Below median and above median refer to the median split on overall leadership ratings.

At the team level (team-level scores aggregated as team mean), overall leadership, the composite of emergent leadership behaviors, and all eight emergent leadership behaviors were significantly positively correlated with positive attitudes about the team, but displayed different patterns of associations with specific measures (collective efficacy, team satisfaction, team viability, and team potency; see Table 18).

Table 18. Emergent leadership and team outcomes

Item parameters	Collective efficacy T1	Collective efficacy T2	Team sat. T1	Team sat. T2	Team viability T1	Team viability T2	Team potency T1	Team potency T2
Overall leadership ratings			.36		.28		.26	
Behavioral composite			.52		.36	.26	.47	.26
Suggests new ideas	.35		.48		.28	.29	.34	
Kept team focused			.35				.30	
Coordinated other team members			.40	.28	.40	.29	.52	.32
Monitored team progress			.42				.40	

(*continued*)

Table 18. (*continued*)

Item parameters	Collective efficacy T1	Collective efficacy T2	Team sat. T1	Team sat. T2	Team viability T1	Team viability T2	Team potency T1	Team potency T2
Prompted info sharing			.50		.37		.44	
Initiated conversation about plan	.26		.45		.34	.29	.39	
Facilitated team agreement			.44		.34		.34	
Helped team members		.27	.32	.28	.33		.37	.33

Note. All $p < .05$. Only significant correlations presented. Team Sat. = Team satisfaction.

Teams with more coordination leadership behaviors displayed better team performance as indicated by their final scores on Mission 1, $r = .33$, $p = .006$, as did teams with more information sharing leadership behaviors, $r = .24$, $p = .049$, and teams with more planning leadership behaviors, $r = .24$, $p = .047$.

Leadership structure varied substantially across teams, with shared leadership being most common. When identifying the presence of emergent leaders as participants scored above the median on the emergent leadership behavior composite, 25% of teams had no emergent leaders, 20% of teams had a sole emergent leader, and 55% of teams had two (30 teams) or three (7 teams) leaders.

Teams with leadership (sole or shared) reported higher levels of collective efficacy, team satisfaction, and team potency following the first trial, compared to teams with no emergent leaders (Table 19).

Table 19. Leadership presence and team outcomes

Item parameters	t	df	SE	95%CI lower	95%CI upper	Mean diff	Mean: no lead	Mean: yes lead
Collective efficacy T1	−2.16	65	0.21	−0.88	−0.03	−0.46	3.65	4.11
Team satisfaction T1	−3.20	65	0.16	−0.81	−0.19	−0.50	2.82	3.32

(*continued*)

Table 19. (*continued*)

Item parameters	*t*	df	SE	95%CI lower	95%CI upper	Mean diff	Mean: no lead	Mean: yes lead
Team potency T1	−2.46	65	0.25	−1.12	−0.16	−0.62	5.10	5.72

Note. All $p < .05$. Only significant ($p < .05$) differences presented. No lead = no emergent leader; yes leader = emergent leader (either single or shared) present. Presence of emergent leader determined by number of team members rated above the median on the composite peer-report behavioral measure of emergent leadership.

Overall, teams with shared leadership reported the most positive attitudes towards their team on these same measures, but teams with single leaders reported higher levels of real-time task behaviors (Tables 20, 21 and 22).

Table 20. Leadership presence and team outcomes

Item parameters	*F*	df	SSIII	MS	EM no leader	EM single leader	EM shared leader
Collective efficacy T1	3.48	2	3.90	1.95	3.65*	3.85	4.21*
Error		64	35.91	0.56			
Team satisfaction T1	5.62	2	3.50	1.75	2.82*	3.19	3.37*
Error		64	19.92	0.31			

Note. All $p < .05$. Only significant ($p < .05$) differences presented. SSIII = sums of squares type III, MS = mean square, EM = estimated marginal mean. * denotes significant subgroup difference.

Table 21. Leadership presence and real-time task behaviors

Item Parameters	*T*	df	SE	95%CI lower	95%CI upper	Mean diff	Mean: no lead	Mean: yes lead
Compensatory helping	−3.05	50	0.21	−1.08	−0.22	−0.65	0.71	1.36
Talk about actions	−2.14	53	31.34	−129.77	−4.07	−66.92	190.89	257.81

(*continued*)

Table 21. (*continued*)

Item Parameters	T	df	SE	95%CI lower	95%CI upper	Mean diff	Mean: no lead	Mean: yes lead
Talk about Plans	−2.65	53	13.03	−60.60	−8.35	−34.47	73.62	108.10

Note. All $p < .05$. Only significant ($p < .05$) differences presented. No lead = no emergent leader; yes leader = emergent leader (either single or shared) present. Presence of emergent leader determined by number of team members rated above the median on the composite peer-report behavioral measure of emergent leadership.

Table 22. Leadership structure and real-time task behaviors

Item parameters	F	df	SSIII	MS	EM no leader	EM single leader	EM shared leader
Compensatory helping	6.19	2	10.22	5.11	0.71*	1.97*	1.13**
Error		52	42.93	0.83			
Talking about actions	3.43	2	71798.86	35899.43	190.89*	296.70*	243.06
Error		52	544789.60	10476.72			
Talk about contingent plans	5.48	2	61.41	30.71	2.00*	4.70*	2.09*
Error		52	291.25	5.60			
Talk about plans	4.45	2	16219.52	8109.76	73.62*	122.74*	102.54*
Error		52	94857.47	1824.18			

Note. All $p < .05$. Only significant ($p < .05$) differences presented. SSIII = sums of squares type III, MS = mean square, EM = estimated marginal mean. * denotes significant subgroup difference.

3.2 Behavioral Markers of Emergent Leadership

At the individual level, the initial NLP behavioral markers were significantly and positively correlated with overall leadership ratings, overall leadership behaviors (composite), and the eight peer-reported leadership behaviors, $rs = .16–.30$, all $p < .05$ (Table 23).

Table 23. Emergent leadership behavior markers and peer-report leadership behaviors

Item parameters	Initiate conversations	Last word in conversation	Taking responsibility
Overall leadership ratings	.27	.23	
Behavioral composite	.30	.31	
Suggests new ideas	.27	.23	
Kept team focused	.27	.23	
Coordinated other team members	.16	.16	
Monitored team progress	.31	.31	.16
Prompted info sharing	.24	.25	.16
Initiated conversation about plan	.30	.33	
Facilitated team agreement	.19	.24	
Helped team members	.18	.24	

Note. All $p < .05$. Only significant correlations presented.

Those who emerged as leaders (above the median on composite of emergent leadership behaviors) demonstrated significantly higher levels on behavioral markers (Table 24).

Table 24. Emergent leaders: mean differences on behavioral markers

Item parameters	t	df	SE	95%CI lower	95%CI upper	Mean diff	Below median	Above median
Initiate conversations	−3.99	174	2.82	−16.79	−68.03	−11.23	32.78	44.01
Last word in conversations	−4.45	174	8.50	−54.51	−54.74	−37.76	113.92	151.69
Taking responsibility	−2.25	174	0.50	−2.11	−0.85	−1.24	2.35	3.47

Note. All $p < .05$. Only significant ($p < .05$) differences presented. Below = below median on composite behavioral measure of emergent leadership; above = above the median.

The behavioral markers of emergent leadership were positively associated with extraversion (e.g., initiating conversations, having the last word, and taking responsibility), $rs = .18–.29$, all $p < .05$. In addition, having the last word was negatively associated with conscientiousness, $r = −.16, p = .039$ (Table 25).

Table 25. Emergent leadership behavioral markers and five factor personality traits

Item parameters	Initiate conversations	Last word in conversation	Taking responsibility
Extraversion	.27	.18	.24
Agreeableness			
Conscientiousness		.16	
Emotional stability			
Openness			

Note. All $p < .05$. Only significant correlations presented.

The behavioral markers of emergent leadership were also positively correlated with features of gregariousness, $rs = .16–.24$, all $p < .05$, and leadership, $rs = .16–.23$, all $p < .05$, and negatively correlated with domineering, $rs = -.16–.17$, all $p < .05$. Attitudes on the measure of sociable dominance (Table 26).

Table 26. Emergent leadership behavioral markers and sociable dominance traits

Item parameters	Initiate conversations	Last word in conversation	Taking responsibility
At school I found it easy to talk in front of the class	.21		
I am not shy with strangers	.18		.20
I can lie without anybody noticing it			.17
I find it important to get my way		−.16	

Note. All $p < .05$. Only significant correlations presented.

NLP behavioral markers of emergent leadership were also significantly positively correlated with real-time task behaviors of explicit coordination, compensatory helping, transactive memory, motivating and confidence building, clarifying roles, clarifying information to share, and clarifying timing and sequencing. Those who were higher on the behavioral markers of leadership also spoke more about team members, their actions, and their roles, as well as about plans (Tables 27, 28).

At the team level, teams higher on these leadership markers also displayed higher levels of important task behaviors. Teams that displayed more leadership according to these markers reported higher levels of team viability after the first mission, $r = .26$, $p = .047$.

Table 27. Emergent leadership behavioral markers and real-time task behaviors

Item parameters	Initiate conversations	Last word in conversation	Taking responsibility
Explicit coordination	.76	.93	.37
Clarifying roles	.41	.59	.23
Clarifying information	.34	.40	
Clarifying timing and sequencing	.33	.47	.17
Transactive memory	.29	.43	
Motivating and confidence building	.43	.48	.24
Compensatory helping	.23	.41	.36

Note. All $p < .05$. Only significant correlations presented.

Table 28. Emergent leadership behavioral markers and real-time communication behaviors

Item parameters	Initiate conversations	Last word in conversation	Taking responsibility
Talking about people	.83	.69	.61
Talking about roles	.56	.47	.48
Talking about actions	.76	.67	.67
Giving approval	.73	.64	.52
Talking about plans	.67	.62	.65
Talking about contingent plans	.35	.39	.40
Talking about deliberate plans	.33	.26	.59

Note. All $p < .05$. Only significant correlation presented.

4 Discussion

4.1 Key Findings and Implications

Overall, the item and scale-level analyses support the psychometric integrity of the peer-report emergent leadership scale. Correlations to perceptions of leadership, behavior-al differentiation of leaders, and associations with team processes, outcomes, and attitudes further support the validity of this measure.

Initial behavioral markers of emergent leadership show concordance with peer report measures of emergent leadership as well as important real-time task behaviors, indicating the utility of even simple NLP extractions for developing behavioral measures of emergent leadership. Leaders could also be differentiated on a number of additional NLP-extracted behavioral/speech markers.

Despite previous research regarding personality traits and emergent leadership (e.g., extraversion, Bono and Judge 2004; Hoch and Dulebon 2017; conscientiousness, Cogliser et al. 2012), and sociable dominance (Kalma et al. 1993), only very limited support was found for the relevance of these traits in the current study. Overall, leaders appeared to be individuals who were more gregarious and less aggressive and domineering in their attitudes towards leadership (i.e., sociable, Kalma et al. 1993); it is unclear if this is context-specific.

Leadership structure of teams did in fact show evidence of being relevant to team processes and attitudes towards the team. As expected teams with leadership displayed higher levels of several important team processes and more positive team attitudes; teams with shared leadership seemed to fair the best according to these measures.

Together, findings support that at both the individual level and team level, emergent leadership is in fact relevant to real-time task- and team-oriented behaviors, as well as task- and team-related outcomes, independent of method of assessment (peer-report or behavioral).

4.2 Future Directions

The research presented here represents a first step in exploring the available data from this experiment. As part of this ongoing research, we are still continuing to evaluate our measure of emergent leadership behaviors and NLP behavioral markers, as well as their relationships to additional team processes, real-time behaviors during the mission, shared mental models, and team outcomes.

Several efforts to add additional behavioral markers of emergent leadership using NLP are currently underway. Some current extractions include the number of times participants say the next to last word followed by team-mate approval, the number of times each participant responds to communications initiated by others (as indication of network centrality) and the number of times participant takes responsibility (e.g. I can do that, I'll take care of it, let me). Other extractions are also being discussed, with the understanding that these will ultimately be used to inform computational NLP for machine agents. In the future, additional qualitative coding of the emergent leadership behaviors may help to identify additional targets for extraction.

Given our relatively sparse findings in this area, one particular focus in future research should be identifying the characteristics that predict who may assume leadership roles within teams; this will be helpful to machine agents integrating with teams, such as in making recommendations for members to take on leadership roles within teams.

Finally, the current findings will be used to make preliminary recommendations for building analytic agents and designing potential interventions that machine agents can engage in to help improve team effectiveness. These agents and interventions will need to be evaluated and refined based on further experimentation in this task environment, and ultimately generalized to other settings.

Ultimately, insofar as optimizing team performance is a fundamental purpose of integrating machine agents into human-machine teams, optimizing task behaviors is instrumental to their purpose. Our work towards developing the concept of emergent leadership into operationalizable measures and inputs presents important progress towards supporting the theory of mind, artificial social intelligence, and general knowledge base necessary for agents in this capacity.

Appendix

```
Vars: "org/clulab/quickstart/grammars/ASIST/vars.yml"
    rules:
      - name: "Entity"
        label: Entity
        priority: 1
        type: token
        pattern: |
          [entity="PERSON"]
          |
          [tag=/^N|PR*/ & !tag=/^V/]
      - name: "Action"
        label: Action
        priority: 2
        pattern: |
          trigger = [tag=/^V/]
          agent: Entity? = /${agents}/
          theme: Entity? = /${objects}/
      - name: "Medic"
        label: Roles
        priority: 1
        type: token
        pattern: |
          /(?i)medic/
          |
          [lemma=/medic|medical/]
      - name: "Hammer"
        label: Roles
        priority: 1
        type: token
        pattern: |
          /(!?)hammer/
      - name: "Specialist"
        label: Roles
        priority: 1
        type: token
        pattern: |
          /(!?)specialist/
      - name: "Search"
        label: Roles
        priority: 1
```

```
   type: token
   pattern: |
     /(!?)search/
 - name: "Obstacle"
   label: stuck
   priority: 1
   type: token
   pattern: |
     [lemma=/immobilize|frozen|stuck/]
     |
     [lemma=can] [lemma=not] [lemma=move]
     - name: "Approval"
   label: Approval
   priority: 2
   example: Sure, Bob!
   pattern: |
     trigger = [lemma=/yes|ok|okay|sure|alright|good|excellent|great|terrific|copy/]
     |
     /(?i)Sounds/ /good/
     |
     /(?i)I/ /agree/
     agent: Entity? = /${agents}/
     - name: "Responsibility"
   label: Responsibility
   priority: 2
   type: token
   example: I can do that.
   pattern: |
     [lemma=/(?i)I\'ll/]
     |
     /(?i)Can/ /do/
     |
     /(?i)Take/ /care/
     |
     /(?i)Let/ /me/
     |
     /(?i)I/ /will/
     # Planning Rules #
###############################
 - name: "ConditionalIF"
   label: ContingentPlan
   priority: 3
   pattern: |
     trigger = [lemma=if]
     condition: Action = <mark
```

```
    solution: Action = <mark <advcl_if
  - name: "PlanTrig"
    label: Planning
    priority: 1
    type: token
    pattern: |
      /(?i)should|need/
      |
      [lemma=/plan|goal|bring|come|gather|get|be/]
  - name: "DeliberateFut"
    label: DeliberatePlan
    priority: 3
    pattern: |
      trigger = (?<= [tag=VBP & lemma=be]) [tag=VBG]
```
the first thing in the parantheses is a look behind so it's going to look at everything that came before.
both inside the square brackets are constraints applied to a single token. A token comes before that is the tag restraints
and the verb "to be"
the second is capturing the gerund "am going"
```
      |
      (?<= [tag=MD & lemma=will]) [tag=VB]
```
to make this useful we need to know who is doing the planning.
```
      agent: Entity = >/${agents}/
```
agent is the name of the argument while Entity is the type.
the pattern is right hand side of the colon and is applied to the sentence.
from the trigger, follow an outgoing agent and it would need to be in previously found entity.
```
      theme: Param? = >/${objects}/
  - name: "HelpRequests"
    label: coordination
    example: Can someone help me?
    pattern: |
      trigger = /(?i)could|would|can/
      actor: Entity = <aux >/${agents}/
```
person doing the helping (someone)
```
      request: Action = <aux
```
not about linear order, we are traversing against an incoming aux to land on the end of the aux (from can to help)
```
      recipient: Entity? = <aux dobj
```
now, we're traversing against an incoming aux to land on the dobj (from help to me).
```
  # - name: "Response"
  # label: coordination
  # example: I can help you.
```

```
# type: token
# pattern: |
# /(?i)could|would|can/ [tag=/PRP|N*/]
- name: "Unless"
  label: coordination
  type: token
  pattern: |
    /(?i)unless/ [tag=/PRP|N*/]
      # My Rule #
# 5. Taking responsibility: Number of times participant takes responsibility #
# (keywords: I can do that, Iâ€™ll take care of it, let me). #
```

References

Bono, J.E., Judge, T.A.: Personality and transformational and transactional leadership: a meta-analysis. J. Appl. Psychol. **89**(5), 901–910 (2004)

Carson, J.B., Tesluk, P.E., Marrone, J.A.: Shared leadership in teams: an investigation of antecedent conditions and performance. Acad. Manag. J. **50**(5), 1217–1234 (2007)

Carte, T.A., Becker, A.: Emergent leadership in self-managed virtual teams: a replication. AIS Trans. Replication Res. **3**(5), 1–10 (2006)

Carte, T.A., Chidambaram, L., Becker, A.: Emergent leadership in self-managed virtual teams: a longitudinal study of concentrated and shared leadership behaviors. Group Decis. Negot. **15**(4), 323–343 (2006)

Cogliser, C.C., Gardner, W.L., Gavin, M.B., Broberg, J.C.: Big Five personality factors and leader emergence in virtual teams: relationships with team trustworthiness, member performance contributions, and team performance. Group Org. Manag. **37**(6), 752–784 (2012)

Cohen, S.G., Bailey, D.E.: What makes teams work: group effectiveness research from the shop floor to the executive suite. J. Manag. **23**(3), 239–290 (1997)

Day, D.V., Gronn, P., Salas, E.: Leadership capacity in teams. Leadersh. Q. **15**(6), 857–880 (2004)

Denison, D.R., Hooijberg, R., Quinn, R.E.: Paradox and performance: toward a theory of behavioral complexity in managerial leadership. Organ. Sci. **6**(5), 524–540 (1995)

Dulebohn, J.H., Hoch, J.E.: Virtual teams in organizations. Hum. Resour. Manag. Rev. **27**(4), 569–574 (2017)

Gerpott, F.H., Lehmann-Willenbrock, N., Voelpel, S.C., van Vugt, M.: It's not just what is said, but when it's said: a temporal account of verbal behaviors and emergent leadership in self-managed teams. Acad. Manag. J. **62**(3), 717–738 (2019)

Hoyt, C.L., Blascovich, J.: Transformational and transactional leadership in virtual and physical environments. Small Group Res. **34**(6), 678–715 (2003)

Kalma, A.P., Visser, L., Peeters, A.: Sociable and aggressive dominance: personality differences in leadership style? Leadersh. Q. **4**, 45–64 (1993)

Kozlowski, S.W.J., Gully, S.M., Salas, E., Cannon-Bowers, J.A.: Team leadership and development: theory, principles, and guidelines for training leaders and teams. In: Beyerlein, M.M., Johnson, D.A., Beyerlein, S.T. (eds.) Advances in Interdisciplinary Studies of Work Teams: Team Leadership, vol. 3, pp. 253–291. Elsevier Science/JAI Press (1996)

Linacre, J.: What do infit and outfit, mean-square and standardized mean? Rasch Meas. Transm. **16**(2), 878 (2002)

O'Connell, M.S., Doverspike, D., Cober, A.B.: Leadership and semiautonomous work team performance: a field study. Group Org. Manag. **27**, 50–65 (2002)

Quinn, R.E.: Applying the competing values approach to leadership: toward and integrative model. In: Hunt, J.G., Stewart, R., Schriesheim, C., Hosking, D. (eds.) Managers and Leaders: An International Perspective. Pergamon, New York (1984)

Stout, R.J., Cannon-Bowers, J.A., Salas, E., Milanovich, D.M.: Planning, shared mental models, and coordinated performance: an empirical link is established. Hum. Factors **41**, 61–71 (1999)

Valenzuela-Escárcega, M.A., Hahn-Powell, G., Surdeanu, M.: Description of the Odin Event Extraction Framework and Rule Language. arxiv:1509.07513 (2015)

Walliser, J.C., de Visser, E.J., Wiese, E., Shaw, T.H.: Team structure and team building improve human–machine teaming with autonomous agents. J. Cogn. Eng. Decis. Mak. **13**(4), 258–278 (2019)

Yoo, Y., Alavi, M.: Emergent leadership in virtual teams: what do emergent leaders do? Inf. Organ. **14**, 27–58 (2004)

Zaccaro, S.J., Rittman, A.L., Marks, M.A.: Team leadership. Leadersh. Q. **12**(4), 451–483 (2001)

Translating and Modeling Human Theory of Mind for ASI

Should Agents Have Two Systems to Track Beliefs and Belief-Like States?

Irina Rabkina[1](✉) and Clifton McFate[2]

[1] Occidental College, Los Angeles, CA, USA
irabkina@oxy.edu
[2] Elemental Cognition, New York, NY, USA
cjm@ec.ai

Abstract. Adult humans are typically capable of impressive, often recursive, reasoning about the mental states of others, but recent evidence has suggested that said reasoning, called Theory of Mind reasoning (ToM), is not easy or automatic. This has lead to the theory that human ToM reasoning requires two systems. One system, efficient but inflexible, enables rapid judgements by operating without explicit modeling of beliefs, while a separate, effortful system, enables richer predictions over more complex belief encodings. We argue that computational ToM requires a similar distinction. However, we propose a different model: a single process, but with effortful re-representation leading to two phases of ToM reasoning. Efficient reasoning, in our view, occurs over representations that include actions, but not necessarily explicit belief states. Effortful reasoning, then, involves re-representation of these initial encodings in order to handle errors, resolve real-world conflicts, and fully account for others' belief states. We present an implemented computational model, based in memory retrieval and structural alignment, and discuss possible implications for computational agents in human-machine teams.

1 Introduction

While the precise trajectory of human theory of mind (ToM) development continues to be debated [14, 19, 27, 28] it has been well established that young children often fail to take into account the mental states of others when predicting their actions. However, typically developing adults (and older children) are generally considered to be proficient ToM reasoners.

Yet, there is substantial evidence that adults do not always effectively utilize ToM, either—at least not automatically. For example, during diadic conversation, adult participants have been found to consider visual referents that their partner could not be aware of [12]. In a further exploration, participants were asked to give a "director" an object from a table. The names of the objects on the table were polysemous (e.g., a roll of tape and a cassette tape), but, prior to the direction, the participant themselves hid one of the possible referents in a bag, leaving only one visible to the director. Even so, the participants sometimes gave the director the occluded object. This was the case even when they were told the director had a false belief about the contents of the bag that excluded the actual contents as a referent [13].

There is also evidence that ToM reasoning requires cognitive effort. Adults are generally slower to answer questions about another person's false beliefs than about reality, but that this processing difference disappears when the participants were instructed to track beliefs explicitly [2]. Furthermore, there is evidence that working memory impairment degrades ToM reasoning, suggesting that humans are "reflexively mind blind", only explaining behavior with regard to mental states when cognitive resources allow [15].

Such findings have led to the proposal that adult humans have two systems for theory of mind. The first ToM system—efficient but inflexible—enables real time goal recognition but does not explicitly encode mental states. The second system does encode mental states and enables full ToM reasoning, but requires cognitive effort. They suggest that the first system is shared by young children and potentially non-human animals as well, while the latter develops with maturation, thus explaining developmental findings [1].

We propose that this distinction is also beneficial when implementing ToM for machines that work with human teammates, allowing agents to conserve resources and respond in real time while reserving effortful ToM for error correction or particularly important interactions.

However, unlike previous accounts, we suggest that the difference between the two systems is purely representational. That is, a single ToM process is sufficient for both efficient and effortful ToM reasoning, with re-representation accounting for the effort in the latter. We present an existing computational model of ToM, the Analogical Theory of Mind [23], which, we argue, can be used for both types of reasoning, given appropriate representations. We finish by discussing implications of this model to human-machine teaming.

2   Automatic and Effortful ToM in Agents

There is a wide variety of ToM-style tasks that computational agents working with human teammates may need to perform. These vary from interpreting the goals behind the person's actions [4] to understanding the preferences or beliefs that underlie those actions [29] and adapting the agent's own actions in response [9]. Some of these tasks can be completed via automatic processes exclusively, while others require effortful reasoning to do well.

Consider the following example. Our agent sees its teammate, Sam, walking toward the kitchen. It might predict that Sam is getting a coffee. For this inference, an example of goal recognition, the sequence of actions performed by Sam is likely sufficient [17].

However, suppose the agent notices that Sam is not carrying a cup and knows there are none in the kitchen. The agent may conclude that Sam erroneously believes the kitchen has spare cups, or perhaps that Sam is going for another reason. This is no longer pure goal recognition. The agent must now reconcile its observation with Sam's possible belief states. As in humans, belief state ToM reasoning is more difficult and requires richer representations. Whether the agent engages in this effortful action depends on its own goals and resources; maybe a colleague going to the kitchen is not worth further thought.

There are real world use cases where goal recognition, without explicit consideration of belief states, is sufficient for computational agents. For example, a goal recognition algorithm that predicts adversary goals from behavioral observations has been used to model air combat scenarios [3]. Other goal recognition domains range from non-player character gameplay in video games [7] to cooking [25], among others. Often, the step from recognizing a goal to taking action with a human teammate is straightforward and does not require access to mental states. In such situations rich representations and effortful reasoning may be wasted effort.

Other tasks, however, do require deeper representations that encode additional actions, belief states, knowledge states, preferences, or all of the above. For example, the proposed "Watch-And-Help" social reasoning task, in which an agent helps a human teammate complete a task in the home (e.g., set the table, put away groceries, etc.) requires reasoning about a human partner's beliefs. While goal recognition is part of this task (i.e., it is necessary for the agent to recognize which task the human is completing), the agent must also consider the human's beliefs about the environment and the intermediate steps they may take to complete the task. That is, the agent must not only recognize that its teammate wants to set the table, but also consider the fact that they may not know where the forks are located or that dinner has already been moved from the refrigerator to the oven for reheating.

It may not be immediately clear at the onset of a task whether pure goal recognition will be sufficient, or if more effortful representations will be required [20]. In fact, we posit that most real-world tasks for agents, as for humans, will fall somewhere in the middle, requiring automatic representations at the onset and effortful adjustments throughout the interaction. Thus, the ability to easily switch between these representations will be necessary for successful human-machine teaming.

3   Analogical Theory of Mind (AToM) Model

We propose that the Analogical Theory of Mind (AToM) model of ToM reasoning and development can perform both automatic and effortful ToM reasoning using a single iterative process of memory retrieval, analogical inference, and effortful re-representation. We describe that model and the types of representations used here.

3.1   Analogical Theory of Mind

Analogical Theory of Mind [23] is a computational cognitive model of human ToM reasoning and development that has also been used for ToM reasoning in computational agents [21,22]. Importantly, different representations have been used for each of these tasks. For example, [23] encoded stories using explicit representations of belief states to model how children learn ToM from hearing stories about others' true and false beliefs. On the other hand, [24] modeled how children gain ToM from learning a complex grammatical structure; while the nested structure of representations played an important role in that model, belief states were not encoded at all.

Representations also varied when the model was used in agents' reasoning about others. [21] used nested qualitative representations of agents' movement to predict whether they were cooperating with each other, while [22] used flat representations of actions in a more typical goal recognition task. In both cases, AToM performed comparably to state-of-the-art solutions[1].

The AToM algorithm did not differ as representations changed. This was enabled by the implemented processes that underlie AToM's reasoning, analogical retrieval [6] and structural alignment [5].

In particular, AToM relies on a learned or pre-populated memory bank of cases, called a *case library*. In the example of the agent reasoning about Sam walking to the kitchen, the case library would likely include memories of other interactions it has had with humans (hopefully, but not necessarily, including observations of other kitchen trips). In AToM, a representation of the ongoing scenario is used to retrieve a memory. The retrieved memory is aligned to the scenario using structural alignment, and *candidate inferences* are generated. Candidate inferences suggest facts that may be true in the scenario, although they are not guaranteed to be accurate or consistent. Thus, a memory of Jackie going to the kitchen for coffee may lead to the candidate inference that Sam is getting coffee, too.

Retrieval and alignment follow the principles of Structure-mapping Theory [8]. At a high level, these prioritize retrieval of memories that share higher order structure with the scenario being reasoned about. They also enforce hard restrictions on alignment (e.g., that each item in the memory can align to at most one item in the scenario) and suggest soft constraints (e.g., prefer aligning identical predicates to each other).

Consider the example in Fig. 1. The agent is comparing the ongoing scenario (Sam going to the kitchen) to two memories. In one, a teammate, Jackie, believes there to be cups in the kitchen and is surprised that there are none. This could be represented with the nested belief proposition (`believes Jackie` (`locationOf cup kitchen`)) and her state of surprise, (`surprised Jackie`), but no action. The other contains the fact that Alex walked to the kitchen (`walks Alex kitchen`), but no representation of a belief.

If the agent represents Sam going to the kitchen with both (`walks Sam kitchen`) and (`believes Sam` (`locationOf cup kitchen`)) facts, the first memory will align better based on the shared nested belief structure and should

---

[1] Cooperation prediction was compared against [26]'s [26] Bayesian model, while goal recognition was compared against PANDA-Rec [10] and Elixir-MCTS [11].

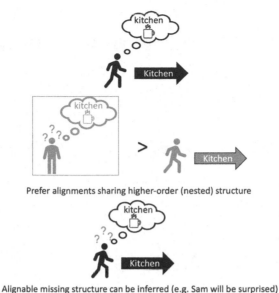

Fig. 1. Analogical alignment and inference

be retrieved. On the basis of the alignment, it can be inferred that Sam will also be surprised.

Different permutations of these facts in memories and scenario representations will lead to different retrievals, and therefore different reasoning outcomes. Note, too, that, while in this toy examples, representations of the scenario and retrieved memories are exactly the same, such exact matching is not required.

3.2 Automatic Encoding and Effortful Re-Representation for AToM

As discussed above, there is evidence that full ToM reasoning is not automatic and in fact requires substantial cognitive effort [1,13,15]. AToM provides a mechanism by which ToM inference occurs, namely analogical retrieval of and mapping from episodic memories. Here we propose that this process underlies both automatic and effortful ToM reasoning, the latter being the result of an iterative sequence of retrieval and re-representation.

When observing a potential ToM reasoning scenario (e.g., Sam going to the kitchen), the agent initially encodes its observation using sparse representations that do not include belief and knowledge states. It then retrieves an analogical experience from memory and infers a potential goal. As in [23], this inference may be incompatible with the real world which triggers a search for explanation via further analogical retrieval.

In our proposed model, the incompatible inference leads to re-representation of the scenario given the false expectations generated by the alignment. This

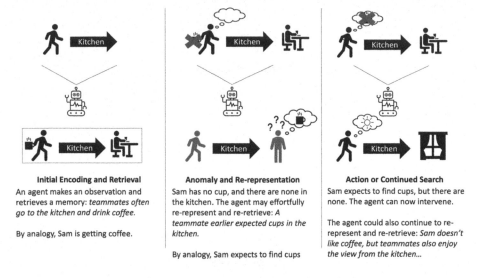

Fig. 2. ToM through successive analogical retreival and re-representation

process of inference evaluation, re-representation, and retrieval requires additional cognitive effort and is subject to executive control.

As an example, consider Fig. 2. Our agent observes their teammate Sam going to the kitchen. This prompts a search for explanation using the agent's initial encoding of the situation. The agent recalls that teammates often go to the kitchen and drink coffee. By aligning Sam to prior teammates, the agent can infer that Sam is likewise getting coffee.

However, in the retrieved memory the teammate needs to bring a cup in order to drink coffee. Sam does not have a cup, triggering what, in analogy literature, is called an alignable difference [16]. This difference is re-represented into the scenario and the agent again searches for explanation. The agent now retrieves a memory that another teammate was surprised to find the kitchen did not have extra cups. So perhaps, by analogy, Sam is also expecting there to be cups in the kitchen.

Now primed with Sam's inferred beliefs, the agent can continue to elaborate. Maybe this belief is inconsistent with reality (i.e., Sam knows there are no cups) or maybe the agent remembers that Sam does not like coffee. The agent can continue to re-reprsent and re-retrieve explanations until satisfied.

In [23] the retrieved memories were encoded from a first person perspective (e.g., "I once got coffee"). In the automatic representations in [22], on the other hand, representations were allocentric (e.g., "My teammate once got coffee"). We note here that, due to analogical alignment, ToM reasoning can arise from both egocentric and allocentric memories. The ToM target could align to oneself or one's mental model of another agent. Interestingly, this suggests that individual encoding biases as well as alignability between the self and the target may play a significant role in ToM prediction. If the target is easily aligned to the self, an agent may be more likely to ascribe its own motivations and beliefs to the target. However if viewed as different, the agent would be more likely to apply its perceived mental model of a more similar analog or even fail to model ToM entirely. Exploring this distinction is one future direction for our modeling work.

4   Implications for Human-Machine Teams

Human agents certainly have the ability to engage in rich ToM modeling, but there is ample evidence that such modeling is both costly and often unnecessary. We believe this lesson can be applied to the ToM reasoning of computational agents collaborating with humans. ToM reasoning need not be complete, and initial reasoning may not even need to explicitly take into account teammates' mental states. Instead, we propose that ToM reasoning ought to progress from efficient reasoning over initial representations to effortful re-representation and reasoning only when there is both need and available cognitive resources.

We suggest that the AToM model provides a single process that naturally allows for this kind of progression in the form of re-representation and retrieval.

Furthermore, as a cognitive model, AToM could provide insight into how and why humans apply or fail to apply their own ToM reasoning to their computational teammates. As we discuss above, the AToM model suggests that the ability to apply ToM and the kinds of judgements made may depend on how alignable the ToM target is to oneself and ones representations of others. If correct, then human teammates may not ascribe a computational agent the same kinds of beliefs and knowledge that they would ascribe themselves (or even other humans) in the same situation. However, they may be more willing to do so if the agent adopts a familiar profile.

Finally, to date, AToM has relied on manually constructed episodic memories or domain-specific training data. This may be possible for online reasoning in some domains, and an agent may be able to accumulate memories through interaction. However, we are also interested in examining how large generative neural models may be used to simulate episodic memory. As an example, [18] collected a large corpus of semi-structured natural language causal explanations which they used to train neural models for causal prediction. Such models may be able to generate plausible beliefs and causal chains as a stand-in for real-life experiences.

5   Conclusion

We have proposed that ToM reasoning for computational agents in human-machine teams should not be one-shot. Rather, following evidence that humans have both a fast automatic and slower effortful system for ToM reasoning, we argue that computational agents should be able to modify initial judgements for more nuanced reasoning. We posit that this distinction can be achieved through automatic initial encodings and effortful re-representation using a single reasoning process. In particular, the Analogical Theory of Mind (AToM) model can be used for this type ToM reasoning. In future work, we plan to empirically test these claims.

References

1. Apperly, I.A., Butterfill, S.A.: Do humans have two systems to track beliefs and belief-like states? Psychol. Rev. **116**(4), 953 (2009)
2. Apperly, I.A., Riggs, K.J., Simpson, A., Chiavarino, C., Samson, D.: Is belief reasoning automatic? Psychol. Sci. **17**(10), 841–844 (2006)
3. Borck, H., Karneeb, J., Floyd, M.W., Alford, R., Aha, D.W.: Case-based policy and goal recognition. In: Hüllermeier, E., Minor, M. (eds.) ICCBR 2015. LNCS (LNAI), vol. 9343, pp. 30–43. Springer, Cham (2015). https://doi.org/10.1007/978-3-319-24586-7_3
4. Eger, M., Martens, C., Chacón, P.S., Córdoba, M.A., Cespedes, J.H.: Operationalizing intentionality to play Hanabi with human players. IEEE Trans. Games (2020)
5. Forbus, K.D., Ferguson, R.W., Lovett, A., Gentner, D.: Extending SME to handle large-scale cognitive modeling. Cogn. Sci. **41**(5), 1152–1201 (2017)
6. Forbus, K.D., Gentner, D., Law, K.: Mac/fac: a model of similarity-based retrieval. Cogn. Sci. **19**(2), 141–205 (1995)
7. Geib, C., Weerasinghe, J., Matskevich, S., Kantharaju, P., Craenen, B., Petrick, R.P.A.: Building helpful virtual agents using plan recognition and planning. In: Proceedings of the 12th AAAI Conference on AIIDE, pp. 162–168 (2016)
8. Gentner, D.: Structure-mapping: a theoretical framework for analogy. Cogn. Sci. **7**(2), 155–170 (1983)
9. Hiatt, L.M., Harrison, A.M., Trafton, J.G.: Accommodating human variability in human-robot teams through theory of mind. In: Twenty-Second International Joint Conference on Artificial Intelligence (2011)
10. Höller, D., Behnke, G., Bercher, P., Biundo, S.: Plan and goal recognition as HTN planning. In: Proceedings of the 30th IEEE International Conference on Tools with Artificial Intelligence, pp. 466–473 (2018)
11. Kantharaju, P., Ontañón, S., Geib, C.W.: Scaling up CCG-based plan recognition via Monte-Carlo tree search. In: Proceedings of the 2019 IEEE-COG, pp. 1–8 (2019)
12. Keysar, B., Barr, D.J., Balin, J.A., Brauner, J.S.: Taking perspective in conversation: the role of mutual knowledge in comprehension. Psychol. Sci. **11**(1), 32–38 (2000)
13. Keysar, B., Lin, S., Barr, D.J.: Limits on theory of mind use in adults. Cognition **89**(1), 25–41 (2003)
14. Kovács, Á.M., Téglás, E., Csibra, G.: Can infants adopt underspecified contents into attributed beliefs? representational prerequisites of theory of mind. Cognition **214**, 104640 (2021)
15. Lin, S., Keysar, B., Epley, N.: Reflexively mindblind: using theory of mind to interpret behavior requires effortful attention. J. Exp. Soc. Psychol. **46**(3), 551–556 (2010)
16. Markman, A.B., Gentner, D.: Commonalities and differences in similarity comparisons. Mem. Cogn. **24**(2), 235–249 (1996)
17. Mirsky, R., Keren, S., Geib, C.: Introduction to symbolic plan and goal recognition. Synth. Lect. Artif. Intell. Mach. Learn. **16**(1), 1–190 (2021)

18. Mostafazadeh, N., et al.: GLUCOSE: generalized and contextualized story explanations. In: Proceedings of the 2020 Conference on Empirical Methods in Natural Language Processing (EMNLP), pp. 4569–4586. Association for Computational Linguistics, Online (2020). https://doi.org/10.18653/v1/2020.emnlp-main.370, https://aclanthology.org/2020.emnlp-main.370

19. Onishi, K.H., Baillargeon, R.: Do 15-month-old infants understand false beliefs? Science **308**(5719), 255–258 (2005)

20. Puig, X., et al.: Watch-and-help: a challenge for social perception and human-AI collaboration. In: International Conference on Learning Representations (2020)

21. Rabkina, I., Forbus, K.D.: Analogical reasoning for intent recognition and action prediction in multi-agent systems. In: Proceedings of the Seventh Annual Conference on Advances in Cognitive Systems, pp. 504–517 (2019)

22. Rabkina, I., Kantharaju, P., Roberts, M., Wilson, J., Forbus, K., Hiatt, L.M.: Recognizing the goals of uninspectable agents. In: Advances in Cognitive Systems (2020)

23. Rabkina, I., McFate, C., Forbus, K.D., Hoyos, C.: Towards a computational analogical theory of mind. In: Proceedings of the 39th Annual Meeting of the Cognitive Science Society (2017)

24. Rabkina, I., McFate, C.J., Forbus, K.D.: Bootstrapping from language in the analogical theory of mind model. In: CogSci (2018)

25. Ramirez, M., Geffner, H.: Goal recognition over POMDPs: Inferring the intention of a POMDP agent. In: Twenty-Second International Joint Conference on Artificial Intelligence (2011)

26. Shum, M., Kleiman-Weiner, M., Littman, M.L., Tenenbaum, J.B.: Theory of minds: understanding behavior in groups through inverse planning. In: Proceedings of the AAAI Conference on Artificial Intelligence, vol. 33, pp. 6163–6170 (2019)

27. Villiers, J.G.: The Role(s) of language in theory of mind. In: Gilead, M., Ochsner, K.N. (eds.) The Neural Basis of Mentalizing, pp. 423–448. Springer, Cham (2021). https://doi.org/10.1007/978-3-030-51890-5_21

28. Wellman, H.M., Liu, D.: Scaling of theory-of-mind tasks. Child Develop. **75**(2), 523–541 (2004)

29. Wilson, J.R., Gilpin, L., Rabkina, I.: A knowledge driven approach to adaptive assistance using preference reasoning and explanation. In: AAAI Fall Symposium on Artificial Intelligence for Human-Robot Interaction (AI-HRI) (2020)

Sequential Theory of Mind Modeling in Team Search and Rescue Tasks

Huao Li[1]([✉])(iD), Long Le[2](iD), Max Chis[1](iD), Keyang Zheng[1](iD), Dana Hughes[3](iD), Michael Lewis[1](iD), and Katia Sycara[3](iD)

[1] Pittsburgh University, Pittsburgh, PA 15260, USA
{hul52,mac372,kez20}@pitt.edu, ml@sis.pitt.edu
[2] University of Pennsylvania, Philadelphia, PA 19104, USA
vlongle@seas.upenn.edu
[3] Carnegie Mellon University, Pittsburgh, PA 15213, USA
danahugh@andrew.cmu.edu, katia@cs.cmu.edu

Abstract. The ability to make inferences about other's mental states is referred to as having a Theory of Mind (ToM). Such ability is fundamental for human social activities such as empathy, teamwork, and communication. As intelligent agents being involved in diverse human-agent teams, they are also expected to be socially intelligent to become effective teammates. In this paper, we propose a computational ToM model which observes team behaviors and infer their mental states in a simulated search and rescue task. The model structure consists of a transformer-based language module and an RNN-based sequential mental state module in order to capture both team communication and behaviors for the ToM inference. To provide a feasible baseline for our ToM model, we present the same inference task to human observers recruited from Amazon MTurk. Results show that our proposed computational model achieves a comparable performance with human observers in the ToM inference task.

Keywords: Theory of mind · Cognitive modeling · Neural networks · Natural language processing

The famous Sally-Anne test has been widely used in developmental psychology to test if children are able to distinguish their own mental states and others. This ability to make inferences about another's mental state is referred to as having a Theory of Mind (ToM). While reasoning about false beliefs is the capability most commonly associated with ToM, other inferences such as preference orderings [1], or affect and empathy [4] have also been linked with ToM along with other explanatory concepts involving mental states such as desires and intentions [6] which have been referred to inclusively as Folk Psychology [19].

In this paper, we propose a sequential Theory of Mind model that reasons about human dynamic beliefs in 3-people urban-search-and-rescue (USAR) teams. The USAR rescuer teams have to navigate through an environment and clear obstacles to locate and triage victims. Multimodal observations, including both team communications and individual actions, are used to infer hidden beliefs of rescuers regarding the meaning of different markers. A team communication module is implemented based on a pre-trained language model to identify marker-related utterances in rescuers' verbal communication. Then those detected timestamps are used as potential transition points of human beliefs about marker meanings. The dynamic belief module is based on recurrent neural networks and capable of mapping observable action sequences to belief sequences. The overall framework of marker ToM inference model is shown in Fig. 1. Each component of the framework is explained in subsequent sections of this paper.

1   Human ToM Inference

The Belief-Desire-Intention model [6], holds that agents form intentions to act in order to bring about desired states, with beliefs describing the allowable states and transitions. Because these mental entities of one human are not known to other humans, an observer must infer them on the basis of very little evidence. Humans do this readily [20] albeit often in error [5,18].

In this paper, we introduce a computational inference model capable of employing ToM reasoning. Because ToM is defined through its role in folk psychology and human commonsense reasoning, the appropriate baseline for guiding development and evaluating a computational ToM model would be a human observer. However, the human observer's accuracy in ToM inference is not necessarily expected to be high. Despite mastery of ToM reasoning in everyday life, people often fail to employ it, in taking directions [18], for example, or fail in reasoning about content of others' minds due to biases toward their own perspectives and knowledge [5]. Nonetheless, it would still be useful to assign the same ToM inference tasks to human observers to provide a performance baseline for our proposed model.

2   Computational ToM Models

Several authors have proposed a computational framework to model human goal inference as a Bayesian inverse planning process, i.e. the Bayesian Theory of Mind (BToM) framework [3]. BToM models have enjoyed success in explaining human ToM inference in goals, desires [15], and (false) beliefs [2]. However, most of the Bayesian-based methods are applied in simple environments with small state space (e.g. grid world) and yet to be tested with real human data in complex task scenarios. Computational ToM models based on neural networks have been shown to successfully reason about both machine agents internals [17] and human mental states [11,12,16]. In this paper, we continue to explore the possibilities of incorporating ToM models with state-of-the-art deep learning techniques.

In the literature, little attention has been paid to modeling human mental states in team settings. When multiple humans form teams, the complexity of their joint mental model increases tremendously. Team members have to intensively communicate about task information to maintain a shared situational awareness. Thus humans in a team have even more dynamic desires, beliefs, and intentions that change over time when compared with humans operating in isolation [8]. In this paper, we take a first step in this direction by investigating human beliefs in 3-person urban-search-and-rescue (USAR) teams.

3   Decision Points

In our work, we analyze three types of human data: verbal communications between team rescuers, rescuer actions, and action prediction, that were collected from human observers to assess our ToM model. ToM inferences involve at least two entities; one team player presumed to have mental states which may on occasion lead to observable actions or communications and an observer who attributes mental states and transitions between them to be the cause of observed actions by the first party. Because human observers are well practiced at making such inferences and making them on the basis of incomplete evidence, human inferences are likely to vary in confidence and accuracy with the ambiguity of observations. The accuracy of our proposed model should vary in a similar way with ambiguity in observations, which makes the comparisons with human 'experts' a good test of inference capabilities.

Because a ToM model is expected to evolve over time but only reveals itself intermittently through observed actions, it needs to be maintained and updated in order to converge to a more accurate model. To choose the decision points for making these updates, it is necessary to consider whether an action is taken or not when an opportunity occurs, for example encountering a door marked by others that could be entered. Those trigger events and consequential behaviors are recorded and fed into a recurrent neural network (RNN) to infer rescuer's beliefs. The other kind of decision points are when team members explicitly communicate about their mental state, for example reporting change of marker meanings. Based on our observation from human teams, we assume that all team belief transitions happened when related communication occurred between team members and use a transformer-based language model to process the communication content. These decision points provide stopping points during a USAR mission, where our ToM computational model can be updated, and inference tasks can be posed to the model and human observers.

4   Simulated Search and Rescue Task

4.1   Task Scenario

[10] describe a Minecraft environment designed to reproduce the uncertainties and hazards of a collapsed building for use in the study of urban search and rescue teams. Using data shared with us by Arizona State University from this task and environment, we built our ToM inference model and collected action predictions at decision points made by Mechanical Turk workers. The search and rescue map developed for this task is shown in Fig. 2. The scenario portrays a

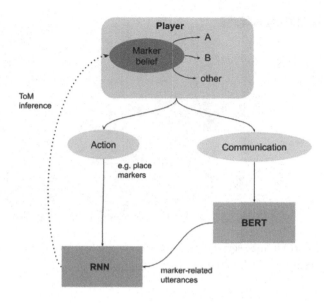

Fig. 1. Overall framework for sequential ToM inference.

structurally damaged office building after an unspecified incident. It contains 54 rooms and multiple connecting corridors. The building layout and connectivity may be changed by perturbations such as rubble. The 3-person team needs to search the building and rescue as many victims as possible within 15 min. Their performance is measured by points earned from saving victims. There are 55 injured victims inside the building. Out of the 55 injured, five are critical victims with severe injures and others are regular victims. Critical victims are worth more points but can not be rescued until all team members are present at the victim's location. This encourages communication, for example about a critical victim's location, and coordination between teammates. The three rescuers in a team are named Red, Blue, Green for easy identification.

4.2   Team Roles

Rescuers can choose from three interdependent roles, each of which have different capabilities and limitations. Teams can choose to have any team composition they would like (e.g., one of each role, all three at the same role). Each role's tools have limited uses before they need to be replenished. Rescuers can change their roles or replenish their tools at any time by returning to the base.

- Heavy Equipment Specialist (a.k.a, engineer): Can remove rubble with a hammer, and move at a slow speed.
- Medical Specialist (a.k.a., medic): Can rescue victims and travel at a medium speed.

Fig. 2. Human participants serving as rescuers see the first-person view on the right and client map and marker block legend on the left.

- Searching Specialist (a.k.a, searcher): Can move regular victims to a different location, making it easier for the medic to rescue multiple victims at one spot, and move at a fast speed, allowing for scouting.

4.3   Information Asymmetry

To provide heterogeneous mental models associated with task knowledge, the participants receive different information when the mission starts. On the client map interface, each rescuer is provided with unique information about a certain map regions. The information includes the room name and locations of rubble and victims divided by regions. Each participant receive a map that provides details in two regions and no information in four regions. In addition, three rescuers each has a set of marker blocks (numbered 1, 2, and 3) that they can put on the ground to indicate the state of a room. Each marker block also indicates the identity of its author (Red, Green, or Blue). In the mission, one rescuer will receive a legend to the meanings of numbered blocks that conflicts with the legend given to the other two rescuers. Two possible semantics are given in Table 1. As such, a rescuer with the marker semantic A would most likely place a marker 1 in front of a room that she believes to contain no victim.

Table 1. The meaning of different marker blocks assigned to players at the beginning of the mission.

Semantics	Marker 1	Marker 2	Marker 3
A	No victim	Regular v.	Critical v.
B	Regular victim	No v.	Critical v.

An example of asymmetrical information received by rescuers is shown in Fig. 3. Note that those rescuers are not aware of this manipulation among team members and will need to communicate to share information.

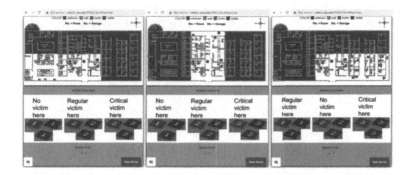

Fig. 3. Asymmetrical information on client map and marker block legend received by each rescuer in the team.

In the present study, we develop a ToM model to predict the marker semantic belief of each rescuer. Note that this belief is inherently dynamic i.e. it can change over time. For example, a rescuer might be initially assigned marker semantic A but later switch to semantic B after the team realize, and communicate about the information asymmetry, and agree to all switch to semantic B.

4.4   Data Set

19 groups, each of 3 participants, took a series of training sessions and surveys before entering the actual search and rescue task. Each team completed two consecutive 15-min missions on two different map configurations. Game state was recorded for in-game events (c.g. rescue victims, switch roles, and place marker blocks) 30 Hz. Rescuer screen recordings and verbal communication audio were saved for post processing.

5   Team Communication Model

Given the experimental setting, rescuers in the team need to intensively communicate about task information to maintain a shared situational awareness among members. Especially for the manipulated marker legends, such information asymmetry can lead rescuers to have different mental models about the meaning of maker blocks, then form false beliefs when seeing makers placed by other rescuers. If such team mental state misalignment is not resolved by communication early in the mission, team performance is harmed severely. Therefore, we propose a natural language processing method to identify team communication entries related to marker blocks. The model takes in a single communication transcription and outputs a binary decision: whether this communication is related to marker blocks or not.

5.1   Model Structure

Our proposed model is based on general language models pre-trained on a large corpus and fine-tuned on our data set. An illustration of the model structure is shown in Fig. 4. Communication transcripts are prepossessed and tokenized then fed into a pre-trained Bidirectional Encoder Representations from Transformers (BERT) [9]. BERT embeddings with a 0.3 dropout rate go through a neural network with two fully connected layers with 64 and 1 hidden neurons each. The ReLU activation function is used between two FC layers. The single output value from neural network is used to determine the binary prediction result.

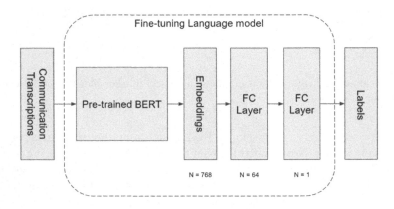

Fig. 4. Communication model structure.

5.2   Training Details

The human data set is divided into two parts, where the training data set consists of 2725 entries from 10 teams and the test dataset consists of 3434 entries from 9 teams. All transcriptions are manually coded by experimenters to serve as ground truth labels of each communication entry. There are in total 67 positive cases out of 2725 entries in the training data. To overcome imbalanced data labels, we oversample positive entries by 20 times to create an augmented training data set. We use binary cross-entropy with logit loss as the loss function and Adam optimizer to regulate the training [13]. Training batch size is 16 and learning rate is set to 1e-05. The whole model including both BERT and FC modules are fine-tuned together for 1 epoch.

5.3   Experimental Results

Cross-validation is used on training set to explore different model structures and hyper-parameters. Specifically, training data from 1 team is held out for validation, and the other 8 teams are used for training. This process repeats 9 times and the average validation result is used to evaluate model performance.

In addition, since the aim of this model is to identify potential mental state transition points, we care more about how relevant returned results are instead of how complete they are. Therefore, precision is used as the performance metric in model evaluation. The average precision of cross-validation on training set is **98.6%** and the test precision is **81.0%**, indicating a good model performance and a reasonable generalization between teams.

Experimental results show that our proposed model is capable of identifying marker-related entries from team communication transcriptions. Those communication points will be used in dynamic belief modeling and human observation experiment as key decision points where rescuers' mental state are highly likely to change.

6   Dynamic Belief Model

The goal of our ToM model is to infer human's dynamic beliefs based on observable behaviors. Here we again concentrate on inferring what marker block meanings each rescuer was using during the mission. Because one rescuer in the team was initially assigned with a different marker legend than other team members and the team may realize and resolve this manipulation at any time during the mission, this ToM model is trying to infer dynamic beliefs of humans that may change over time. By observing an individual rescuer's behaviors for a certain time interval, the model should be able to estimate the most likely marker legend that the rescuer is using. Since we have identified time points where the team communicates about marker blocks, we can assume that the mental state of rescuers remains the same during intervals between those communication points. We make such an assumption based on the observation that it is unlikely for a certain rescuer to suddenly change her marker block meaning without informing other team members. For example, when one rescuer realizes the difference in team marker legends, her first choice is usually confirming with others by asking 'Do we have marker number 1 for regular victims?'. Then the team will further discuss and finalize a common legend for the team to use, e.g. 'Let's use 1 for victims, 2 for rubble and 3 for empty room.' Those communication utterances can be detected by the communication model proposed earlier and served as potential belief transition points for the belief model.

6.1   Data Processing

In total, 16 trials of game data from 9 teams are used in model training and evaluation. We first slice the game log of each trial by marker-related communication points generated by the BERT communication model, then calculate each individual rescuer's actions within those N intervals. Specifically, we count the number of action sequences that potentially reveal the rescuer's belief about marker blocks, in each interval. For example, if a rescuer sees a regular victim and then immediately places a number 2 marker block, it is more likely for her to hold semantics A (the complete action list is shown in Table 2). With a 12-dimension action vector, each time a listed action is observed within a certain time interval following its prerequisite, the count of corresponding dimension adds one. Some actions share the same dimension as they refer to the same semantic meanings in different forms, e.g. perception (marker in FOV – rescue victim) and intention (victim in FOV – place marker). By counting those actions in each observation window, we have an input observation sequence with the shape of $(N, 12)$ per trial per rescuer.

Table 2. List of action sequences tracked as model input.

Prerequisite	Action	Dimension
Other	Place marker 1/2/3	1,2,3
Marker 1/2/3 in FOV	Other	1,2,3
Regular v. in FOV	Place marker 1/2/3	4,5,6
Marker 1/2/3 in FOV	Rescue regular v.	4,5,6
Critical v. in FOV	Place marker 1/2/3	7,8,9
Marker 1/2/3 in FOV	Rescue critical v.	7,8,9
Marker 1/2/3 in FOV	Clean rubble	10,11,12

In addition, the actual marker semantics rescuers were using during the mission are manually coded by experimenters into three categories: semantics A, semantics B, and other. These label sequences are used as the supervised ground truth for model training and evaluation.

6.2   Model Structure and Experimental Results

Figure 5 shows the structure of our dynamic belief model. It uses Gated recurrent units (GRUs) to process input observation sequence and transit hidden state through timestamps [7]. At each timestamp, a fully connected neural network takes in the hidden state and outputs prediction results. Both the GRU and FC module share weights along the timeline. Hyper-parameters used in training is as follows: dropout rate = 0.3, learning rate = 0.001, batch size = 1, loss function = cross entropy loss, optimizer = Adam.

   Values of hyper-parameters are determined by experimenting on small validation set. The model is trained on 12 trials of data and tested on 4 held-out data. We run 20 epochs of training 10 times to balance the influence of random initialization. The average prediction accuracy on test data set is **70.5%**.

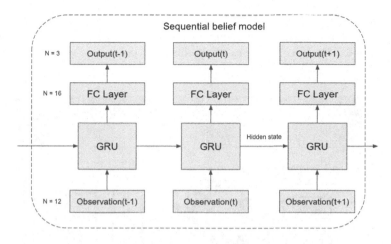

Fig. 5. Belief model structure.

7 Human Observation Experiments

Because the initial goal of our computational ToM model is to replicate human performance at ToM tasks, we have collected predictions from human observers to provide a baseline with which to compare the model performance. Note that our human observer experiment goes beyond just inferring the marker block semantics to include other aspects such as team scores and map. Thus, this data can be used in future studies for other ToM tasks.

We devise a team-focused and an individual-focused experiment. In the team-focused experiment, the observer is asked to predict the final team performance and make inferences about the team mental model such as which rescuer was assigned with different marker semantics than other team members. In the individual-focused experiment, the observer is asked to predict individual rescuer's next action based on potential false belief about marker block semantics.

7.1 Materials

For human experiment materials, we use the same 4 team trials as in the test data set for belief model evaluation. Based on the collected team trajectories, we generated the following materials: game screen video recordings and dynamic mini-map videos. The first person screen recordings provides the situation awareness for human observers to understand what the rescuers were doing, while the dynamic map help locate the rescuers' current location and navigation path. The individual-focused experiment differs from the team-focused in which the observer can have access to only the field of view of one player and the minimap does not include the locations of other players (unless their locations are within the field of view). Without the fully-observable perspective, human observers in the individual-focused experiment have the same amount of information that one individual rescuer has during the mission. Video materials were segmented by 'decision points' at which behaviors occur such as spotting a victim or placing a marker block. The specific types of the decision points are explained below.

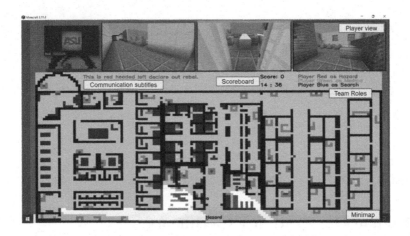

Fig. 6. Game state video presented to human observers

Table 3. List of decision points paused for human observers to make predictions.

Prediction tasks	Decision points	Ground truth
Team performance	Fixed intervals	Final team performance
Map information	Map-related comm.	Initial map assignment
Marker semantics	Marker-related comm./place markers	Initial semantics assignment
Reaction to markers	Markers in FOV	Actual next action

Table 3 defines "decision points" for each experiment. For the team **Performance** prediction task, observers are asked to predict the final team score at different mission stages, i.e. 4, 9, 14 min. Other prediction tasks in the team-focused experiment are triggered at corresponding decision points by communication behaviors between team members. For example, **Map** and **Marker** prediction questions are triggered whenever a rescuer mentions the map or markers in verbal communication, respectively. At those points, observers are required to conduct ToM inference by predicting the initial map/marker semantics assignment of each rescuer. The team communication model introduced earlier is used to detect communication about objects of interest (blocks, maps, ect...).

For the individual-focused prediction task, we concentrate on predicting individual behaviors based on their (false) beliefs. Specifically, the video is paused when a rescuer places or sees a marker block for observers to 1) infer rescuer's interpretation about this marker, and 2) predict rescuer's next action upon seeing this marker. Those **Reaction** predictions require observers to form an accurate mental model about the rescuer to infer her beliefs and actions correctly.

Video segments were presented in chronological order so that prior segments can inform judgments. The actual action taken by the rescuer in the video segments was then presented at the start of the following sequence providing knowledge of results. The total number of decision points in one trajectory is around 300, which is too demanding for human observers to annotate. Thus we sampled a subset of decision points for each type and generated 15 video segments with corresponding prediction questions for each trajectory.

7.2 Procedure

102 human observers were recruited from Amazon Mechanical Turk where 42 participated in the team-focused experiment and 60 participated in the individual-focused experiment. Participants accessed the online survey on their own computer. Observers received detailed instructions about the search and rescue environment and the prediction tasks they were to complete. A quiz was given to the observers to make sure they were familiar with the basic knowledge of the experiment in order to proceed to the experimental task. Each observer was assigned with one trajectory from a rescue team. Each trial of team trajectories were annotated by at least 5 independent observers. In each of the decision points from the trajectory, human observers were presented a video clip and the corresponding prediction questions. The length of this human observation experiment was around 45 min.

7.3 Results

To ensure quality control, we removed data with missing answer entries or extreme completion times (i.e. it took too long for the observers to answer). For team performance prediction, observer's prediction is compared with the discrete actual team performance, thus the average RMSE of observers is calculated as the metric. For other categorical predictions, the majority result of observers is used. For example, if 3 out of 5 observers predict the player will enter the room, this is the result that is compared with ground truth (e.g. actual team performance, initial assignments, and in-game actions). Table 4 show the prediction accuracy of human observers. In addition to the majority voting results, we also calculated the 90th percentile of individual observers indicating the performance of proficient humans in ToM inference tasks.

8 Discussion

In this paper, we propose a sequential Theory of Mind model that reasons about human dynamic beliefs in a team task. Specifically, the model observes team communication and individual actions to infer marker meanings each rescuer used during the search and rescue mission. A team communication module is

Table 4. Human observation accuracy.

Prediction	Human majority voting	Human 90th percentile	Model prediction
Performance	125.2	48.6	N/A
Map	20.29%	44.44%	N/A
Marker	**58.52%**	**77.78%**	**70.5%**
Reaction	32.65%	55.56%	N/A

implemented based on a pre-trained language model to identify marker-related utterances in rescuers' verbal communication. Then those detected timestamps are used as potential transition points of human beliefs about marker meanings. The dynamic belief module is based on recurrent neural networks and capable of mapping observable action sequences (e.g. see a regular victim then place a marker 2) with belief sequences (e.g. hold semantics A). The overall framework of marker ToM inference model is shown in Fig. 1. Both communication and belief models are trained and tested on data previously collected from human teams. Test set results show that the communication model achieves **81.0%** precision in identifying marker-related utterances, and the belief model achieves **70.5%** accuracy in inferring rescuer's marker semantics. To provide a feasible baseline to evaluate our model performance, we assign the same test materials and ToM inference tasks to human observers recruited from Amazon MTurk. Results show that majority populations only achieve **58.52%** in inferring marker semantics and even worse in other ToM inference tasks. Even for the more competent human observers, i.e. the 90th percentile, the inference accuracy is only **77.78%**. This aligns with previous findings in the literature that inferring other humans' mental states in complicated task scenarios is challenging for human observers [14]. We can tell from the above comparison that our proposed computational ToM model achieves a human-level performance in inferring dynamic beliefs in human teams.

This research bears its own limitations that we would like to improve in future steps. First, the current model structure deals with the mental state of each individual in the team separately. Although the communication model considers information shared among all team members, the dynamic belief model only takes in action sequence from one rescuer when inferring her mental state. However, in such a team task, the mental states of three members are dependent on each other and conditioned on team roles, which might lead to more complicated belief structure such as nested second-order beliefs (rescuer Red thinks that rescuer Blue has marker semantic A). A more reasonable method to model team ToM is to incorporate action sequences of all individuals in the team and infer the joint team mental state. In addition, the current model is trained and tested on a relatively small dataset and limited to a narrow belief regarding marker meanings. Further experiments on larger dataset and more general mental beliefs are needed to test the model effectiveness and robustness.

Acknowledgement. This material is based upon work supported by the Defense Advanced Research Projects Agency (DARPA) under Contract No. HR001120C0036 and by the AFRL/AFOSR award FA9550-18-1-0251. Any opinions, findings and conclusions or recommendations expressed in this material are those of the author(s) and do not necessarily reflect the views of the Defense Advanced Research Projects Agency (DARPA).

References

1. Baker, C., Saxe, R., Tenenbaum, J.: Bayesian theory of mind: modeling joint belief-desire attribution. In: Proceedings of the Thirty-Third Annual Conference of the Cognitive Science Society (2011)
2. Baker, C.L., Jara-Ettinger, J., Saxe, R., Tenenbaum, J.B.: Rational quantitative attribution of beliefs, desires and percepts in human mentalizing. Nat. Hum. Behav. **1**(4), 1–10 (2017)
3. Baker, C.L., Saxe, R., Tenenbaum, J.B.: Action understanding as inverse planning. Cognition **113**(3), 329–349 (2009)
4. Baron-Cohen, S., Leslie, A.M., Frith, U.: Does the autistic child have a "theory of mind"? Cognition **21**(1), 37–46 (1985)
5. Birch, S.A.: When knowledge is a curse: children's and adults' reasoning about mental states. Curr. Dir. Psychol. Sci. **14**(1), 25–29 (2005)
6. Bratman, M.: Intentions, Plans, and Practical Reason. Harvard University Press, Cambridge (1987)
7. Cho, K., et al.: Learning phrase representations using RNN encoder-decoder for statistical machine translation. arXiv preprint arXiv:1406.1078 (2014)
8. DeChurch, L.A., Mesmer-Magnus, J.R.: The cognitive underpinnings of effective teamwork: a meta-analysis. J. Appl. Psychol. **95**(1), 32 (2010)
9. Devlin, J., Chang, M.W., Lee, K., Toutanova, K.: BERT: pre-training of deep bidirectional transformers for language understanding. arXiv preprint arXiv:1810.04805 (2018)
10. Fiore, S., Bracken, B., Demir, M., Freeman, J., Lewis, M., Huang, L.: Transdisciplinary team research to develop theory of mind in human-AI teams. In: Proceedings of the Sixty-Fourth Annual Conference of the Human Factors and Ergonomics Society (2020)
11. Guo, Y., Jena, R., Hughes, D., Lewis, M., Sycara, K.: Transfer learning for human navigation and triage strategies prediction in a simulated urban search and rescue task. In: 2021 30th IEEE International Conference on Robot & Human Interactive Communication (RO-MAN), pp. 784–791. IEEE (2021)
12. Jain, V., et al.: Predicting human strategies in simulated search and rescue task. In: Accepted at NeurIPS 2020; Workshop on Artificial Intelligence for Humanitarian Assistance and Disaster Response (AI+HADR 2020) (2020)
13. Kingma, D.P., Ba, J.: Adam: a method for stochastic optimization. arXiv preprint arXiv:1412.6980 (2014)
14. Li, H., Zheng, K., Sycara, K., Lewis, M.: Human theory of mind inference in search and rescue tasks. In: Proceedings of the 65th Annual Meeting of the Human Factors and Ergonomics Society. Human Factors and Ergonomics Society (2021)
15. Liu, S., Ullman, T.D., Tenenbaum, J.B., Spelke, E.S.: Ten-month-old infants infer the value of goals from the costs of actions. Science **358**(6366), 1038–1041 (2017)

16. Oguntola, I., Hughes, D., Sycara, K.: Deep interpretable models of theory of mind. In: 2021 30th IEEE International Conference on Robot & Human Interactive Communication (RO-MAN), pp. 657–664. IEEE (2021)

17. Rabinowitz, N., Perbet, F., Song, F., Zhang, C., Eslami, S.A., Botvinick, M.: Machine theory of mind. In: International Conference on Machine Learning, pp. 4218–4227. PMLR (2018)

18. Samson, D., Apperly, I.: There is more to mind reading than having theory of mind concepts: new directions in theory of mind research. Infant Child Dev. **19**(5), 443–454 (2010)

19. Stich, S., Ravenscroft, I.: What is folk psychology? Cognition **50**(1–3), 447–468 (1992)

20. Wimmer, H., Perner, J.: Beliefs about beliefs: representation and constraining function of wrong beliefs in young children's understanding of deception. Cognition **13**(1), 103–128 (1983)

Integrating Machine Learning and Cognitive Modeling of Decision Making

Taher Rahgooy[1]([✉]), K. Brent Venable[1,2], and Jennifer S. Trueblood[3]

[1] University of West Florida, Pensacola, FL, USA
trahgooy@students.uwf.edu
[2] Institute for Human and Machine Cognition (IHMC), Pensacola, FL, USA
bvenable@ihmc.org
[3] Department of Psychological and Brain Sciences and Cognitive Science Program,
Indiana University, Bloomington, IN, USA
jstruebl@iu.edu

Abstract. Modeling human decision making plays a fundamental role in the design of intelligent systems capable of rich interactions and effective teamwork. In this paper we consider the task of choice prediction in settings with multiple alternatives. Cognitive models of decision making can successfully replicate and explain behavioral effects involving uncertainty and interactions among alternatives but are computationally intensive to train. ML approaches excel in terms of choice prediction accuracy, but fail to provide insights on the underlying preference reasoning. We study different degrees of integration of ML and cognitive models for this task. We show, via testing on behavioral data, that our hybrid approach, based on the integration of a neural network and the Multi-alternative Linear Ballistic Accumulator cognitive model, requires significantly less time to train, and allows to capture important cognitive parameters while maintaining similar accuracy to the pure ML approach.

Keywords: Cognitive models · Decision making · Machine learning · Preferential choice prediction · Artificial neural networks · Behavioral effects

1 Introduction

Decision making is a core capability which is central in describing how humans function in everyday life. The ability to understand and predict how humans make choices is also key to the design of artificial agents capable to provide rich interactions, for example, in the context of teamwork [3,9,17,20]. Understanding human decision processes has been a topic of intense study in different disciplines including psychology, economics, and artificial intelligence. Yet, accurate and general models of human choice behavior are, for the most part, still work in progress. In the area of psychology, cognitive computational models (e.g., [2,7,15,19,26]) have been designed to replicate fundamental aspects of human decision making such as, for example, violations of transitivity, and the well

© The Author(s), under exclusive license to Springer Nature Switzerland AG 2022
N. Gurney and G. Sukthankar (Eds.): AAAI-FSS 2021, LNCS 13775, pp. 173–193, 2022.
https://doi.org/10.1007/978-3-031-21671-8_11

known contextual effects of similarity, attraction and compromise [5]. Contextual effects have practical implications for areas such as recommender systems, consumer choice and human-machine teaming. They are also important from a theoretical standpoint, since they exemplify violations to the principle of simple scalability [28], entailing, for example, independence to irrelevant alternatives, and underlying many preference theories [14].

In this paper we propose a way to integrate machine learning and a cognitive model of decision making into an accurate, yet explainable, model of human choice behavior. In particular, we consider the Multi-alternative Linear Ballistic Accumulator (MLBA) [27], one of the most recent and successful dynamic models of decision making. MLBA is an ideal candidate as it has been shown to outperform the state of the art in terms of accuracy on both choice prediction and deliberation time prediction across all context effects. It is designed for more realistic tasks including multiple (i.e., non-binary) choices described via multiple attributes. It strikes a unique balance between cognitive plausibility and computational complexity and comes with a well developed implementation [10,27]. **Our contribution** can be summarized as follows: (i) we present a pure machine learning method, namely an MLP (multi-layer perceptron), and show how strong prediction accuracy can be achieved without relying on cognitive mechanisms; (ii) we then propose two hybrid architectures integrating a neural network with MLBA allowing us to examine the accuracy/explainablity tradeoff for different cognitive priors; (iii) we perform an extensive experimental comparison of the models (including MLBA) on human behavioral data.

Our results suggest that the integration of ML and cognitive models of decision making can indeed achieve strong accuracy while retaining explainability in terms of cognitive foundations underlying the deliberation processes. This is an important step forward in the design of intelligent agents equipped with a realistic model of human behavior. Indeed, a natural application of our hybrid approach would be to provide members of a team with a model of the preferences and decision making process of other team members. Our integration method also shows how ML can be used as a tool in the development of cognitive models to isolate and study the impact of different cognitive assumptions on prediction performance.

2   Multi-attribute Linear Ballistic Accumulator (MLBA)

The Multi-attribute Linear Ballistic Accumulator (MLBA) [27] is a prominent cognitive model of value-based decision making designed to capture choice distributions in settings with multi-attribute and multi-alternative choices.

More formally, we define a choice problem p as tuple $\langle \mathbb{O}, \mathbb{A}, \mathbb{E} \rangle$, where $\mathbb{O}$ is a set of K options, $\mathbb{O} = \{o_1, \ldots, o_K\}$, $\mathbb{A}$ is a set of J attributes, $\mathbb{A} = \{A_1, \ldots, A_J\}$, and $\mathbb{E}$ is the set containing the evaluation of each option in $\mathbb{O}$ with respect to each attribute in $\mathbb{A}$, denoted $\mathbb{E} = \{a_i^{[j]} | i \in \{1, \ldots, K\}, j \in \{1 \ldots J\}\}$. For example, in a scenario where a car must be chosen, $\mathbb{O}$ would be the set of considered models, and a plausible attribute set might be $A = \{A_1, A_2\}$, where A_1 corresponds to price and A_2 to performance. Then given car model o_i, we could have, for example, $a_i^1 = 20,000\$$ would be an evaluation of its price and $a_i^2 = 150$ mph be an evaluation of its performance in terms of maximum speed.

Given a choice problem $p = \langle \mathbb{O}, \mathbb{A}, \mathbb{E} \rangle$ in input, the output of MLBA is a choice probability distribution over $\mathbb{O}$ with the aim of replicating observed human behavior. MLBA is structured into a front-end and a back-end. Similarly to other successful models of decision making, MLBA is based on the principle of *accumulation to threshold* [7], by which deliberation consists in a cumulative gathering of evidence until a certain threshold is reached. This accumulation process is modeled by the back-end of MLBA, while as a linear process where, given an initial point selected within a given interval and a drift rate, the preference of an option "races" linearly towards a threshold. The front-end models the mapping of the raw stimuli (the evaluations in $\mathbb{E}$) into the parameters driving the accumulation (a distribution of drift rates). Consider the example of choosing a car based on two attributes: cost and performance. Given a set of cars under consideration, each described by their retail price and, say, maximum speed, MLBA would model the choice distribution among them by mapping their values into drift rates and simulating the linear accumulation of preferences to the threshold.

We now provide more details on both components, as they are essential to the understanding of our approach. The back-end of MLBA is based on its precursor the Linear Ballistic Accumulator (LBA) [4], a dynamic-cognitive approach for single-attribute choice problems. LBA assumes that the decision maker accumulates information linearly for each option over time but at different rates. The final decision is made when the accumulated preference for one of the options exceeds a specific threshold. In Fig. 1 we depict a scenario with three options: $\mathbb{O} = \{o_1, o_2, o_3\}$.

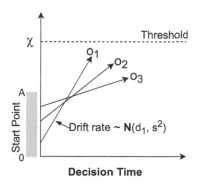

Fig. 1. Example of LBA (back-end of MLBA) with three options o_1, o_2, and o_3.

At the beginning of a trial each option is associated with an initial preference value sampled from a uniform distribution $\mathcal{U}(0, A)$, where A is a parameter of the model. The accumulation speed of the preference is determined by a drift rate chosen randomly from a normal distribution defined by a mean drift rate associated to the option and a standard deviation. In the example in Fig. 1, drift rates would be sampled in $\mathcal{N}(d_1, s^2)$, $\mathcal{N}(d_2, s^2)$, and $\mathcal{N}(d_3, s^2)$ where s is the standard deviation and d_i denotes the mean drift rate for option o_i. The race continues until one of the preference accumulators reaches threshold χ, which can, thus, be seen as modeling how cautious the individual is in making decisions.

The front-end component of MLBA maps the raw objective inputs, $a_i^{[j]}$ (such as price, quality, or performance) to subjective values representing psychological magnitudes, denoted $u_i^{[j]}$, and then computes the mean drift rates, d_i, by combining pairwise comparisons of subjective values.

The objective-to-subjective mapping accounts for how humans may perceive rationally indifferent options as distinct and is achieved by curving the indifference line $\sum_{j=1}^{J} \left(\frac{a^{[j]}}{b_j} \right) = 1$, i.e. the line connecting two indifferent options, via a power function defined by a parameter m:

$$\sum_{j=1}^{J} \left(\frac{u^{[j]}}{b_j} \right)^m = 1. \tag{1}$$

The b_j values define the space and are computed from the objective evaluations of indifferent options (see Appendix C), m is, instead, a parameter of the model [27] estimated from experimental data. The mapping is exemplified in Fig. 2 for the case with two attributes where the indifference line is in green and its power function is depicted in red. Notice how the relationship between extreme and intermediate alternatives is governed by the m parameter. If the curve is concave (i.e., $m > 1$), then intermediate options (i.e., those with less attribute dispersion) are preferred to extreme options, while, the opposite is true when the curve is convex ($m < 1$). When $m = 1$, the curve reduces to a straight line and subjective and objective values coincide.

Let $u_i^{[j]}$ and $u_h^{[j]}$, $j \in \{1, \ldots, J\}$ be the subjective values, determined by the mapping, for options o_i and o_h, respectively. MLBA uses these subjective values to quantify how o_i compares to o_h:

$$V_{ih} = \sum_{j=1}^{J} w_{ih}^{[j]} (u_i^{[j]} - u_h^{[j]})$$

Intuitively, comparison value V_{ih} represents the advantage (or disadvantage) that o_i has w.r.t. o_h, and weight $w_{ih}^{[j]}$ reflects the amount of attention given in this comparison to the jth attribute. Weight $w_{ih}^{[j]}$ is defined as

$$w_{ih}^{[j]} = \begin{cases} exp\left(-\lambda_1 \left| u_i^{[j]} - u_h^{[j]} \right| \right), & \text{if } u_i^{[j]} - u_h^{[j]} \geq 0 \\ \\ exp\left(-\lambda_2 \left| u_i^{[j]} - u_h^{[j]} \right| \right), & \text{otherwise} \end{cases}$$

where λ_1 and λ_2 are decay constants for attention weights with positive and negative differences respectively. This definition of the attention weights relies on two assumptions. The first one is that attention weight should be larger when attribute values are difficult to discriminate and smaller when they are clearly different. The second assumption is that similarity judgment in humans often violates symmetry thus requiring two different decay parameters, λ_1 and λ_2 [29].

Comparison values are used by the front-end of MLBA to define the mean drift rate for each option as follows:

$$d_i = \sum_{j \neq i} V_{ij} + I_0$$

where $I_0 > 0$ is introduced to ensure at least one positive drift rate. As an example, for option o_1 in Fig. 1 we would have $d_1 = V_{12} + V_{13} + I_0$.

Choice Probability Distribution. So far we have described how, given a choice problem p, MLBA's front-end first maps objective evaluations into subjective evaluations, computes the comparison between the different options, and then uses these comparisons to define mean drift rates for preference accumulators. After sampling initial preferences and drift rates, MLBA's back-end selects an option by launching the accumulators. By running the back-end a sufficient number of times, one can obtain a choice probability distribution over $\mathbb{O}$. However, the choice distribution emerging from the LBA component has also been described in analytical form [4]. First, the cumulative distribution function for the time taken for the ith accumulator to reach threshold χ can be defined as:

$$
\begin{aligned}
F_i(t) = 1 &+ \frac{ts\phi\left(\frac{\chi - A - td_i}{ts}\right) - ts\phi\left(\frac{\chi - td_i}{ts}\right)}{A} \\
&+ \frac{(\chi - A - td_i)\Phi\left(\frac{\chi - A - td_i}{ts}\right) - (\chi - td_i)\Phi\left(\frac{\chi - td_i}{ts}\right)}{A}
\end{aligned}
\tag{2}
$$

where $\phi(.)$ and $\Phi(.)$ are the probability density function and cumulative distribution function of the normal distribution. Informally, $F_i(t)$ represents the likelihood that option o_i's linear accumulator will reach threshold χ before or at time t. The associated probability density function is:

$$
\begin{aligned}
f_i(t) = \frac{1}{A}\Bigg[&- d_i\Phi\left(\frac{\chi - A - td_i}{ts}\right) + s\phi\left(\frac{\chi - A - td_i}{ts}\right) \\
&+ d_i\Phi\left(\frac{\chi - td_i}{ts}\right) - s\phi\left(\frac{\chi - td_i}{ts}\right)\Bigg].
\end{aligned}
\tag{3}
$$

Finally, the defective probability density function modeling option o_i being chosen at or before time t as the likelihood that its accumulator reaches threshold χ by time t while the other accumulators do not, is:

$$PDF_i(t) = f_i(t) \prod_{j \neq i}(1 - F_j(t)).
\tag{4}$$

We note that the term "defective" signifies that the distribution is normalized to the probability of the choice with which it's associated. We denote this distribution for problem $p = \langle \mathbb{O}, \mathbb{A}, \mathbb{E} \rangle$ and option $o_i \in \mathbb{O}$ as $PDF_{p,i}$. We can now define the overall choice probability for option o_i as the integral over time of the defective probability density function:

$$\pi_{p,i} = \int_0^\infty PDF_{p,i}(t)dt. \tag{5}$$

Fitting MLBA Parameters to Behavioral Data. To assess how well a model can replicate human behavior its parameters are fitted and its accuracy is tested using behavioral data. In this paper we consider as a baseline the implementation of MLBA proposed in [10] where it is converted using a stochastic differential equation formalism and a hierarchical Bayesian method is used for parameter fitting. We call it MLBA-HB and we refer to [10] for more details[1].

3   Context Effects

Several studies in cognitive science have shown that preferences over a set of options can be influenced by adding different alternatives to the choice set [11,22,28]. In some extreme cases it can lead to preference reversal. These so called "context effects" have significant implications from both an applied and theoretical perspective and their modeling has been one of the major thrusts behind the development of dynamic models of decision making like MLBA.

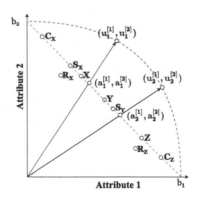

Fig. 2. Mapping of objective values (green line) to subjective values (red line) for the case with two attributes (resp. **x** and **y** axis) and $m > 1$. Options $\mathbf{X}, \mathbf{Y}, \mathbf{Z}$, $\mathbf{C_X}, \mathbf{S_X}, \mathbf{R_X}, \mathbf{S_Y}, \mathbf{R_Z}$, and $\mathbf{C_Z}$, exemplify the effects described in Sect. 3. (Color figure online)

---

[1] The code for MLBA-HB was shared by the authors of [10].

We illustrate the effects with the options in Fig. 2.

- *The Attraction Effect* enhances the probability of choosing an option (X) over another one (Z) by introducing a similar, but inferior "decoy" (R_X), formally, as depicted in Fig. 2 options R_X and R_Z are similar but inferior to option X and Z respectively. The attraction effect happens when having R_X in the choice set improves the chance of choosing X compared to having R_Z and vise versa: $P(X|\{X, Z, R_X\}) > P(X|\{X, Z, R_Z\})$ and $P(Z|\{X, Z, R_X\}) < P(Z|\{X, Z, R_Z\})$.
- *The Similarity Effect* occurs when the introduction of an option similar and competing with another option increases the probability of selecting the dissimilar option. For example, consider two competitive options X and Y and two decoy options S_X and S_Y from Fig. 2. We encounter a similarity effect if adding S_X reduces the chance of choosing X compared to the case where we add S_Y and vice versa: $P(X|\{X, Y, S_X\}) < P(X|\{X, Y, S_Y\})$ and $P(Y|\{X, Y, S_X\}) > P(Y|\{X, Y, S_Y\})$.
- *The Compromise Effect* occurs when an extreme option is introduced and makes one of the existing options appear as a more appealing compromise in the choice set. For example, in Fig. 2, Y is a compromise option in choice set $\{X, Y, Z\}$ whereas Z is an extreme option. On the other hand Y is an extreme option in choice set $\{Y, Z, C_Z\}$ and Z is a compromise. The compromise effect occurs when the probability of choosing Y is bigger in the first choice set compared to the second one and vise versa: $P(Z|\{X, Y, Z\}) < P(Z|\{Y, Z, C_Z\})$.

The main goal of cognitive models of decision making is to capture human decision behavior, including these deviations to rationality [6]. MLBA outperforms other state of the art models in terms of providing superior choice (and deliberation time) predictions when tested on behavioral data collected to elicit context effects [10]. The results of MLBA-HB on data sets described in Sect. 9 are shown in Fig. 5 in green.

4   Related Work

The integration of machine learning in the context of cognitive modeling of decision making has recently attracted the interest of researchers in psychology and artificial intelligence [3,8,18,21,23]. Of particular interest here, is the line of work generated around the choice prediction competitions CPC-15 and CPC-18 [3,9,17], where cognitive models and ML competed to accurately predict average human choice behavior. While we share a similar goal, the task considered there was quite different as it involved only binary choices among gambles. In the more recent paper [3], the authors propose a system integrating the CPC-18 winner (an enhanced version of cognitive model BEAST [9,17]) and an ML approach by using the cognitive model to label training data. In this way they, indirectly, introduce a cognitive bias that allows ML to outperform both approaches taken in isolation. This integration is radically different from ours since it does not include the design of a hybrid architecture and the ML component is not used to learn any cognitive parameters. We also note that a similar approach designed to address the scarcity of data labeled by humans by producing large quantities of synthetic data using a cognitive architecture, is described in [23] for a more complex supervisory control task involving planning. Also related to our work is the one presented in [18], where the authors use a recurrent neural network to learn some of the parameters of a Multi Decision Field Theory (MDFT) model [19]. While belonging to the same family of accumulation-to-threshold decision making models, MLBA and MDFT are radically different in their underlying preference structure. Moreover, the goal of the ML approach in [18] is to extract the MDFT equivalent of the MLBA evaluations and attention weights, rather than to model the choice probability distribution as done here.

5   Learning Task Formulation

Our overall goal is to be able to predict and analyze aggregate decision maker's behavior in the presence of contextual effects given examples of past choices. In the following sections we will present a pure ML approach and two hybrid ML-MLBA approaches and will compare their performance to that of MLBA on this task. Our problem setup assumes that various combinations of options has been presented to the decision makers and their final choices has been recorded. Our goal is to model the aggregate decision maker's behavior.

This task can be formalized as follow. Let $\mathbb{P} = \{p_1, \ldots, p_m\}$ be a set of choice problems with K options and sharing the same attribute set $\mathbb{A}$. Different subsets of these problems has been presented to a set of decision makers multiple times and their choices have been recorded. For example, in [25] a perceptual data set is introduced where each problem involves choosing among three rectangles and attributes are their height and width, while in [26] an inference data set is described where each problem concerns three suspects and the attributes are the eyewitnesses (see Sect. 9). Given collection of N (*problem, choice*) pairs, $\mathbb{C} = \{\langle p_{\pi_1}, c_1 \rangle, \ldots, \langle p_{\pi_N}, c_N \rangle\}$, where $p_{\pi_l} \in \mathbb{P}$ for every $l \in \{1, \ldots, N\}$, our goal is to learn aggregate choice probability distributions, $\pi_p = \langle \pi_{p,1}, \ldots \pi_{p,K} \rangle$, for problems $p \in \mathbb{P}$, where $\pi_{p,i}$ represents the probability of option $o_i \in \mathbb{O}_p$ to be chosen. Each sample $\langle p_{\pi_i}, c_i \rangle$ in $\mathbb{C}$ denotes the choice $c_i \in \mathbb{O}_{p_{\pi_i}}$ that has been made by a decision maker for problem $p_{\pi_i} \in \mathbb{P}$. In our perceptual example, c_i is the rectangle selected as largest among three by the participant and the goal is to learn a model which, given in input a triplet of rectangles described by their heights and width, outputs, for each, the probability of being chosen according to average human behavior. The inference case is similar.

6   Pure ML Baseline

The task formulated in the previous section can be treated as standard multi-class classification to obtain class probability distributions. Machine learning algorithms are natural candidates for learning this task and making accurate predictions and we start with a pure ML method to investigate its efficacy while not relying on any cognitive priors. In particular, we choose multi-layer neural networks given their expressive power in approximating complex functions.

More in detail, let us assume the problems in set $\mathbb{P}$ have K options and J attributes. We use a four-layered feed-forward neural network, namely MLP, as our baseline with $K \times J$ inputs, one for each subjective evaluation $a_i^{[j]}$, and K outputs estimating the choice probability for each option. The choice probability distribution is obtained by passing the outputs of the final layer through a *softmax* function [16]. This architecture implies that the probability $\pi_{p,i}$ of choosing option o_i given problem p, is determined via logistic function

$$\pi_{p,i} = \frac{\exp\left(y_i\right)}{\sum_{j=1}^{K} \exp\left(y_j\right)}$$

where y_i is the ith output of the feed-forward neural network.

7   ML-MLBA Hybrids

A pure ML approach fails, however, to provide any explanation about the underlying deliberation process. On the other hand, one can argue that models, such as MLBA, suffer from high bias due to over-simplification of the cognitive underpinnings of decision making. For example, the front-end component of MLBA imposes inductive biases by assuming that the objective-to-subjective mapping is a power function and by fixing the way mean drift rates are computed. This structure is useful for explaining how a decision emerges from the raw stimuli. However, it may also cause the model to under-fit the data (see Fig. 5). We propose to relax some of these constraints by using a feed-forward NN to increase flexibility and explore the accuracy/explainability trade-off in two different ways. In the first model, denoted MLBA-NN, we integrate the back-end of MLBA on top of a multi-layer NN (see Fig. 3). In the second model, we extend the MLBA parameters learned by the NN component to m which governs the objective-to-subjective mapping. This architecture is denoted by MLBA-NN-m and is shown in Fig. 4.

MLBA-NN: As shown in Fig. 3, the NN's inputs are the objective evaluations $a_i^{[j]}$ which are, then, passed through four hidden layers with *tanh* activation functions [16] alongside three other free variables filtered by a *sigmoid* × 10 function [16] to yield back-end parameters $\langle d_1, \ldots, d_K, s, A, \chi - A \rangle$ with values in $[0, 10]$ in accordance with original MLBA model constraints (see [10]).

At this point we could use the estimated parameters to run the ballistic accumulators for the options and obtain the choice distribution. However, we opt for a more efficient solution, avoiding simulation, and we use the Gauss-Legendre quadrature to approximate the solution of Eq. 5, obtaining:

$$\pi_{p,j} \approx \frac{1}{2} \sum_{i=1}^{n} \frac{w_i PDF_{p,j}\left(\frac{(x_i+1)/2}{1-(x_i+1)/2}\right)}{\left(1 - (x_i + 1)/2\right)^2} \tag{6}$$

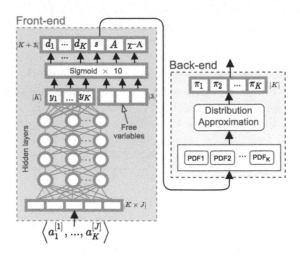

Fig. 3. The MLBA-NN architecture. The front-end is a 4-layer feed-forward neural network. The back-end approximates the choice distributions using LBA-model.

where the x_i's and w_i's are respectively discrete time points and parameters of the approximation method [1]. While we defer the details of this derivation to Appendix A, we note that, given a particular time t, Eqs. 2, 3 and 4 show how PDF_i can be expressed in terms of parameters χ, A, s, and d_i which are, in turn, the output of the NN component of MLBA-NN. Moreover, since Eq. 6 contains a differentiable approximation of the choice distribution, it can be used for computing the loss (see Sect. 8) and for training the model.

MLBA-NN-m: As depicted in Fig. 4, in this model the objective evaluations $a_i^{[j]}$ are first passed through the objective-to-subjective mapping described in Sect. 2 before feeding them to a NN similar to MLBA-NN. This is possible since the objective-to-subjective mapping (Sect. 2) is a differentiable function and can easily be integrated in the training allowing for the estimation of the m parameter. We apply a *soft-plus* function [16] to ensure positive values for m. Note that m is represented by a free variable in the model making it independent of the inputs. The back-end of this model is identical to the back-end of MLBA-NN.

8   Parameter Estimation

Both the baseline and hybrid models output a choice probability distribution which is differentiable (Sect. 6 and Eq. 6). We can thus minimize the negative-log-loss over the training data using standard gradient-descent (Appendix B). The training process for MLBA-NN and MLBA-NN-m is performed in an end-to-end fashion, meaning that the forward pass goes through the front-end and back-end in one go and we keep track of all computations by building the computation

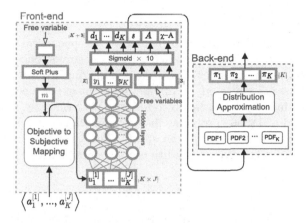

Fig. 4. The MLBA-NN-m architecture. The objective values are mapped to subjective values before feeding them to a 4-layer feed-forward NN in the front-end. The back-end approximates the choice distributions using the LBA model.

graph using an off-the-shelf software package (e.g. PyTorch). Next, we calculate the loss from the outputs of the forward pass. Finally, we use the obtained computation graph to calculate the gradients and propagate back the loss to the parameters for adjustment.

9 Experiment Design

All models were trained and tested on the following data sets.

Perceptual Dataset

Participants performed a simple perceptual decision making task involving the selection of the largest rectangle among three. Attributes correspond to height and width. The data is structured into two main subsets, collected in separate experiments ([25] and [24]). The first subset $E1$, involved 178 participants and consists of 1440 trials based on 12 conditions, for a total of 82646 (problem, choice) pairs divided into 3 parts (E1a, E1b, and E1c) each targeting one of the effects. A *condition* is a base problem designed to elicit a specific context effect and a trial for that condition is a problem generated by adding some random variation to the base problem while preserving the expected choice proportions. The second subset, E2, contains 480 trials from 6 conditions performed by 75 participants for a total of 35135 (problem, choice) pairs, spanning all three effects.

Inference Dataset

Participants were asked to infer which of three suspects was the most likely culprit, based on two eyewitnesses. Each eyewitness corresponds to an attribute and the evaluations are guilt evidence ratings ranging from 0 to 100. Also in this case the data was collected during two different experiments. The first set [26], E3, consists in 360 trials from 13 conditions, performed by 150 participants, generating a total of 18000 (problem, choice) pairs divided into 3 subsets (E3a, E3b, E3c) corresponding to the three effects. The second set, E4, involved 68 participants for 120 trials from 8 conditions and contains 8160 (problem, choice) pairs [27].

Evaluation

Similarly to [10], we group the choice problems based on their condition and compare the probability distributions generated by MLBA-HB, MLP, MLBA-NN, and MLBA-NN-m on each group using the Mean Squared Error (MSE) and Jensen-Shannon Divergence (JS-Divergence) [13]. For all models, except MLBA-HB, we report the average of 50 runs with their 95% confidence intervals.

Training Specifications and Hyper-parameters

All models were trained on E2, resp. E4, and tested on E1, resp. E3, depending on the data set. We further split E2 and E4 to validation/training sets with ratio of 33/67. Each model was trained for 200 epochs using the *Adam* [12] optimizer with weight decay of 10^{-6}, mini-batches of size *batchSize*, and learning rate $10^{-5} \times batchSize$, with *batchSize* = 1024 for the perceptual data and *batchSize* = 512 for the inference data. The validation set was used for early stopping and hyper-parameter tuning. The size of hidden layers in all models was set to 50 with *tanh* activation functions.[2]

Results

Figure 5 shows the choice distribution predicted by each model compared to the observed choice proportions for both experiments.

The first observation is that the choice proportions generated by MLP and the hybrid methods on all of the conditions are very similar despite using different approximations of the choice distributions in the loss function. Furthermore, we see that MLP and the hybrid methods significantly outperform MLBA-HB in predicting attraction effects in both datasets. Similarly for the compromise effect, which, however, seams to be more challenging for all models in the inference set. It also appears that, for MLP and the hybrid models, the source of error in this case is concentrated on one condition (represented by a circle in Fig. 5), and that, otherwise, they predict the other conditions very well. For the similarity effect, MLBA-HB performs slightly better than the other models in the perceptual data, but much worse on the inference data. As shown in Figs. 6 and 7, the overall accuracy of all of the ML-based methods is significantly better than MLBA-HB. This proves that our hybrid methods are successful in maintaining

---

[2] All the codes are publicly available at https://github.com/Rahgooy/mlba_ml.

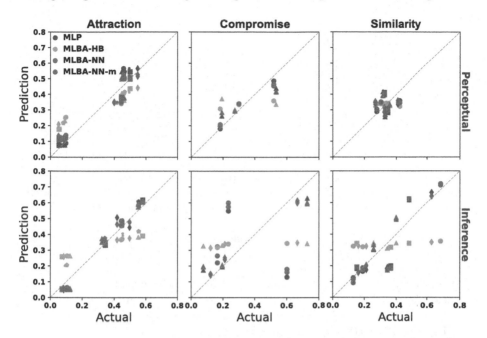

Fig. 5. Probability-Probability plots for the empirical (x-axis) and model (y-axis) predicted response for the Perceptual (top) and Inference (bottom) data on the three effects (columns). Symbols (e.g., circle, triangle) represent experimental conditions, colors represent different models. The closer to the diagonal the better. (Color figure online)

prediction accuracy while also capturing important cognitive priors. As an example regarding drift-rates, on an attraction instance similar to that described in Sect. 3, MLBA-NN-m correctly captured the decrease in X's drift rate and choice probability when shifting from $\mathbb{O}_1 = \{X, Z, R_X\}$ to $\mathbb{O}_2 = \{X, Z, R_Z\}$, with d_X going from 7.31 to 7.17 and the choice probability going from 0.49 to 0.37. We also note that the training and test sets in both datasets were obtained from different experiments with different participants. This further supports the ability of our proposed models to generalize the average user behavior.

The MLBA-NN success in making predictions, in comparison with MLBA-HB, provides evidence that the back-end of MLBA is expressive enough for this problem and is not a source of under-fitting in MLBA-HB. Similarly, MLBA-NN-m's very strong performance, suggests that MLBA's objective-to-subjective mapping also doesn't restrict the expressiveness of the model. Interestingly, by comparing the average predicted m values for the perceptual and inference data, namely (2.02, 4.08) for MLBA-NN-m and (1.08, 1.09) for MLBA-HB, we see that MLBA-NN-m captures a stronger deviation of subjective values from objective values, which may be a reason for its superior performance. Also open for inves-

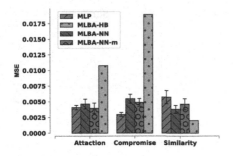
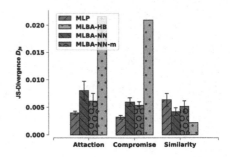

(a) Average of Mean Squared Error of the predictions over 50 runs. The error margins depict 95% confidence intervals.

(b) Average of JS-Divergence of the predictions over 50 runs. The error margins depict 95% confidence intervals.

Fig. 6. Performance of the models on the Perceptual Data.

tigation, is whether the lack of accuracy of MLBA-HB may be related to how attention is modeled and to the way the subjective values are combined to generate the drift rates in MLBA, or by limitations of the actual fitting method used in the MLBA-HB implementation.

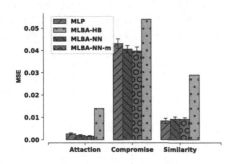

(a) Average of Mean Squared Error of the predictions over 50 runs. The error margins depict 95% confidence intervals.

(b) Average of JS-Divergence of the predictions over 50 runs. The error margins depict 95% confidence intervals.

Fig. 7. Performance of the models on the Inference Data.

We also investigate the effect of reducing the training data on the performance of the models. The results are shown in Table 1. We see that MLP and the hybrid models perform extremely well even with less data. Even with 30% of the training set they are performing better than MLBA-HB. However, unsurprisingly, they are more sensitive to the size of the training set compared to MLBA-HB. The steeper drop in performance on the inference data is due to its already limited size. Also, according to the results, the inference problems are more challenging to predict than the perceptual ones.

Table 1. Overall MSE ×100 results for models trained on 100%, 50%, and 30% of the training data.

Model	Perceptual			Inference		
	100%	50%	30%	100%	50%	30%
MLBA-HB	0.94	0.93	0.89	3.29	3.05	2.84
MLP	0.44	0.49	0.47	1.86	2.05	2.55
MLBA-NN	0.45	0.44	0.47	1.78	2.11	2.87
MLBA-NN-m	0.44	0.44	0.47	1.73	2.01	2.74

Finally we note that, on average, it takes less than an hour to train any of the ML based models, the MLP being the fastest and MLBA-NN-m the slowest. This is significantly faster than fitting MLBA-HB for which training, via the hierarchical Bayes approach, takes more than 10 h. Summarizing, our experimental results show that our hybrid methods are performing extremely well on a prediction task involving behavioral effects while explaining major parts of the decision making process, such as, sequential accumulation to threshold and subjective mapping of preferences.

10 Conclusion and Future Work

In this paper, we investigated incorporating machine learning into one of prominent cognitive models of decision making, MLBA, in an incremental way. This approach allowed us to study the prediction accuracy versus explainablity in our models to examine the expressiveness of different components of MLBA for the prediction task. We followed this approach on two experimental datasets and showed that the back-end and also the objective-to-subjective mapping components of MLBA are perfectly capable of producing accurate prediction when they are embedded in our ML architecture. Therefore, we need to look for sources of error in other parts of the model or the method of fitting MLBA to understand the shortcomings of MLBA. The experimental results also show that our hybrid methods are performing extremely well in the prediction task while explaining major parts of the decision making process namely, sequential accumulation to threshold, subjective mapping, pairwise comparison of alternatives, and the context effects through the inherited parts from MLBA. In the near future we plan to address learning the MLBA parameters governing attention and preference aggregation (i.e., λ_1 and λ_2) to better understand their role in modeling performance. We also plan to investigate our method in the context of predicting individual behavior and of more complex decision tasks. Our research agenda also includes the application of our general methodology to other cognitive models of deliberation, such as MDFT [19].

Acknowledgement. Jennifer S. Trueblood was supported by National Science Foundation grant 1846764 / 2305559.

Appendix A: Choice Probability Approximation

In this section we describe the details of approximating the following improper integral, which describes the choice probability distribution, using the Gauss-Legendre quadrature method:

$$\pi_{p,j} = \int_0^\infty PDF_{p,j}(t)dt. \tag{7}$$

According to the Gauss-Legendre quadrature method, integral of function f in $[-1,1]$ interval is approximated by:

$$\int_{-1}^1 f(x)dx \approx \sum_{i=1}^n w_i f(x_i) \tag{8}$$

where n is the number of samples, w_i are the quadrature weights, and x_i are the roots of the nth Legendre polynomial.

A change of interval from $[0,\infty]$ to $[-1,1]$ is needed to write Eq. 7 in the form of Eq. 8. We do this in two steps. First, we use substitution $x = \frac{t}{1-t}$, $dx = \frac{1}{(1-t)^2} dt$:

$$\int_0^\infty f(x)dx = \int_0^1 f\left(\frac{t}{1-t}\right) \frac{1}{(1-t)^2} dt \tag{9}$$

applying this to Eq. 7 results in

$$\pi_{p,j} = \int_0^1 \frac{PDF_{p,j}\left(\frac{t}{1-t}\right)}{(1-t)^2} dt \tag{10}$$

we define $h(t)$ to be

$$h(t) \equiv \frac{PDF_{p,j}\left(\frac{t}{1-t}\right)}{(1-t)^2} \tag{11}$$

and, thus,

$$\pi_{p,j} = \int_0^1 h(t)dt \tag{12}$$

next, we change the interval from $[0,1]$ to $[-1,1]$ using:

$$\int_0^1 f(x)dx = \frac{1}{2} \int_{-1}^1 f\left(\frac{x+1}{2}\right) dx \tag{13}$$

taking this step for Eq. 12 results in:

$$\pi_{p,j} = \frac{1}{2} \int_{-1}^1 h\left(\frac{t+1}{2}\right) dt \tag{14}$$

substitution of h with $PDF_{p,j}$ using Eq. 11 leads to

$$\pi_{p,j} = \frac{1}{2} \int_{-1}^{1} \frac{PDF_{p,j}\left(\frac{(t+1)/2}{1-t}\right)}{(1-(t+1)/2)^2} dt \qquad (15)$$

Finally, we can approximate it using Eq. 8 as follows

$$\pi_{p,j} \approx \frac{1}{2} \sum_{i=1}^{n} \frac{w_i PDF_{p,j}\left(\frac{(x_i+1)/2}{1-(x_i+1)/2}\right)}{(1-(x_i+1)/2)^2}. \qquad (16)$$

Appendix B: Parameter Estimation of Models

In this section we describe the details of parameter estimation for MLP, MLBA-NN, and MLBA-NN-m models. We utilize the differentiable likelihood functions of these models to formulate the parameter estimation as a maximum likelihood optimization. More formally, let $\mathcal{L}(\theta; D)$ be the likelihood of a parametric distribution function $f(y; \theta)$ with parameters θ over sample D, the maximum likelihood estimation is defined as:

$$\theta^* = \arg\max_{\theta} \mathcal{L}(\theta; D).$$

In this paper we assume the samples are independent and identically distributed (iid). Thus, we can write:

$$\mathcal{L}(\theta; \mathcal{D}) = \prod_{y \in D} f(y; \theta)$$

and we can use the log-likelihood for simplicity:

$$log(\mathcal{L}(\theta; \mathcal{D})) = \sum_{y \in D} \log(f(y; \theta)).$$

In the MLP model the choice distribution function $\pi_{p,i}^{MLP}$ is defined as a *soft-max* function and the parameters are the weights of the neural network denoted here by W_{MLP}. The likelihood function is defined as

$$\mathcal{L}_{MLP}(W_{MLP}; D) \equiv \prod_{\langle p,c \rangle \in D} \pi_{p,i=c}^{MLP}$$

which is the product of the probability of ground-truth choices. Finally, we find the optimal weights W_{MLP}^* by solving

$$W_{MLP}^* = \arg\min_{W} -\log(\mathcal{L}_{MLP}(W; D)).$$

In the MLBA-NN model, the inputs are passed through a neural network with weights W_{NN} to generate the $\langle d_1, \ldots, d_K, s, A, \chi - A \rangle$ parameters as described in the model Sect. 7 of the paper. Note that these parameters are functions of W_{NN} subsequently, $PDF_{p,i}$ is a function of W_{NN}. To calculate the choice distributions we use the approximation approach in Appendix A using $PDF_{p,i}$. As a result the approximated choice distribution function π_p^{NN} is a function of W_{NN}. Finally, the likelihood of this model $\mathcal{L}_{NN}$ is a function of the same weights:

$$\mathcal{L}_{NN}(W_{NN}; D) \equiv \prod_{\langle p,c \rangle \in D} \pi_{p,i=c}^{NN}.$$

Therefore, we can find these weight by solving

$$W_{NN}^* = \arg\min_W - \log(\mathcal{L}_{NN}(W; D)).$$

MLBA-NN-m model passes the inputs through a mapping with parameter m first. Next, it follows the same approach as MLBA-NN. So, the parameters of this model can be defined as the concatenation of the neural network weights and the m parameter, $W_m = \langle m | W_{NN} \rangle$, leading to:

$$\mathcal{L}_{NNm}(W_m; D) \equiv \prod_{\langle p,c \rangle \in D} \pi_{p,i=c}^{NNm}.$$

Consequently, we can estimate these parameters by solving

$$W_m^* = \arg\min_W - \log(\mathcal{L}_{NNm}(W; D)).$$

All of these likelihood functions are differentiable and we use gradient descent algorithm to estimate their solutions.

Appendix C: Mapping Objective to Subjective Values

Consider a pair of options o_1, o_2 objectively defined as indifferent by the additive rule $\sum_j a_1^{[j]} = \sum_j a_2^{[j]}$. The line connecting these two options is defined as:

$$\sum_{j=1}^{J} \left(\frac{a^{[j]}}{b_j} \right) = 1$$

In the case of our experimental data we have two attributes. The indifference rule in the inference experiment is defined as:

$$a_1^{[1]} + a_1^{[2]} = a_2^{[1]} + a_2^{[2]}. \tag{17}$$

In the perceptual experiment, two options are indifferent if their areas are equal, in order to make them additive we use the logarithm of their values, that is:

$$a_1^{[1]} \times a_1^{[2]} = a_2^{[1]} \times a_2^{[2]} \implies$$
$$\log(a_1^{[1]}) + \log(a_1^{[2]}) = \log(a_2^{[1]}) + \log(a_2^{[2]}).$$

The indifference line for two attributes is written as:

$$\frac{a^{[1]}}{b_1} + \frac{a^{[2]}}{b_2} = 1.$$

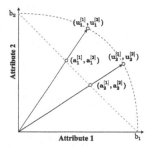

Fig. 8. Mapping of objective values (green line) to subjective values (red line) for the case with two attributes (resp. **x** and **y** axis) and $m > 1$. (Color figure online)

Using the additive rule in 17 we can find b_1 and b_2, x-intercept and y-intercept respectively, as follows:

$$b_1 = a_1^{[1]} - a_1^{[2]} \times \frac{a_2^{[1]} - a_1^{[1]}}{a_2^{[2]} - a_1^{[2]}}$$

$$b_2 = a_1^{[2]} - a_1^{[1]} \times \frac{a_2^{[2]} - a_1^{[2]}}{a_2^{[1]} - a_1^{[1]}}$$

Note that when both attribute values are in the same metric, $b_1 = b_2 = a_1^{[1]} + a_1^{[2]}$, as it is the case in our experiments. At this point we use these parameters and the m parameter to map the objective value a_1 to subjective value u_1 defined on the following curve and depicted in Fig. 8:

$$\sum_{j=1}^{J} \left(\frac{u^{[j]}}{b_j} \right)^m = 1.$$

For two attributes we can write this formula as:

$$\left(\frac{u^{[1]}}{b_1} \right)^m + \left(\frac{u^{[2]}}{b_2} \right)^m = 1. \tag{18}$$

Now, let θ be the angle between the x-axis and $a_1 = (a_1^{[1]}, a_1^{[2]})$, which can be written as:

$$\theta = \arctan \left(\frac{a_1^{[1]}}{a_1^{[2]}} \right),$$

As you can see in Fig. 8 a subjective vector u is a multiple of its corresponding objective vector a, hence they produce the same angle with the x-axis. Therefore, we can write:

$$u_1^{[2]} = u_1^{[1]} \tan(\theta).$$

Substituting this in Eq. 18 results in:

$$\left(\frac{u_1^{[1]}}{b_1} \right)^m + \left(\frac{u_1^{[1]} \tan(\theta)}{b_2} \right)^m = 1.$$

We now, obtain the subjective values by solving above equation which gives us:

$$u_1^{[1]} = \frac{b_2}{\left(\tan(\theta)^m + \left(\frac{b_2}{b_1} \right)^m \right)^{\frac{1}{m}}}$$

$$u_1^{[2]} = u_1^{[1]} \tan(\theta)$$

References

1. Abramowitz, M., Stegun, I.A.: Handbook of Mathematical Functions with Formulas, Graphs, and Mathematical Tables, vol. 55. US Government Printing Office (1948)
2. Bhatia, S.: Associations and the accumulation of preference. Psychol. Rev. **120**(3), 522 (2013)
3. Bourgin, D.D., Peterson, J.C., Reichman, D., Russell, S.J., Griffiths, T.L.: Cognitive model priors for predicting human decisions. In: Proceedings of the 36th International Conference on Machine Learning, ICML 2019. Proceedings of Machine Learning Research, vol. 97, pp. 5133–5141. PMLR (2019)
4. Brown, S.D., Heathcote, A.: The simplest complete model of choice response time: linear ballistic accumulation. Cogn. Psychol. **57**(3), 153–178 (2008)
5. Busemeyer, J.R., Diederich, A.: Survey of decision field theory. Math. Soc. Sci. **43**(3), 345–370 (2002)
6. Busemeyer, J.R., Johnson, J.G.: Computational models of decision making. In: Blackwell Handbook of Judgment and Decision Making, pp. 133–154 (2004)
7. Busemeyer, J., Gluth, S., Rieskam, P., Turner, B.: Cognitive and neural bases of multi-attribute, multi-alternative, value-based decisions. Trends Cogn. Sci. **23**(3), 251–263 (2019)
8. Chandiok, A., Chaturvedi, D.K.: Machine learning techniques for cognitive decision making. In: 2015 IEEE Workshop on Computational Intelligence: Theories, Applications and Future Directions (WCI), pp. 1–6 (2015). https://doi.org/10.1109/WCI.2015.7495529
9. Erev, I., Ert, E., Plonsky, O., Cohen, D., Cohen, O.: From anomalies to forecasts: toward a descriptive model of decisions under risk, under ambiguity, and from experience. Psychol. Rev. **124**(4), 369–409 (2017)
10. Evans, N.J., Holmes, W.R., Trueblood, J.S.: Response-time data provide critical constraints on dynamic models of multi-alternative, multi-attribute choice. Psychon. Bull. Rev. **26**(3), 901–933 (2019). https://doi.org/10.3758/s13423-018-1557-z

11. Huber, J., Payne, J.W., Puto, C.: Adding asymmetrically dominated alternatives: violations of regularity and the similarity hypothesis. J. Consum. Res. **9**(1), 90–98 (1982)
12. Kingma, D.P., Ba, J.: Adam: a method for stochastic optimization. arXiv preprint arXiv:1412.6980 (2014)
13. Lin, J.: Divergence measures based on the Shannon entropy. IEEE Trans. Inf. Theory **37**(1), 145–151 (1991)
14. Luce, R.: Individual Choice Behavior: A Theoretical Analysis. Wiley (1959)
15. Noguchi, T., Stewart, N.: Multialternative decision by sampling: a model of decision making constrained by process data. Psychol. Rev. **125**(4), 512 (2018)
16. Nwankpa, C., Ijomah, W., Gachagan, A., Marshall, S.: Activation functions: comparison of trends in practice and research for deep learning. arXiv preprint arXiv:1811.03378 (2018)
17. Plonsky, O., Erev, I., Hazan, T., Tennenholtz, M.: Psychological forest: predicting human behavior. In: Proceedings of the Thirty-First AAAI Conference on Artificial Intelligence (AAAI-17), pp. 656–662. AAAI Press (2017)
18. Rahgooy, T., Venable, K.B.: Learning preferences in a cognitive decision model. In: Zeng, A., Pan, D., Hao, T., Zhang, D., Shi, Y., Song, X. (eds.) IIBAI 2019. CCIS, vol. 1072, pp. 181–194. Springer, Singapore (2019). https://doi.org/10.1007/978-981-15-1398-5_13
19. Roe, R.M., Busemeyer, J.R., Townsend, J.T.: Multialternative decision field theory: a dynamic connectionist model of decision making. Psychol. Rev. **108**(2), 370 (2001)
20. Rosenfeld, A., Kraus, S.: Predicting Human Decision-Making: From Prediction to Action. Synthesis Lectures on Artificial Intelligence and Machine Learning. Morgan & Claypool Publishers (2018)
21. Rosenfeld, A., Zuckerman, I., Azaria, A., Kraus, S.: Combining psychological models with machine learning to better predict people's decisions. Synthese **189** (2012). https://doi.org/10.1007/s11229-012-0182-z
22. Simonson, I.: Choice based on reasons: the case of attraction and compromise effects. J. Consum. Res. **16**(2), 158–174 (1989)
23. Trafton, J.G., Hiatt, L.M., Brumback, B., McCurry, J.M.: Using cognitive models to train big data models with small data. In: Proceedings of the 19th International Conference on Autonomous Agents and Multiagent Systems, AAMAS 2020, pp. 1413–1421. IFAAMAS (2020)
24. Trueblood, J.S., Brown, S.D., Heathcote, A.: The fragile nature of contextual preference reversals: reply to Tsetsos, Chater, and Usher. Psychol. Rev. (2015)
25. Trueblood, J.S., Brown, S.D., Heathcote, A., Busemeyer, J.R.: Not just for consumers: context effects are fundamental to decision making. Psychol. Sci. **24**(6), 901–908 (2013)
26. Trueblood, J.S.: Multialternative context effects obtained using an inference task. Psychon. Bull. Rev. **19**(5), 962–968 (2012). https://doi.org/10.3758/s13423-012-0288-9
27. Trueblood, J.S., Brown, S.D., Heathcote, A.: The multiattribute linear ballistic accumulator model of context effects in multialternative choice. Psychol. Rev. **121**(2), 179 (2014)
28. Tversky, A.: Elimination by aspects: a theory of choice. Psychol. Rev. **79**, 281–299 (1972)
29. Tversky, A.: Features of similarity. Psychol. Rev. **84**(4), 327 (1977)

Overgenerality from Inference in Perspective-Taking

Timothy Clausner[1]([⊠]) [iD], Christopher Maxey[1] [iD], Matthew D. Goldberg[1] [iD],
Paul Zaidins[1] [iD], Justin Brody[2] [iD], Darsana Josyula[3] [iD], and Don Perlis[1] [iD]

[1] University of Maryland, College Park, MD 20742, USA
{clausner,mdgold,perlis}@umd.edu
[2] Franklin and Marshall College, Lancaster, PA 17604, USA
[3] Bowie State University, Bowie, MD 20715, USA
darsana@cs.umd.edu

Abstract. The representational and mental processes that support Theory of Mind need greater clarity to guide computational approaches. Perspective-taking is among the key abilities for Theory of Mind. In human visual perspective-taking, two kinds of judgments develop: Level 1 judges whether something can or cannot be seen, and Level 2 aligns perspectives using communication. To investigate these processes, simulated agents with limited visual range, and decentralized active-logic reasoning, moved, saw discrete spatial locations, and communicated locations visited (Level 2); and inferred the locations within other agents' visual range (Level 1). Controlled conditions systematically varied team size and how far agents spread out. The results are consistent with an account in which Level 1 overgeneralizes and Level 2 corrects, and corrects more, as agents interact more frequently, in larger teams, or by spreading out less. This account of perspectival processes suggests that overgenerality might have both benefits and costs in Theory of Mind, and serve an important role in computation approaches.

Keywords: Theory of mind · Perspective-taking · Collective search ·
Multi-agent interaction

1 Introduction

A present challenge for computational approaches to Theory of Mind beyond simulating a collection of functional abilities—e.g., false belief, joint intention, perspective-taking, normativity—is that the representational and mental processes which support these abilities are not clearly understood, and it remains unclear how Theory of Mind arises (Moll and Tomasello 2006, 2007, 2012; Sterck and Begeer 2010). Human and other primate studies continue to illuminate the topic (Premack and Woodruff 1978; Call and Tomasello 2011; Wellman 2018; Tomasello 2019), but the results still offer only general guidance to computational approaches, leaving them to confront choices of assumptions and the need to fill in specifics of designs and implementations. Even amid this need for greater clarity and specificity, prevailing explanations from studies of developmental cognition

N. Gurney and G. Sukthankar (Eds.): AAAI-FSS 2021, LNCS 13775, pp. 194–201, 2022.
https://doi.org/10.1007/978-3-031-21671-8_12

offer that biologically-based abilities serve as scaffolding on which experience serves to promote development toward mature abilities (Tomasello and Rakoczy 2003; Tomasello 2019). Still, the choices for computational approaches to Theory of Mind range from implementation of mature abilities (Tang et al. 2020) to guidance on minimal Theory of Mind (Butterfill and Apperly 2013).

The research presented here builds up from minimal assumptions, toward capabilities of individual agents to interact using representation and reasoning processes thought necessary for visual perspective-taking in Theory of Mind. This approach contrasts with attempts to distinguish between minimal and full-blown Theory of Mind (Butterfill and Apperly 2013). The aim is not to achieve mature abilities, or to bootstrap them (Tang et al. 2020), but to focus on a particular ability of Theory of Mind: perspective-taking (Surtees, Apperly, and Samson 2013; Palmer et al. 2009).

This study focused on visual perspective-taking, an ability widely acknowledged as fitting in the broad context of social interaction across diverse theoretical approaches to Theory of Mind (Barnes-Holmes et al. 2004; Moll and Kadipasaoglu 2013), and in which visual tasks can serve to investigate perspectival cognition. In visual perspective-taking, there are two kinds of judgements about another's perspective (Michelon and Zacks 2006; Moll and Meltzoff 2011; Tomasello 2019). Level 1: *what* can be seen, is a judgement about whether something can or cannot be seen. Level 2: *how* something is seen, is a judgement that accounts for rotating into the other's angle of view, where self and other use communication to align perspectives. Charactering levels of visual perspective-taking suffers from some ambiguity: e.g., whether to split them into three levels (Moll and Meltzoff 2011), and how tasks engaged levels by manipulating object appearance, e.g., with barriers (McGuigan and Doherty 2002), or by altering perceived color (Moll and Tomasello 2012; Moll and Kadipasaoglu 2013). A recent proposal broadly characterizes the tracking of perspectives to account for non-linear development of successes and difficulties across various social-cognitive tasks of false-belief, appearance-reality, and aspectuality in language (Tomasello 2019).

Computational approaches to visual perspective-taking that endow agents with full overhead views of their environment (e.g., Chen et al. 2021) contrast with ego-centric camera views in the present study.

2 Method

The Active Logic MAchine (ALMA) (Perlis et al. 2017) ran decentralized reasoners for teaming agents. Agents had 360° field of view with limited range, which required them to be within range of seeing each other to interact during a search task.

As an agent moved in the simulated environment, its present locations were successively encoded as visited locations (dark color paths, Fig. 1). From any visited location an agent saw discrete spatial locations within its field of view (light color disks and locations, Fig. 1). This distinction between locations visited and locations seen had two purposes. Communicating only visited locations, and then inferring seen locations compressed information sharing. An agent used the locations it knew to have been seen to move toward locations known to have not yet been seen (white locations one move beyond the current field of view, and their quantity per movement direction, Fig. 1).

Simple active-logic axioms encoded the knowledge for Theory of Mind, enabling an agent, upon seeing another agent, to react on two levels: 1. infer spatial locations the other agent could potentially see from its present position; 2. communicate all of the spatial locations the agent knows to have to been visited thus far.

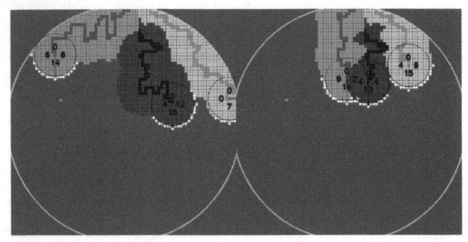

Fig. 1. Example of Unlimited spread (left) and Limited spread (right). 3-Agents searching for a target (gray dot). Agent field-of-view history (lighter colors) and path history (darker colors). White dots represent locations that agents believe are unseen.

An agent's knowledge base maintained a set of unique locations visited, from which locations seen were inferred. Agents' 360° views, and sparsity of the environment, motivated an approach in which spatial locations were the unit of what an agent could see. Perspective-taking operated in Level 1, not based on whether a barrier occluded objects, but whether spatial locations were within field of view range. Level 2, operated, not with spatial rotations for perspectival alignment, but by using communication. The Level 1 mechanism was sensitive to the locations within the range of the other agent's field of view, but not to occluded locations from the other agent's position. The Level 2 mechanism was sensitive to another agent's perspective, in that, the locations known to have been visited by another agent were communicated between agents, if the other agent was within visual range and not occluded.

Within ALMA, commonsense active logic reasoning extended the ability to nest formulas via quotation (Goldberg et al. 2020), which enabled reasoning about the locations contained in communications. A separate Level 1 perspective-taking mechanism, operated outside of ALMA, within an agent's decentralized wrapper, to calculate the locations within an (unoccluded) field of view. When an agent saw another agent at a location, it geometrically inferred the locations within the other agent's field of view. This Level 1 perspective-taking was sensitive to the spatial locations an agent could potentially see (within its visual range) and could not see (beyond its visual range), but not to occlusions. Level 2 was sensitive to occlusions, dependent on the spatial alignment between agents.

In summary, seeing another agent triggered two perspective-taking levels: Level 1 enabled an agent to infer from that other agent's present location, all the locations within the other agent's field of view. Level 2 used peer-to-peer communication to send all the locations an agent believed had been visited thus far (by self or others). Upon receiving a communication containing visited locations, the agent applied each one to the Level 1 mechanism, which inferred all of the locations within the range of field of view centered on each visited location. Levels 1 and 2 shared a single inference mechanism for inferring the locations another agent could see. These two levels of perspective-taking operated as distinct process, as surmised from human cognitive development (Michelon and Zacks 2006).

The search task axioms and custom physical simulator were implemented to enable agents to search for a single target within a time deadline. The experiment infrastructure allocated processing timeslices (distinct from the timesteps within active logic) to agents, enabling asynchronous decentralized reasoning. Each agent could sense the simulated environment (look for the target and see other agents), draw inferences (running its own copy of ALMA), and act (move one step). Spatial movements were limited to discrete orthogonal steps forward, back, left, right. Communications encoded only locations, enabling agents to share information about locations searched.

Agents moved by self-avoiding random walks, which allowed for study of agent per-formance without complications of spatial reasoning and navigation strategies. Agents were randomly assigned to start locations in a pair or triad configuration. The two levels of perspective-taking operated as a Theory of Mind mechanism. These designs of agents, environment, reasoning, and experimental conditions allowed for comparisons of agent performance between experimental conditions. The design was originally focused on the broader topic of cooperation, not only perspective-taking, and included conditions in which agent movements had Limited and Unlimited spread (Fig. 1). In the Limited condition, agents spread no farther than three times the field of view radius.

This design and method investigated the cost of overgeneralization in visual perspective-taking. Level 1 judgements were expected to incur overgeneralizations, in that the inference that "you can see what I could see from your location" does not account for your alignment with me, nor for the locations occluded from your view. Whereas, Level 2 perspective-taking, was expected to be indirectly sensitive to occlusions, because agents communicated only if unoccluded, thus indirectly guiding movement choices.

Overgeneralizations were operationalized as follows. Each agent inferred locations seen by others. The number of unique locations that were inferred collectively by all agents was counted, and of those, the number of unique locations not seen due to occlu-sions collectively by all agents was counted. Overgeneralizations were measured as the mean proportion of unique locations occluded out of the total number of unique locations inferred as having been seen (Fig. 2). This proportion of inferred locations to occluded locations measured how much the Theory of Mind inferences overgeneralized. That is, agents searched for the target by moving to locations known to have not been seen, based on knowledge of locations that have been seen, from two sources: observations by self (sensitive to occlusions), and inferences about what others have seen (not sensitive to occlusions). This study focuses on those inferences, which overly encoded locations as seen that were not actually seen.

Agents were run in four separate teaming conditions: Group size (2-Agents and 3-Agents) and Spread (limited and unlimited). In each condition, 512 trials were run.

3 Results and Analysis

Results for overgeneralization are shown in Fig. 2. An ANOVA compared proportional overgeneralization across group size and spread. Effect sizes were calculated for F-tests as partial eta-squared, and for t-tests as Cohen's d. The ANOVA found significant main effects of group size (F(1, 2047) = 196.38, p < .0001, η_p^2 = 0.085) and spread (F(1, 2047) = 113.66, p < .0001, η_p^2 = 0.053). Overgeneralizations were proportionally higher for 3-agents (M = 0.128, SD = 0.084) than for 2-agents (M = 0.067, SD = 0.083), a significant effect (t(2046) = 14.0, p < .0001, d = 0.31). This comparison of proportional overgeneralizations indicates a 40.3% increase for 3-agents over 2-agents. Overgeneralizations were proportionally higher for limited spread (M = 0.122, SD = 0.091) than for unlimited spread (M = 0.082, SD = 0.079), a significant effect (t(2046) = 10.7, p < .0001, d = 0.24). This comparison of proportional overgeneralizations indicates a 32.7% increase for limited over unlimited spread.

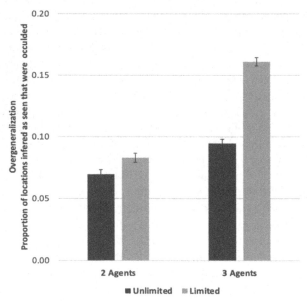

Fig. 2. Theory of Mind overgeneralizations by 2-Agents and 3-Agents, and in Limited and Unlimited spread conditions. Overgeneralization was measured as the mean proportion of unique locations occluded out of the total number of unique locations inferred as having been seen. Bars represent one standard error above and below the mean.

Individual tests of spread were conducted for 2-agents and 3-agents. For 2-agents, overgeneralizations were proportionally no different in unlimited spread (M = 0.083, SD = 0.082) than in limited spread (M = 0.070, SD = 0.082), not a sizable effect (t(1022) =

2.6, p = 0.0094, d = 0.08). For 3-agents, overgeneralizations were proportionally higher in limited spread (M = 0.161, SD = 0.081) than in unlimited spread (M = 0.095, SD = 0.073), a significant effect (t(1022) = 13.8, p < .0001, d = 0.43). This comparison of proportional overgeneralizations indicates a 41.3% increase when 3-agents were limited to stay closer together than when 3-agents were free to spread out.

The mains effects of number of agents and spread are each driven by the 3-Agent limited spread condition. These results exemplify the importance of not relying solely on p-values but also including effect sizes as more reliable indicators of potentially meaningful results.

In addition to assessing overgeneralizations (i.e., occlusions that agents failed to infer), corrections to them were roughly assessed as occlusions eventually seen during a search. Two set sizes were counted: unique locations seen by all agents, and unique inferred locations. The set sizes were equal, in each condition, which suggests that nearly, if not all, locations overgeneralized as occlusions were eventually seen.

The relative efficiency of Levels 1 and 2 was roughly assessed. Level 2 communicated non-unique locations that agent(s) had thus far visited, then Level 1 inferred the locations seen within the other agent's field of view, as if from the vantage point of each visited location. The overall mean ratio of visited locations encoded in communications to locations inferred as seen, was M = 2.6, SD = 2.9, ranging from minimum 0.3 to maximum, 66.5. Within spread conditions, limited spread tended to have the largest ratios: limited (2-Agents: M = 3.0, SD = 3.1; 3-Agents: M = 3.1, SD = 1.6); unlimited (2-Agents: M = 2.3, SD = 5.0; 3-Agents: M = 2.1, SD = 1.8). As an agent saw and communicated locations known to have been visited thus far, it did not keep track of previous communications. Over the course of a search trial, many locations communicated were redundant. The ratio of these non-unique locations visited to non-unique inferences of locations seen, represents the efficiency of not communicating every location seen. Even though redundant (non-unique) locations were communicated, the mean ratios were greater than 1, which represents greater efficiency of Level 2 communications and inferences over Level 1 inferences only.

4   Conclusions and Discussion

Overgeneralizations occurred when agents inferred that some locations were seen by others, but those locations were not seen, due to occlusion. The pattern of overgeneralizations in the results supports competing explanations. When agents' spread was limited, they were expected to interact more frequently than when they were free to spread out. So, limited spread increased opportunities for agents to occlude other's views, which increased overgeneralizations. A similar explanation might apply to the increased overgeneralizations for 3-agents compared to 2-agents. Larger numbers of agents interact and occlude one another more frequently than smaller numbers of agents, which would tend to increase overgeneralizations. This explanation of the results treats Levels 1 and 2 as a single combined mechanism, but does not explain why overgeneralizations were (nearly) all corrected.

An alternative explanation treats Level 2 as indirectly sensitive to actual occlusions as agents directly avoided locations known to have been seen, by moving toward unseen locations. The results are consistent with an account in which Level 1 overgeneralizes and Level 2 corrects, and corrects more, as agents interact more frequently, in larger teams, or by spreading out less. This explanation is consistent with a dual-level theory of visual perspective-taking. It does not explain whether the levels should or should not share a common inference mechanism. The contribution of the results isn't that the Level 1 inferences were implemented to have overgeneralizations, it's that overgeneralizations from inferences can operate dually with Level 2, such that more general information (Level 1) and more specific information (Level 2) were mediated by agent observation and communication, respectively.

The present study cannot distinguish between these two alterative explanations of the results. Presently, human and other primate studies of cognitive development, also cannot conclude whether Level 1 is replaced by dual-processes which share a legacy Level 1 inference mechanism, or if Level 2 is added to Level 1, or how the two levels interact. In the absence of a more detailed specification of perspectival processes, computational approaches can explore the processes requisite for Theory of Mind.

The importance of studying perspective-taking in the context of movement and target search, is that any one missed location (any single overgeneralized location) could mean missing the target. Surprisingly, the assessment of overgeneralizations found that the agents collectively corrected them all (or nearly all). Future analyses are required to more fully understand that result. The assessment of the communications has importance for the role of human language in Level 2, for efficiently sharing information. The 2.6 ratio results of communicated locations to inferred locations is consistent with this theorized compressive functionality in Theory of Mind (Tomasello 2019), and with the idea that abstract knowledge can guide reasoning from incomplete information (Tenenbaum et al. 2011).

This investigation focused on perspective-taking, with the acknowledgement that perspectival processes operate together with others, e.g., that "the notions of objective reality, subjective beliefs, and intersubjective perspectives thus form a logical net that can only fully be grasped as a whole" (Tomasello and Rakoczy 2003). Another consideration is whether computational approaches treat levels as an amalgam (e.g., Stacy et al. 2021), or distinguish specific processes as in the present study.

Computational approaches to theory of mind tend to focus on tasks or models of behavior, even if processes are explicitly acknowledged (e.g., Vinciarelli et al. 2015). The present study's approach implemented knowledge and processes to test behaviors and measure performance. The results could be used to inform computational theory of mind approaches because the alternate explanations of the results are stated in terms of processes that could be implemented to test between the alternatives. This process-focused approach has potential importance for theory-testing, as well as, for applications to integrated human-machine teams. The human cognitive processes that enable Theory of Mind are some of those which guide human social interactions, which in turn bear on task performance. For computational theory of mind to socially interact with human theory of mind, a detailed understanding is required of the processes which cause social behaviors and task performance.

Acknowledgements. This research was partly supported by DARPA-PA-19-03-01-01-FP-037 to DP, TC, DJ, and JB.

References

Barnes-Holmes, Y., McHugh, L., Barnes-Holmes, D.: Perspective-taking and Theory of Mind: a relational frame account. Behav. Anal. Today **5**(1), 15 (2004)

Butterfill, S.A., Apperly, I.A.: How to construct a minimal theory of mind. Mind Lang. **28**(5), 606–637 (2013)

Call, J., Tomasello, M.: Does the chimpanzee have a theory of mind? 30 years later. In: Human Nature and Self Design, pp. 83–96 (2011)

Chen, B., Vondrick, C., Lipson, H.: Visual behavior modelling for robotic theory of mind. Sci. Rep. **11**(1), 1–14 (2021)

Goldberg, M.D., Josyula, D., Perlis, D.: Quotation for real-time metacognition. In: Advances in Cognitive Systems, vol. 8 (2020)

McGuigan, N., Doherty, M.J.: The relation between hiding skill and judgment of eye direction in preschool children. Dev. Psychol. **38**(3), 418–427 (2002)

Michelon, P., Zacks, J.M.: Two kinds of visual perspective taking. Percept. Psychophys. **68**(2), 327–337 (2006)

Moll, H., Kadipasaoglu, D.: The primacy of social over visual perspective-taking. Front. Hum. Neurosci. **7**, 558 (2013)

Moll, H., Meltzoff, A.N.: How does it look? Level 2 perspective-taking at 36 months of age. Child Dev. **82**(2), 661–673 (2011)

Moll, H., Tomasello, M.: Level 1 perspective-taking at 24 months of age. Br. J. Dev. Psychol. **24**(3), 603–613 (2006)

Moll, H., Tomasello, M.: How 14-and 18-month-olds know what others have experienced. Dev. Psychol. **43**(2), 309 (2007)

Moll, H., Tomasello, M.: Three-year-olds understand appearance and reality—Just not about the same object at the same time. Dev. Psychol. **48**(4), 1124 (2012)

Palmer, E.M., Brown, C.M., Bates, C.F., Kellman, P.J., Clausner, T.C.: Perceptual cues and imagined viewpoints modulate visual search in air traffic control displays. In: Proceedings of the 53rd Annual Human Factors and Ergonomics Society Meeting, San Antonio, TX, pp. 1111–1115, October 2009

Perlis, D., Brody, J., Kraus, S., Miller, M.J.: The internal reasoning of robots. In: Commonsense-17 (2017)

Premack, D., Woodruff, G.: Does the chimpanzee have a theory of mind? Behav. Brain Sci. **1**(4), 515–526 (1978)

Surtees, A., Apperly, I., Samson, D.: Similarities and differences in visual and spatial perspective-taking processes. Cognition **129**(2), 426–438 (2013)

Stacy, S., et al.: Modeling Communication to Coordinate Perspectives in Cooperation. arXiv preprint arXiv:2106.02164 (2021)

Sterck, E.H., Begeer, S.: Theory of mind: specialized capacity or emergent property? Eur. J. Dev. Psychol. **7**(1), 1–16 (2010)

Tang, N., Stacy, S., Zhao, M., Marquez, G., Gao, T.: Bootstrapping an imagined we for cooperation. In: Denison, S., Mack, M., Xu, Y., Armstrong, B. (eds.) Proceedings of the 42nd Annual Meeting of the Cognitive Science Society, pp. 2453–2458. Cognitive Science Society, Austin (2020)

Tenenbaum, J.B., Kemp, C., Griffiths, T.L., Goodman, N.D.: How to grow a mind: statistics, structure, and abstraction. Science **331**(6022), 1279–1285 (2011)

Tomasello, M.: Becoming Human: A Theory of Ontogeny. Belknap Press of Harvard University Press (2019)

Tomasello, M., Rakoczy, H.: What makes human cognition unique? From individual to shared to collective intentionality. Mind Lang. **18**(2), 121–147 (2003)

Vinciarelli, A., et al.: Open challenges in modelling, analysis and synthesis of human behaviour in human–human and human–machine interactions. Cogn. Comput. **7**(4), 397–413 (2015)

Wellman, H.M.: Theory of mind: the state of the art. Eur. J. Dev. Psychol. **15**(6), 728–755 (2018)

Tools for Improving ASI

Using Features at Multiple Temporal and Spatial Resolutions to Predict Human Behavior in Real Time

Liang Zhang[(✉)] [iD], Justin Lieffers [iD], and Adarsh Pyarelal [iD]

University of Arizona, Tucson, AZ 85721, USA
{liangzh,lieffers,adarsh}@email.arizona.edu

Abstract. When performing complex tasks, humans naturally reason at multiple temporal and spatial resolutions simultaneously. We contend that for an artificially intelligent agent to effectively model human teammates, i.e., demonstrate computational theory of mind (ToM), it should do the same. In this paper, we present an approach for integrating high and low-resolution spatial and temporal information to predict human behavior in real time and evaluate it on data collected from human subjects performing simulated urban search and rescue (USAR) missions in a Minecraft-based environment. Our model composes neural networks for high and low-resolution feature extraction with a neural network for behavior prediction, with all three networks trained simultaneously. The high-resolution extractor encodes dynamically changing goals robustly by taking as input the Manhattan distance difference between the humans' Minecraft avatars and candidate goals in the environment for the latest few actions, computed from a high-resolution gridworld representation. In contrast, the low-resolution extractor encodes participants' historical behavior using a historical state matrix computed from a low-resolution graph representation. Through supervised learning, our model acquires a robust prior for human behavior prediction, and can effectively deal with long-term observations. Our experimental results demonstrate that our method significantly improves prediction accuracy compared to approaches that only use high-resolution information.

Keywords: Theory of mind · Urban search and rescue · Neural networks

This research was conducted as part of DARPA's Artificial Social Intelligence for Successful Teams (ASIST) program, and was sponsored by the Army Research Office and was accomplished under Grant Number W911NF-20-1-0002. The views and conclusions contained in this document are those of the authors and should not be interpreted as representing the official policies, either expressed or implied, of the Army Research Office or the U.S. Government. The U.S. Government is authorized to reproduce and distribute reprints for Government purposes notwithstanding any copyright notation herein.

N. Gurney and G. Sukthankar (Eds.): AAAI-FSS 2021, LNCS 13775, pp. 205–219, 2022.
https://doi.org/10.1007/978-3-031-21671-8_13

1   Introduction

Artificially intelligent (AI) teammates should have a number of capabilities to be effective [1], including inferring the internal states of other agents [2–4], solving problems collaboratively with them [5–7], and communicating with them in a socially-aware manner [8,9]. While these capabilities have been developed to some extent for simple domains (e.g., 2D gridworlds) and simulated agents, current state of the art approaches still face significant challenges when it comes to dealing with complex domains and modeling actual human teammates (as opposed to simulated agents). We attempt to address some of these challenges in the context of an experiment involving humans conducting a simulated urban search and rescue (USAR) mission set in a Minecraft-based environment [10].

   This domain is significantly more complex than the domains previously studied in the literature on computational theory of mind (ToM) [2,3]. Enabling AI agents to understand human behavior in complex domains will be essential to achieve the goal of better human-AI teaming. The complexity of the domain and the emphasis on analyzing human subjects lead to a few unique challenges, which we describe below.

- **Limited data.** Since collecting human subjects data is expensive and time-consuming, the amount of training data available to us is very limited. This rules out using certain classes of modern machine learning approaches (e.g., transformer architectures) that require a large amount of training data.
- **Noisy data.** Human subjects data is typically noisy, especially in the short term, with participants frequently violating assumptions of rationality that are used in existing works on computational ToM [2,3,11]. This expresses the need for a two resolution approach as rationality can often be recovered when the domain is represented at a lower resolution and the noise is averaged over, yet the high resolution is required for real-time predictions.
- **Long horizon.** In contrast to earlier works on computational ToM [2,3,11] that study domains with $\approx 10^2$ primitive actions per episode[1], our work considers a domain with episodes containing $\approx 10^3$ primitive actions and a far larger observation space including more than 20 areas and complex connectivity. This requires us to implement a long-term memory mechanism and the ability to extract key features from large amounts of noisy data, both of which are challenging in their own right.
- **Complex dynamics.** Our domain is large and possesses a complex topological structure, coupled with a complex rescue mechanism setting (for details, please refer to the approach section), which require us to consider human behavior at different levels of spatial and temporal granularity. Our model simultaneously takes into account both the *short-term goal preference* in a local area and the *long-term rescue strategy*.

---

[1] We use the term *episode* to denote a sequence of actions taken by an agent to perform a given task. We also use the term *trial* elsewhere in the paper to denote the same thing.

To address the above challenges, we propose a two-level representation. The first is a *low-resolution* level that contains information about the topology of the environment (i.e. which areas are connected to each other) and the status of victims in each area. The second is a *high-resolution* level that contains more granular information about the environment, such as the Cartesian coordinates corresponding to the agent's current location, walls, openings, and victims inside the rooms.

For the low-resolution representation, we build a matrix that encodes key historical information, which helps our model learn high-level features of human behavior, such as long-term search and rescue strategies. In contrast, for the high-resolution representation, we organize the input vector to our proposed model based on the latest short-term observations, which are more conducive to recognizing short-term goal preferences. Using the high and low level resolutions simultaneously aligns with the way humans reason about complex tasks, and also results in better performance on our prediction tasks, compared to considering only a single resolution.

2   Related Work

There exist a number of other approaches to computational ToM in the literature. In this section, we describe some of them, along with their advantages and disadvantages compared with our approach.

Bayesian Theory of Mind (BToM) models [3,12,13] calculate the probabilities of potential goals of an agent and other's beliefs. These models are primarily based on Markov Decision Process (MDP) formalisms and thus suffer from high computational costs for complex domains.

Zhi-Xuan et al. [11] proposed an online Bayesian goal inference algorithm based on sequential inverse plan search (SIPS). This approach allows for real-time predictions on a number of different domains. Notably, their approach models agents as *boundedly rational planners*, thus making them capable of executing sub-optimal plans, similar to humans. However, this approach cannot be directly applied to our domain due to the fact that our agents (i.e., humans) have incomplete knowledge of their domain and thus the short term planning would suffer without added hierarchical complexity or longer term planning. In our proposed approach, we use a similar idea of calculating the probabilities of potential goals, but we use neural networks which allow for the automatic extraction of features and correlations from the data without having to hand-craft conditional probability distributions.

Our supervised learning approach considers both long-term historical and real-time high-resolution features in a robust fashion, dramatically reducing the computational costs of training and deployment in online settings even for complex domains.

Inverse reinforcement learning (IRL) methods [14–17] make real-time predictions about an agent from learning the agent's reward function by observing its behavior. However, IRL methods suffer in online settings for complex domains because they are based on MDP formalisms, similar to BToM approaches [18,19].

Approaches based on plan recognition as planning (PRP), which use classical planners to predict plan likelihoods given potential goals, can also give real-time predictions for complex domains [20–25]. However, these methods require labor-intensive manual knowledge engineering, which can be prohibitive for environments that have complex dynamics. Additionally, these methods struggle with the noisy and sub-optimal nature of human behavior. In contrast, our neural network based approach requires minimal manual knowledge engineering and our two levels of resolutions allow for an effective treatment of noisy/sub-optimal behavior.

Guo et al. [26] study the same domain as the one in this paper, and use a graph-based representation for their model as well. However, they focus on transfer learning as a way to improve training when dealing with a limited amount of training data. Additionally, their agent predictions are focused on navigation. The techniques developed in their work are applicable to us and could be useful to further expand our model in the near future.

Lastly, Rabinowitz et al. [2] used meta-learning to build models of the agents from observations of their behavior alone. This resulted in a prior model for the agents' behavior and allowed for real-time predictions. However, this approach only studied situations where the agents followed simple policies, and the dynamics of their domain are much simpler than ours.

3   Approach

3.1   Domain and Task

The domain we consider is that of a USAR mission simulated in a Minecraft-based environment [10]. In this scenario, the participants must navigate an office building that has suffered structural damage and collapse due to a disaster. The original building layout is altered by the collapse, with some passages being closed off due to rubble, and new openings being created by walls collapsing.

The goal of the mission is to obtain as many points as possible by triaging victims of the building collapse within a 10-minute time limit. There are 34 victims in the building, among whom 10 are seriously injured and will expire 5 minutes into the mission. These *critically injured* victims take 15 seconds to triage and are worth 30 points each. These victims are represented by *yellow* blocks. The other victims are considered *non-critically injured*, take 7.5 s to triage, and are worth 10 points each. These victims are represented by *green* blocks.

Each participant conducts three versions of the mission, with different levels of difficulty (easy, medium, and hard). On higher difficulty levels, the victims are less clustered, further away from the starting point, and are more difficult to find. Higher difficulty levels also have more alterations from the original static map that the participants are provided at the beginning of the mission (i.e., more blockages and openings).

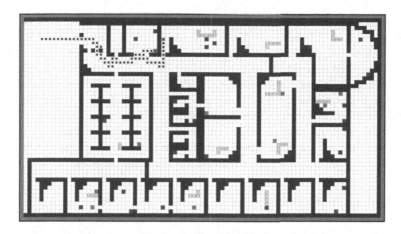

Fig. 1. A visualization of the high-resolution representation for our domain. The red dot represents the agent (i.e., the human's Minecraft avatar), and the grey dots represent grid cells that the agent has traversed in the past. Green and yellow squares represent untriaged victims, blue squares represent triaged victims, brown squares represent walls, and grey squares represent obstacles. Walls and obstacles are not traversable, and the blank (white) squares are walkable areas. (Color figure online)

3.2   Representation

High-Resolution Representation. We use a highly simplified 2D gridworld environment representation for the high resolution representation. In this representation, we encode different objects and store them in a 51×91 integer matrix. The specific encodings are shown in Table 1.

Table 1. Encodings for objects in the high resolution representation.

Object	Value
Empty	1
Wall	4
Critical victim	81
Non-critical victim	82
Unavailable victim (triaged or expired)	83
Obstacle	255
Agent	0

In Fig. 1, we show a visualization of the high-resolution representation[2]. Our primitive action space consists of two types of actions: *move* and *triage*. The

[2] Our high-resolution visualization code implementation is based on this repository: https://gitlab.com/cmu_asist/gym_minigrid.

'move' action can be carried out in four directions: up, down, left, and right, moving one cell at a time when the direction of moving is not obstructed. The 'triage' action can only be performed when the agent reaches locations cells where victims are located.

In this high-resolution representation, we can analyze human behavior based on discrete primitive actions combined with the layout of the building, which enables modeling real-time changes in short-term goal preferences. However, these actions also introduce noise, and inference based on them alone is not conducive to extracting high-level features and organizing long-term memory due to the large number of primitive actions per trial ($\approx 10^3$).

Low-Resolution Representation. To facilitate the extraction of high-level features from human behavior and the organization of long-term historical information, we construct a graph-based representation to simplify our domain further. The nodes of the represent areas (e.g., rooms, hallways, etc.) of the building, the edges represent connections between areas, and each node has three integer-valued attributes:

- Number of green victims in the area.
- Number of yellow victims in the area.
- Visited status. This attribute can take one of four possible values:
  - 0: The node has not been previously visited by the agent.
  - 1: The node has been previously visited by the agent.
  - 2: The agent is currently located at the node.
  - 3: The node was the previous node the agent was at.

For 'visited status' attribute, if two conditions are met at the same time, the higher encoding value has a higher priority. For example, if the agent returns to a previously visited room, the visited status of the current room defaults to 2 instead of 1 even though both are applicable. The visited status in the memory matrix is updated according to the above rules when the agent moves from one area to the next. In addition, when the agent successfully triages a specific type of victim, the number of victims of that type in the current area is reduced by one. Therefore, the updates to this matrix record the historical behavior of the current agent.

This is a dramatic simplification of our domain, since we ignores many details from the environment, such as the specific locations of agents and victims, the detailed layout of the building, etc. Therefore, the low-resolution representation provides a more concise encoding of crucial historical information, making it easier for the model to extract high-level features in human behavior. We organize this information into a matrix. However, the time interval for state updates is longer than that in the high-resolution representation, since we are not encoding primitive actions for this representation, and it cannot grasp real-time changes in human intentions. Figure 3 shows an example sketch of the time intervals for updates to the state in the two resolutions. In order to leverage the complementary strengths of these two resolutions, we propose a model that uses both as inputs simultaneously.

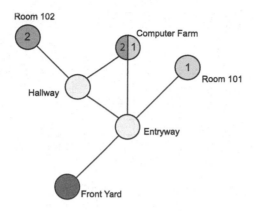

Area ID	Yellow victims	Green victims	Visited status
Room 101	1	0	0
Room 102	0	2	1
Front Yard	0	0	2
Entryway	0	0	3
Hallway	0	0	1
Computer Farm	1	2	0

Fig. 2. Visualization of an example low resolution graph representation and the corresponding memory matrix. The nodes represent the areas in the building, and the edges the connections between them. The number and type of victims in each area are recorded as attributes on each node, and are shown using a color and number indicating the type and quantity of victims. The red node represents the node the agent is in. The matrix below the graph is the corresponding low resolution memory matrix. (Color figure online)

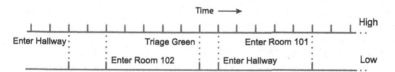

Fig. 3. An example sketch showing the different time intervals of state updating for the two resolutions. Each tick line indicates an update to the state, and the red dotted lines connect ticks with the same timestamp The high resolution input is updated for every primitive action, while the low resolution input is only updated when the agent leaves a node or changes the attributes of a node (triaging a victim), hence the lesser number of ticks. (Color figure online)

3.3   Model

Our model produces two types of outputs: (i) *goals*, i.e., objects/locations that the agent is trying to get to, and (ii) the *next type of victim* (green or yellow) that the agent will attempt to triage.

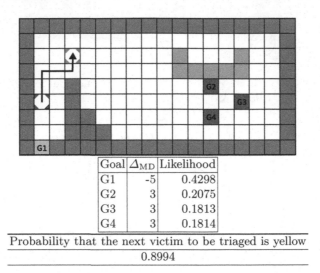

Goal	Δ_{MD}	Likelihood
G1	-5	0.4298
G2	3	0.2075
G3	3	0.1813
G4	3	0.1814

Probability that the next victim to be triaged is yellow
0.8994

Fig. 4. An example of how we deal with the data from the high resolution representation. The arrows represent the agent's last six movements. The quantity $\Delta_{MD}(g, 6)$ (see Eq. 1) is computed for $g \in \{G1, G2, G3, G4\}$ and shown in the table below the figure, along with the predictions of the model for each potential goal g in the area. The window of 'move' actions is from when the agent moves from the magenta outlined square to the blue outlined square. (Color figure online)

Goals. The primary outputs of our model are similar to methods based on Bayesian ToM approaches [3,12,13]. We consider victims and portals connecting adjacent areas as potential goals, and aim to predict which goal the agent is currently pursuing. See Fig. 4 for an example set of goals available to an agent when entering a particular room.

Next Triaged Victim Type. In addition to predicting the probability of the agent pursuing a potential goal, we also predict the type of victim to be triaged next, which helps us identify the agent's strategy or long term behavior. For example, we observed that some players prioritize triaging yellow victims because they are worth more points and expire sooner, while some players are more opportunistic, triaging victims in the order they appear in their field of view. Note that the next victim to be triaged may not be in the current area that the player is in. Thus, we need to leverage information from both the high and low resolution representations to make this prediction, making it an important output that takes advantage of our multi-resolution architecture.

3.4   Architecture

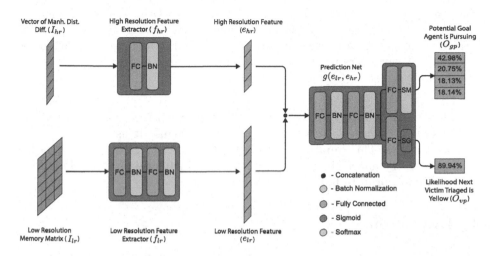

Fig. 5. This is our network architecture. Our inputs are fed into features extractors for each resolution and then those extracted features are concatenated and fed into the prediction net which produces our goal and victim type predictions. The values shown for O_{gp} and O_{vp} are taken from the example in Fig. 4 for illustrative purposes.

The architecture of the model is shown in Fig. 5. First, the information from the high and low resolution representations are used as inputs. The high-resolution input I_{hr} is a vector of Δ_{MD} values, one for each goal. The low-resolution input I_{lr} is the memory matrix described earlier. The corresponding features $e_{hr} = f_{hr}(I_{hr})$ and $e_{lr} = f_{lr}(I_{lr})$ are extracted by the feature extractor networks f_{hr} and f_{lr}, respectively. Then, these two features from the two different resolutions are concatenated and fed into the prediction net g. The next goal and victim type to be triaged predictions O_{gp} and O_{vp} take the form of estimating the two probabilistic outputs with $g(e_{hr}, e_{lr})$. Since the inputs consider state differences rather than the entire state, the size of the input observation space is significantly reduced, thereby reducing the training difficulty of our deep learning model. We use a fully connected (FC) layer combined with a batch normalization layer as a basic building block for our three neural networks. The output FC layers in the prediction network ($g(e_{lr}, e_{hr})$) are passed through softmax and sigmoid functions to obtain the probabilities of the agent's goal (O_{gp}) and the likelihood that the next victim is triaged (O_{vp}), respectively.

High-Resolution Input. Similar to the setting of the BToM [3], we infer the probability of pursuing a goal. As shown in Fig. 4, we compute the quantity Δ_{MD}, defined as follows:

$$\Delta_{MD}(g, m) = D(x_i^m, x_g) - D(x_f^m, x_g) \tag{1}$$

where x_i^m and x_f^m are the initial and final positions of the agent computed with respect to a window of the past m 'move' primitive actions, x_g is the location of the goal g for which Δ_{MD} is being calculated, and $D(a, b)$ is the Manhattan distance between locations a and b. We found that setting $m = 6$ to be the best fit choice, which still gives real-time predictions, while also handling some noise in the agent's actions. See Table 4 for a comparison of results with different values of m.

Low-Resolution Input. As shown in Fig. 2, we record the victim status and area visitation status of each area in a matrix and use it as an input to the proposed model. This input helps us extract long-term historical information to form memory and facilitate the extraction of high-level features (long term strategies) as a prior to human behavior predictions.

4   Evaluation

Our model is trained in an end-to-end manner via supervised learning using an Nvidia V100S GPU and the Adam optimization algorithm [27]. We calculate the softmax cross entropy loss for goal prediction and the binary cross entropy loss for victim type prediction. The training loss L_{total} is the sum of the goal prediction loss L_{gp} and the victim type loss L_{vp} as seen in Eq. 2, where the victim type loss weight, W, is given in Table 2, along with the rest of the training hyperparameters after tuning.

$$L_{total} = L_{gp} + W * L_{vp} \tag{2}$$

Figure 4 illustrates how our proposed model works. As shown in Fig. 1, in the room that the agent searched just prior to the room that it is currently in, the agent only triaged the yellow victim and left the two green victims, which hints that the agent is likely following a strategy that prioritizes rescuing all the yellow victims first. Our model encodes this behavior as prior knowledge and predicts that the probability that the next victim to be triaged will be yellow is ≈ 0.9.

Without a prior about the rescue strategy we may naively expect that the agent will move from G2 to G3 or G4 (i.e., to the next closest victim) with a high probability. In contrast, our model predicts that the most likely next short-term goal is the room's exit, with a probability of ≈ 0.43. In Fig. 6 (similar to Fig. 4), the same player finally chose to leave after finding there is no yellow victims in this room. The probability of the agent returning to G1 to try and find a yellow victim to triage next can be seen to increase from about 0.90 to 0.95.

Table 2. Hyperparameters for our model training.

Hyperparameter	Value
Learning rate	0.001
Low resolution feature size	64
High resolution feature size	4
Hidden size for prediction net	64
Batch size	16
Random seed	0
Victim type loss weight (W)	0.3

This demonstrates that our model can learn about high-level strategies that a player is following, and can also detect instantaneous changes in the short-term goals of human players.

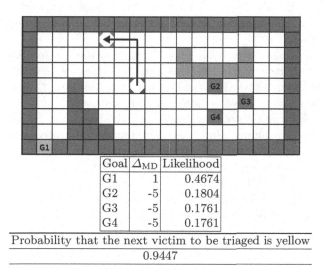

Goal	Δ_{MD}	Likelihood
G1	1	0.4674
G2	-5	0.1804
G3	-5	0.1761
G4	-5	0.1761

Probability that the next victim to be triaged is yellow
0.9447

Fig. 6. The high resolution representation at a later time than the example shown in Fig. 4. Here we see the probabilities of the agent heading to goal G1, and that the next victim triaged will be yellow are increasing, showing that our model is correctly predicting the agent's goals in real-time, in addition to showing our prediction at an earlier timestep was correct. (Color figure online)

In Table 3, we compare our multi-resolution method to two baseline approaches based solely on high-resolution information[3]. The first baseline uses

---

[3] We do not compare with an approach based solely on low-resolution information, as it would be not be sufficient to differentiate between multiple short-term goals within a single area/node.

Table 3. Results for 6-fold cross-validation for our approach and two baselines based on high-resolution inputs. In the first method, we encode the high resolution input as the destination locations of the agent's most recent six 'move' actions. For the second method, we concatenate the high resolution input vector I_{hr} with an integer representing which area the agent is in. We find that our multi-resolution approach significantly outperforms the baselines that only use high resolution inputs.

	Easy		Medium		Hard	
Model - Cross Val	Goal Acc	Vic. Acc	Goal Acc	Vic. Acc	Goal Acc	Vic. Acc.
High Res. (Locations)	0.6313	0.7060	0.6232	0.6874	0.6031	0.6838
High Res. (Δ^i_{MD})	0.6526	0.7315	0.6412	0.7037	0.6251	0.6881
High + Low Res	**0.7208**	**0.9008**	**0.7146**	**0.8803**	**0.6780**	**0.8881**

the 2D coordinates of the destination cells of the six most recent 'move' actions as the input. The second baseline considers the high-resolution input based on Δ_{MD} and includes only a small portion of the information from the low-resolution representation. Specifically, since the current area cannot be encoded if only Δ_{MD} is considered, we encode each area with a unique integer and append this integer to the input vector I_{hr}.

We have 66 trials for each difficulty level, and use a 6-fold cross-validation procedure to evaluate our model[4]. As shown in Table 3, we see that the baseline using Δ_{MD} performs better than the baseline that uses only the past six destination cells of the agent's 'move' actions, and our approach that uses both high and low resolution information outperforms both the baselines. Compared to using location information alone, using Δ_{MD} (or more specifically, a vector of Δ_{MD} values, one for each goal, i.e., I_{hr}) as an input can lead to better features being extracted, thus improving prediction accuracy. Our proposed method based on the combination of high and low-resolution information allows our model to effectively learn the relationship between features at multiple resolutions in the data, further improving the accuracy of behavior prediction.

Table 4. Results for 6-fold cross-validation for our approach in which the high resolution inputs are based on different numbers of 'move' actions.

	Easy		Medium		Hard	
last m moves	Goal Acc.	Vic. Acc.	Goal Acc.	Vic. Acc.	Goal Acc.	Vic. Acc.
3	0.7181	**0.9037**	0.7071	0.8816	0.6712	0.8857
6	**0.7208**	0.9008	**0.7146**	0.8803	0.6780	**0.8881**
12	0.7151	0.9001	0.7118	**0.8835**	**0.6801**	0.8845

---

[4] We evaluate the accuracy of the victim type prediction only in the first five minutes of each trial because yellow victims expire after five minutes, leaving only green victims to triage.

We also investigated the sensitivity of our approach to the choice of the parameter m (the number of moves in our window when we compute $\Delta_{\mathrm{MD}}(m, g)$). The results are shown in Table 4. The performance of our proposed method is not overly sensitive to the number of moves, and thus we choose $m = 6$ after comprehensively considering the results for the three tasks.

5   Conclusion

In this paper, we proposed a real-time human behavior prediction model that uses multi-resolution features. In the high-resolution input, the model observes the Manhattan distance difference between the agent and each potential goal during recent behavior, which is robust to obtain the agent's short-term intention. The low-resolution historical state matrix effectively organizes the long-term memory and helps the model extract the high-level feature. In addition, the supervised learning-based training provides a straightforward and automatic way to organize and learn the internal correlations from the human subjects data. After training, the experimental results demonstrated that our method is robust and accurate at effectively utilizes prior knowledge to predict human behavior.

References

1. Seeber, I., et al.: Machines as teammates: a research agenda on AI in team collaboration. Inf. Manage. **57**(2), 103174 (2020)
2. Rabinowitz, N., Perbet, F., Song, F., Zhang, C., Eslami, S.A., Botvinick, M.: Machine theory of mind. In: Proceedings of the 35th International Conference on Machine Learning, pp. 4218–4227, July 2018
3. Baker, C.L., Jara-Ettinger, J., Saxe, R., Tenenbaum, J.B.: Rational quantitative attribution of beliefs, desires and percepts in human mentalizing. Nat. Hum. Behav. **1**(4), 0064 (2017)
4. Wu, Y., Baker, C.L., Tenenbaum, J.B., Schulz, L.E.: Rational inference of beliefs and desires from emotional expressions. Cogn. Sci. **42**(3), 850–884 (2018)
5. Galescu, L., Teng, C.M., Allen, J., Perera, I.: Cogent: a generic dialogue system shell based on a collaborative problem solving model. In: Proceedings of the 19th Annual SIGdial Meeting on Discourse and Dialogue, pp. 400–409, July 2018
6. Allen, J.F., Bahkshandeh, O., de Beaumont, W., Galescu, L., Teng, C.M.: Effective broad-coverage deep parsing. In: Proceedings of the Thirty-Second AAAI Conference on Artificial Intelligence, (AAAI 2018), pp. 4776–4783 (2018)
7. Perera, I., Allen, J., Teng, C.M., Galescu, L.: Building and learning structures in a situated blocks world through deep language understanding. In: Proceedings of the First International Workshop on Spatial Language Understanding, pp. 12 20, June 2018. https://doi.org/10.18653/v1/W18-140
8. Zhao, R., Papangelis, A., Cassell, J.: Towards a dyadic computational model of rapport management for human-virtual agent interaction. In: Bickmore, T., Marsella, S., Sidner, C. (eds.) IVA 2014. LNCS (LNAI), vol. 8637, pp. 514–527. Springer, Cham (2014). https://doi.org/10.1007/978-3-319-09767-1_62

9. Zhao, R., Sinha, T., Black, A.W., Cassell, J.: Socially-aware virtual agents: automatically assessing dyadic rapport from temporal patterns of behavior. In: Traum, D., Swartout, W., Khooshabeh, P., Kopp, S., Scherer, S., Leuski, A. (eds.) IVA 2016. LNCS (LNAI), vol. 10011, pp. 218–233. Springer, Cham (2016). https://doi.org/10.1007/978-3-319-47665-0_20

10. Huang, L., et al.: ASIST Experiment 1 Study Preregistration, December 2020. https://doi.org/10.17605/OSF.IO/ZWAU

11. Zhi-Xuan, T., Mann, J.L., Silver, T., Tenenbaum, J., Mansinghka, V.: Online Bayesian goal inference for boundedly rational planning agents. In: Proceedings of Annual Conference on Neural Information Processing Systems 2020 (2020)

12. Jara-Ettinger, J., Schulz, L.E., Tenenbaum, J.B.: The naïve utility calculus as a unified, quantitative framework for action understanding. Cogn. Psychol. **123**, 101334 (2020). https://doi.org/10.1016/j.cogpsych.2020.10133

13. Baker, C., Saxe, R., Tenenbaum, J.: Bayesian theory of mind: modeling joint belief-desire attribution. In: Proceedings of the 33th Annual Meeting of the Cognitive Science Society (2011)

14. Ng, A.Y., Russell, S.J.: Algorithms for inverse reinforcement learning. In: Proceedings of the 17th International Conference on Machine Learning (ICML 2000), pp. 663–670 (2000)

15. Abbeel, P., Ng, A.Y.: Apprenticeship learning via inverse reinforcement learning. In: Proceedings of the 21st International Conference (ICML 2004) (2004). https://doi.org/10.1145/1015330.101543

16. Ramachandran, D., Amir, E.: Bayesian inverse reinforcement learning. In: Proceedings of the 20th International Joint Conference on Artificial Intelligence, pp. 2586–2591 (2007)

17. Hadfield-Menell, D., Russell, S.J., Abbeel, P., Dragan, A.: Cooperative inverse reinforcement learning. CoRR (2016)

18. Brown, D.S., Niekum, S.: Deep Bayesian reward learning from preferences. CoRR (2019)

19. Michini, B., How, J.P.: Improving the efficiency of Bayesian inverse reinforcement learning. In: Proceedings of IEEE International Conference on Robotics and Automation, pp. 651–3656. (2012). https://doi.org/10.1109/ICRA.2012.622524

20. Ramírez, M., Geffner, H.: Plan recognition as planning. In: Proceedings of the 21st International Joint Conference on Artificial Intelligence, pp. 1778–1783 (2009)

21. Ramírez, M., Geffner, H.: Probabilistic plan recognition using off-the-shelf classical planners. In: Proceedings of the 24th AAAI Conference on Artificial Intelligence (2010)

22. Sohrabi, S., Riabov, A.V., Udrea, O.: Plan recognition as planning revisited. In: Proceedings of the 25th International Joint Conference on Artificial Intelligence, pp. 3258–3264 (2016)

23. Höller, D., Bercher, P., Behnke, G., Biundo, S.: Plan and goal recognition as HTN planning. In: Proceedings of the Workshops of the 32th AAAI Conference on Artificial Intelligence, pp. 607–613 (2018)

24. Kaminka, G.A., Vered, M., Agmon, N.: Plan recognition in continuous domains. In: Proceedings of the 32th AAAI Conference on Artificial Intelligence, pp. 6202–6210 (2018)

25. Vered, M., Pereira, R.F., Magnaguagno, M.C., Meneguzzi, F., Kaminka, G.A.: Online goal recognition as reasoning over landmarks. In: Proceedings of the Workshops of the 32th AAAI Conference on Artificial Intelligence, pp. 638–645 (2018)

26. Guo, Y., Jena, R., Hughes, D., Lewis, M., Sycara, K.: Transfer learning for human navigation and triage strategies prediction in a simulated urban search and rescue task. In: Proceedings of 30th IEEE International Conference on Robot & Human Interactive Communication, pp. 784–791, August 2021
27. Kingma, D.P., Ba, J.: Adam: a method for stochastic optimization. In: Proceedings of the 3rd International Conference on Learning Representations (2015)

Route Optimization in Service of a Search and Rescue Artificial Social Intelligence Agent

Yunzhe Wang[1]([✉]) [iD], Nikolos Gurney[3] [iD], Jincheng Zhou[2,3] [iD],
David V. Pynadath[3] [iD], and Volkan Ustun[3] [iD]

[1] USC Dornsife College of Letters, Arts and Sciences, Los Angeles, USA
yunzhewa@usc.edu
[2] Computer Science Department, USC Viterbi School of Engineering,
Los Angeles, USA
[3] USC Institute for Creative Technologies, Los Angeles, USA
{gurney,pynadath,ustun}@ict.usc.edu

Abstract. The success and safety of a Search and Rescue (SAR) team hinge on routing, making it an integral part of any SAR mission. Consequently, an Artificial Social Intelligence (ASI) agent aware of the "good" available routes in a mission is a very desirable asset for a SAR team. Such awareness is contingent on having superior knowledge of the environment and understanding the dynamics of the SAR team. An ASI agent equipped with this capability can utilize it while reasoning about the mission, similar to how a human may use real-time GPS route suggestions from a navigation application. This feature was historically infeasible for real-time ASI agents because the problems were computationally intractable. However, recent advances in Graph Neural Networks, transformers, and attention models make them candidates to be leveraged as neural heuristics in routing problems to quickly generate near-optimal routes. This paper describes a sequential decision framework based on neural heuristics to devise such routes for participants in the DARPA ASIST Minecraft SAR Task and reports our initial findings.

1 Introduction

The success and safety of a SAR team hinge on routing, making access to a trusted advisor an indispensable asset. Although many factors impact trust in advisors, expertise is fundamental [2,7]. Thus, a SAR ASI agent must have demonstrable expertise in the real-time routing of teams.

A trusted SAR ASI that is equipped with routing technology is similar to a driver with a real-time GPS navigation application. The recommendations that an app provides are based on critical information which it can easily access and process, such as road conditions, traffic jams, accidents, etc. Obviously, this is not something a driver can readily do while traveling—but drivers are also privy to their own private information, such as preferences and physiological states. A driver with a car full of hungry kids, for example, may choose to stop and eat dinner early after the app recommends a re-route rather than following the recommendation. Critically, this decision does not make the re-routing recommendation any less valuable. The driver *trusted* the app, but used private information to make a personal and rational decision. Just like the app performs real-time path planning and provides options to the user based on the current information state, the SAR ASI agent ingests routing suggestions and combines them with other information that it has for the mission and the SAR team it is assisting. Then, the SAR ASI agent makes informed recommendations to the SAR team.

SAR missions burden rescuers with continual decisions about how to traverse an environment. These decision are frequently made under extreme conditions and often from very limited information, both of which place significant stress on humans and impact their decision making capacity [14]. One of these stressers is enough to warrant technological help, but more troublesome is the NP Hard nature of routing in SAR missions. SAR routing is akin to the family of Traveling Salesman Problems (TSPs) which are also NP Hard and studied extensively in Operations Research. However, the most advanced Operations Research methodologies cannot generate real-time guaranteed optimal solutions for TSP problems (save for small networks). There are a number of heuristics available to find candidate solutions [3], and many practical applications utilize such heuristics.

An insight from studying TSPs is that the problem instances often share key characteristics or patterns. Cappart et al. (2021) illustrate this with a trucking company routing problem in which the company needs to generate daily routes for the same city, but with slight differences due to traffic conditions. Such similarities bring opportunities for the data-dependent machine learning approaches that exploit these patterns [1]. Recently, Graph Neural Networks (GNNs) with attention mechanisms have become strong heuristic alternatives for combinatorial optimization problems [4]. We leverage such an approach as a neural heuristic to quickly generate good paths that exploit the similarities in routing requirements of a Minecraft SAR task. A real-time ASI agent prototype can utilize this capability to explore the routing options available to the SAR team under different conditions.

2   Background

Combinatorial optimization (CO) is a well-established interdisciplinary area with many critical real-world applications including routing [12]. For a given problem, CO tries to optimize a cost (or objective) function by selecting a subset from a finite set which is subject to constraints on the selection. The goal of CO is to find a unique, optimal solution to each problem. This is not always practical, however, due to the complexity of problems. Practitioners turn to problem-specific heuristic methodologies in such instances [3].

Graph Neural Networks (GNNs) are a powerful machine learning architecture that leverages structural, relational, and compositional biases to facilitate geometric deep learning [8]. GNNs aggregate information into simpler representations of nodes and edges from structural and feature-based (e.g. node or edge type) graph data. By parameterizing this aggregation, they can be trained in an end-to-end fashion against a loss function. What differentiates GNNs from their predecessors, convolutional and recurrent neural networks, is the ability to operate on higher complexity data than what can be represented in regular Euclidean structures, e.g., a picture (2D) or text (1D). GNNs accomplish this by being order-invariant—they propagate on each node in the graph independently and ignore the input order—and by using the graph structure to guide propagation. These innovations empower GNN models to "reason" about a graph, that is, draw general inferences, and then use those inferences to successfully make predictions and classifications [17]. Recently, GNNs have also been utilized as neural heuristics to generate solutions for CO problems [16]. The central promise of GNNs in this role is that the learned vector representations encode crucial graph structures to help solve a CO problem more efficiently [4].

Kool et al. (2018) proposed a transformer-like encoder-decoder architecture based on Graph Attention Networks [15], a well-known GNN architecture with attention, for general routing problems. In this framework, an encoder-decoder neural network is trained on randomly generated routing problems with network sizes similar to a target problem. The training leverages an actor-critic reinforcement learning approach that circumvents the need for the optimal solutions to the training instances. Although the training needs to be done in advance, with a trained model it is possible to quickly generate very good solutions to SAR routing problems. The work depicted in this paper leveraged the Kool et al.'s codebase (2018) (ALSR codebase) and augmented it for our task.

3   DARPA ASIST Minecraft SAR Task

The DARPA ASIST Minecraft SAR task ("our" task) is a game-based simulated training environment designed with the explicit purpose of developing ASI agents. The task places participants in a Minecraft environment where they attempt to save victims of an urban disaster and earn points for doing so. Victims are either non-critical or critical, the latter of which are worth more points but take a team effort to save. The environment includes risks, which are locations where a player is frozen until a teammate rescues them. There is also rubble, which can be cleared, that may block access to victims. Teams consist of three participants, and each participant can select one of three roles: medical specialist (medic), hazardous material specialist (engineer), and search specialist (transporter). Medics can triage victims and rescue frozen teammates, engineers can clear rubble, and transporters can transport victims. Each role is associated with a tool that expires after so many uses and must be renewed. Further details about the environment are available in the preregistration [9].

4   Solution Approach

Participants in a Minecraft SAR experiment face routing decisions akin to a Vehicle Routing Problem (VRP), which is a type of TSP in the Operations Research literature. A VRP is a combinatorial optimization problem with an objective to identify optimal routes for each vehicle in a delivery fleet. For example, in the Minecraft SAR environment, triaging victims, clearing rubble, deactivating freezing plates, and converging at critical victims are all demand points (customer locations) that the participants need to visit to complete the SAR task. Consequently, VRP models can provide routing decisions for planning a participant's path. Different VRP models can assist in capturing different aspects of the Minecraft SAR task. For example, the capacitated VRP (CVRP) model, which defines vehicle capacities, can model tool durability, whereas the CVRP with Profits (CVRPP) model can assign unique rewards to different demand points.

We address routing for the Minecraft SAR teams in a sequential decision-making framework via defining separate VRP models for each team member. Each team composition, e.g., one medic - two engineers or one medic - one engineer - one transporter, defines a different sequence of VRP models. Suggested routes for one model informs the definition of the next model. For example, suppose that we generated paths for the medic with the CVRP model under the assumption that there is no rubble. An engineer must clear the rubble blocking a victim before the medic arrives at this location for the paths to be valid. This forms the basis for the engineer routing model definition, which is akin to the CVRPP. In this definition, we set up rewards if the engineer can clear path rubble before it is needed or if the engineer can be at a critical victim location near the same time as the medic so that triage can start.

Each team composition defines a different sequential decision-making problem. When we have completed the model definitions for all team compositions, we can compare the results across teams. Here, we only define a (medic, engineer, engineer) team for demonstration purposes. One of the main assumptions made with this team composition is that the second engineer switches to the medic role if time permits and starts triaging victims in reverse order from the medic routing solution. Figure 1 depicts the routing problem definition process for this team composition in detail.

Our sequential decision-making framework can start at any arbitrary point during an experiment. Thus, it is possible to run the framework and generate solutions for any combination of victims, rubble, and freezing plates. Additionally, the framework can also be initialized with the information that participants have (or should have), yielding solutions representative of participant knowledge states. Such a capability also allows the ASI agent to compose what-if type of questions to develop a better intuition on the routing options available to the team under different assumptions.

4.1   Solution Pipeline

Our framework adapts the ALSR codebase. We trained separate models for the medic and engineer roles using various network sizes so that the solution generation process can utilize the appropriate model to produce routes. Save a few modifications to set up the routes correctly, we directly utilized a CVRP model native to the ALSR codebase for training medic routes. We had to update the

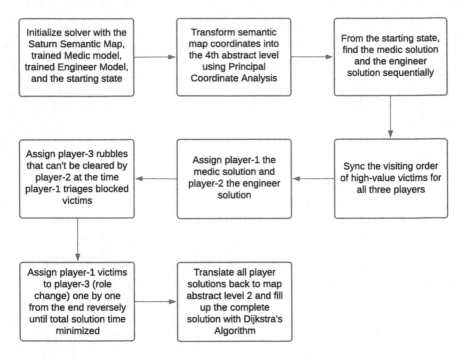

Fig. 1. The sample process to generate a complete routing solution for a (medic, engineer, engineer) team

ALSR codebase for training CVRPP models for the engineer role. For instance, we added timing-based penalties to the objective function to make the engineer route better aligned with the medic route. We defined two types of penalties: (1) Being late, e.g., there is a penalty if the engineer clears rubble later than the medic needs it; and (2) Being off-sync, e.g., there is a penalty if the engineer visits critical victims or freezing plates before or after the medic's visits. Algorithm 1 presents the CVRPP model generation in detail. In this model, parameters control the weights for each type of penalty and the length of the proposed route in the objective function.

The ALSR codebase strictly requires using 2D coordinates (between 0 and 1), not distances between nodes, as input. We addressed this requirement by setting up four abstraction levels of the Minecraft SAR task maps. The lowest abstraction is the original task map (Saturn) (Fig. 2a). Our second abstraction level is a semantic graph that captures all the main map features and structures (rooms, victims, rubble, and the connection of them) needed for navigation decisions (Fig. 2b). Each role has objective nodes, e.g., the medic role needs only the victim nodes, whereas the engineer role requires the rubble nodes directly blocking victims, the critical victims, and the freeze plates. The third abstraction level is a distance matrix capturing pairwise distances for all objective nodes (Fig. 2c), where Dijkstra's algorithm [6] is utilized to calculate the distances

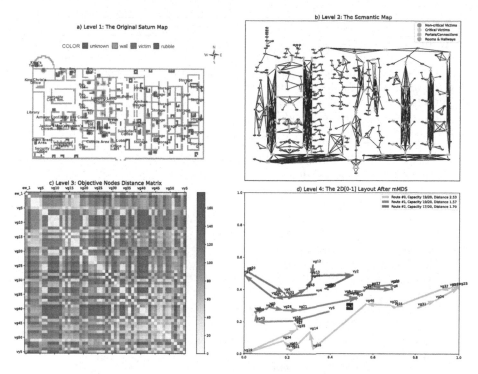

Fig. 2. Four Abstract Levels of the Saturn Map. a) Plan view of a representative Saturn map in its original form. b) Semantic map with victims/rooms/connections extracted. Note: the map structures are consistent with that in (a), but victim distribution is different. c) Distance matrix (in meters) of objective nodes extracted. d) An euclidean 2-dimensional layout transformed from the distance matrix using mMDS and JLT. Coordinates are scaled to [0–1]. A sample routing solution with three routes is shown.

between objective nodes directly based on the semantic graph representation (Fig. 2b). The fourth abstraction level is a set of 2D coordinates between 0 and 1 dictated by the ALSR codebase. Because the distance matrix generated in the third abstraction level is non-euclidean, we performed Metric Multidimensional Scaling (mMDS) [5,13], also known as Principal Coordinate Analysis (PCoA), to transform the distance matrix into coordinates in high-dimensional space (~36 dim). We then used the John-Lindenstrauss Transform (JLT) [11] to generate 2D coordinates from those in the high-dimensional space while preserving distance information from the initial matrix [10]. As the last step, the output coordinates from JLT are scaled to [0, 1] to finalize the fourth abstraction level of the map (Fig. 2d). We perform route planning via neural heuristics on the fourth abstraction level and convert the generated routes back to the semantic map representation for visualization, analysis, and interfacing purposes.

Algorithm 1: Training Pipeline for the Engineer's Routing Model

---

Input: trained medic model $model_m$, normal victims V_n, high-value victims V_h,
      rubbles R, freezing plates F, medic tool life T_m, engineer tool life T_e,
      mismatch penalty coefficient α, rubble penalty coefficient β

Output: Trained Engineer model $model_e$

Initialize Engineer model $model_e$

Initialize Medic Graph G_m and Engineer Graph G_e

repeat

    $G_m \leftarrow$ `RandUnif2D`$(|V_n| + |V_h| + 1)$

    Medic Route $R_m \leftarrow model_m(G_m, T_m)$

    foreach *node* $u \in G_m$ **do**

        if $u \in V_h \cup R \cup F$ **then**

            $G_e \leftarrow G_e \cup \{u\}$

        end

    end

    Engineer Route $R_e \leftarrow model_e(G_e, T_e)$

    Mismatch Penalty $P_m \leftarrow 0$

    Rubble Penalty $P_r \leftarrow 0$

    foreach *node* $u \in G_e$ **do**

        $t_m^u \leftarrow$ `time`(R_m, u), $t_e^u \leftarrow$ `time`(R_e, u)

        if $u \in V_h \cup F$ **then**

            $P_m \leftarrow P_m + l_2(t_m^u, t_e^u)$

        end

        if $u \in R$ **and** $t_e^u > t_m^u$ **then**

            $P_r \leftarrow P_r + 1$

        end

    end

    $cost \leftarrow |R_e| + \alpha \cdot P_m + \beta \cdot P_r$

    Update $model_e$ parameters based on $cost$

until *convergence*

4.2 Exploratory Results

We ran two experiments with our task on the Saturn_B map (see Huang et al. 2021). Both assumed the team composition described in the Solution Approach section. The first experiment focused on generating a complete solution for the task. Our sequential decision-making framework generated a solution with a perfect score of 750, an average distance traveled per participant of 1646 blocks, and completed the mission in 802 s. In comparison, the four teams from the Human Subjects Research (HSR) trials which started with the same team composition—trials 416, 450, 508, and 523—averaged 392.5 points and a distance of 2974 blocks per participant during their 900 s missions. The second experiment focused on selecting an arbitrary point in a trial and running our pipeline from that point onward. For this experiment, we selected trial 416, and we ran our pipeline given the scenario state at time 10:44 (when a role change from an engineer to medic happens). Our pipeline suggests a solution for the remaining 4:16 of the mission that improves the total score from 480 to 620 points.

5   Discussions and Future Work

Our pipeline generated superior routes to those followed by HSR teams. This is expected since the framework had access to the maps and victim locations, meaning it had the required information to generate near-optimal routes. Nevertheless, these results showed that our framework has the potential to be a *trusted* tool to service a SAR ASI agent. The ability to quickly generate routing solutions under different conditions would allow the ASI agent to better reason about what routes are available to the SAR team while intervening.

We plan to complete our framework for all possible team compositions and run experiments to compare them in the short term while setting up an interface for interaction with the real-time ASI agent prototype. We will also exploit the decoding stage of our framework by augmenting the masking component in the ALSR codebase to better handle CO model constraints and resolve potential deadlocks, e.g., a medic waits for the engineer to clear rubble, where the engineer waits for the medic at a critical victim. In the medium term, we will explore avenues to generate solutions concurrently for all team members directly on the third abstraction level—the distance matrices based on the semantic map.

6   Conclusions

We depicted a sequential decision-making framework leveraging neural heuristics to quickly inform a real-time ASI agent on routing options available to a SAR team under different conditions given the state of the SAR mission. Such an agent could leverage this framework as a trusted tool for routing when reasoning about how to assist the SAR teams better in Minecraft SAR experiments.

Acknowledgements. Part of the effort depicted is sponsored by the U.S. Army Research Laboratory (ARL) under contract number W911NF-14-D-0005 and by the Defense Advanced Research Projects Agency (DARPA) under contract number W911NF2010011, and that the content of the information does not necessarily reflect the position or the policy of the Government or the Defense Advanced Research Projects Agency, and no official endorsements should be inferred.

References

1. Bengio, Y., Lodi, A., Prouvost, A.: Machine learning for combinatorial optimization: a methodological tour d'horizon. Eur. J. Oper. Res. **290**(2), 405–421 (2021)
2. Bonaccio, S., Dalal, R.S.: Advice taking and decision-making: an integrative literature review, and implications for the organizational sciences. Organ. Behav. Hum. Decis. Process. **101**(2), 127–151 (2006)

3. Boussaïd, I., Lepagnot, J., Siarry, P.: A survey on optimization metaheuristics. Inf. Sci. **237**, 82–117 (2013)
4. Cappart, Q., et al.: Combinatorial optimization and reasoning with graph neural networks. arXiv preprint arXiv:2102.09544 (2021)
5. Cox, M., Cox, T.: Multidimensional scaling. In: Handbook of Data Visualization, pp. 315–347. Springer, Heidelberg (2008). https://doi.org/10.1007/978-3-540-33037-0_14
6. Dijkstra, E.W.: A note on two problems in connexion with graphs. Numer. Math. **1**(1), 269–271 (1959)
7. French, J.R., Raven, B., Cartwright, D.: The bases of social power. Classics Organ. Theory **7**, 311–320 (1959)
8. Gilmer, J., Schoenholz, S.S., Riley, P.F., Vinyals, O., Dahl, G.E.: Neural message passing for quantum chemistry. In: International Conference on Machine Learning, pp. 1263–1272. PMLR (2017)
9. Huang, L., et al.: ASIST study 2 June 2021 exercises for artificial social intelligence in minecraft search and rescue for teams (2021). https://doi.org/10.17605/OSF.IO/GXPQ5
10. Indyk, P., Matoušek, J., Sidiropoulos, A.: 8: low-distortion embeddings of finite metric spaces. In: Handbook of Discrete and Computational Geometry, pp. 211–231. Chapman and Hall/CRC, London (2017)
11. Johnson, W.B., Lindenstrauss, J.: Extensions of Lipschitz mappings into a Hilbert space. Contemp. Math. **26**, 189–206 (1984)
12. Korte, B., Vygen, J.: The traveling salesman problem. In: Combinatorial Optimization. Algorithms and Combinatorics, vol. 21, pp. 557–592. Springer, Heidelberg (2012). https://doi.org/10.1007/978-3-642-24488-9_21
13. Kruskal, J.B.: Multidimensional scaling. No. 11, Sage (1978)
14. Starcke, K., Brand, M.: Effects of stress on decisions under uncertainty: a meta-analysis. Psychol. Bull. **142**(9), 909 (2016)
15. Veličković, P., Cucurull, G., Casanova, A., Romero, A., Lio, P., Bengio, Y.: Graph attention networks. arXiv preprint arXiv:1710.10903 (2017)
16. Vesselinova, N., Steinert, R., Perez-Ramirez, D.F., Boman, M.: Learning combinatorial optimization on graphs: a survey with applications to networking. IEEE Access **8**, 120388–120416 (2020)
17. Zhou, J., et al.: Graph neural networks: a review of methods and applications. AI Open **1**, 57–81 (2020)

Author Index

Ainooson, James   53

Banerjee, Aditya   85
Barnard, Kobus   85
Brody, Justin   21, 194

Cauffman, Stephen J.   72
Chis, Max   158
Clausner, Timothy   21, 194

Debusk-Lane, Les   118
Diego-Rosell, Pablo   118

Freeman, Jared   72

Goldberg, Matthew D.   194
Goldberg, Matthew   21
Gonzalez, Cleotilde   102
Gulati, Aditya   102
Gurney, Nikolos   3, 220

Herron, Anthony   21
Huang, Lixiao   72
Hughes, Dana   158

Josyula, Darsana P.   21
Josyula, Darsana   194

Kress, Nathan   118
Kunda, Maithilee   53

Le, Long   158
Lewis, Michael   158
Li, Huao   158
Lieffers, Justin   205

Maese, Ellyn   118
Marsella, Stacy   3
Maxey, Christopher   21, 194
McFate, Clifton   149
Michelson, Joel   53

Nguyen, Thuy Ngoc   102

Pavlovic, Vladimir   30
Perlis, Don   21, 194
Pyarelal, Adarsh   85, 205
Pynadath, David V.   3, 220

Rabkina, Irina   149
Rahgooy, Taher   173

Sanyal, Deepayan   53
Sycara, Katia   158

Trueblood, Jennifer S.   173

Ustun, Volkan   3, 220

Venable, K. Brent   173
Viola, Alexander   30

Wang, Yunzhe   220
Wood, Matt   72

Yang, Yuan   53
Yoon, Sejong   30

Zaidins, Paul   21, 194
Zhang, Liang   205
Zheng, Keyang   158
Zhou, Jincheng   220

Printed in the United States
by Baker & Taylor Publisher Services